The Politics
of Popular Representation

The Politics
of Popular Representation

Reagan, Thatcher,
AIDS, and the Movies

Kenneth MacKinnon

Rutherford ● Madison ● Teaneck
Fairleigh Dickinson University Press
London and Toronto: Associated University Presses

Associated University Presses
440 Forsgate Drive
Cranbury, NJ 08512

Associated University Presses
25 Sicilian Avenue
London WC1A 2QH, England

Associated University Presses
P.O. Box 39, Clarkson Pstl. Stn.
Mississauga, Ontario,
L5J 3X9 Canada

The paper used in this publication meets the requirements
of the American National Standard for Permanence of Paper
for Printed Library Materials Z39.48-1984.

Library of Congress Cataloging-in-Publication Data

MacKinnon, Kenneth, 1942–
   The politics of popular representation : Reagan, Thatcher, AIDS, and the movies / Kenneth Mackinnon.
      p.   cm.
   Includes bibliographical references and index.
   ISBN 0-8386-3474-5 (alk. paper)
   1. AIDS (Disease)—Social aspects—United States.   2. AIDS (Disease)—Social aspects—Great Britain.   3. Reagan, Ronald. 4. Thatcher, Margaret.   5. Motion pictures—Social aspects—United States.   6. Motion pictures—Social aspects—Great Britain.
RA644.A25M23   1992
362.1′969792′001—dc20   91-58581
                                                                              CIP

PRINTED IN THE UNITED STATES OF AMERICA

Contents

Acknowledgments

I am glad to place on record my gratitude to my employers, the Polytechnic of North London, and particularly to the Faculty of Humanities, for continuing to grant me a measure of research relief in straitened times. The price of such relief has to be borne from a budget which has real difficulty in providing even modest financing of all the areas to which the Faculty is committed.

As always, the Kentish Town Library staff has been tireless and quietly efficient in tracking down and securing the interlibrary loan of the vast amount of books and articles which I felt I had to consult. Quite literally, the book could not have been written without that staff's help.

Another debt should be acknowledged—to a recently graduated student of Film Studies, Christopher Barwick, for sharing his enthusiasm for the work of David Cronenberg with me, for educating me in it via his final-year dissertation, but especially for lending me videocassettes of several Cronenberg works which have proved crucial to chapter 12.

Thanks are owed too to Alan Smith of the Polytechnic's Media Services for providing the photograph on this book's back cover.

It is unusual to acknowledge help from a publication that has not, for example, granted the author special permission to use an extract. Nevertheless, I should like to give thanks for the existence of the *Monthly Film Bulletin*. Its existence must lighten the task of any researcher into dominant cinema, in that it provides not only critiques but, invaluably, plot summaries of most of the films released during the period that each particular issue attempts to cover. Especially in light of the complaints which my last publication necessitated, concerning the *MFB*'s seldom-relenting campaign against the work of Brian De Palma, I should like to take this opportunity to confess that, even if the current book could have been written without consultation of the *MFB*, it would in that case have taken much longer to complete. (It may be of interest that the *Monthly Film Bulletin* has been incorporated recently into the new-look *Sight and Sound*.)

1

Introduction

Decades acquire images. This process is helped along by the application of descriptive names to them, so that "the naughty nineties" last century and "the roaring twenties" this epitomize an overall conception of these times. The debate about whether the last decade began in 1980 or 1981 may be of academic interest, but it matters little in itself when concentration is upon the images through which decades are given signification for later generations. The association of the sixties with flower-power love children, more or less public pot smoking, and antiwar protests plays upon images that do relate to that period of ten years. All the same, what was in vogue in terms of clothes and attitudes in San Francisco in the middle of the decade bears little relation to what might have been in vogue in London in 1961, for example. The sharp differences between periods and places are quickly eroded to provide a neatly packaged cluster of impressions that become the folk memory of the sixties.

That images are tenacious and invested with meanings not necessarily of their period's making is further demonstrated in relation to the sixties, a period and name which have been heavily exploited by conservative thinkers, especially in Great Britain. Saddled with all the connotations that the term "permissiveness" summons up when uttered vituperatively, the sixties has been made into a composite by certain politicians and moralists. Since, largely, they lived through the period, they might be expected to recognize the absence of unified meaning and explanation for the various phenomena that are attacked under the sixties umbrella, but they manifestly do not. (Explanations for failure of government in matters of public law and order, or in matters relating to the unceasing claims of "falling educational standards," are still, in 1990, offered in terms of "permissiveness," if not of the period supposed to epitomize that phenomenon.)

Normally, thinking in decades is unhelpful because it leads to oversimplification and historical inaccuracy, however attractive the

11

habit may be to pundits and professional politicians. The eighties, on the other hand, does have a kind of credible unity, one that goes deeper than image (deep as image is made to go at the service of opinion formers), at least insofar as these years have been experienced in the United States and Great Britain. Such unity is discoverable in the consequences of the 1979 general election in Great Britain and of the 1980 presidential election in the United States. The triumph of the Conservative party in Britain and Ronald Reagan's success, followed by conservative achievements on both sides of the Atlantic in the eighties, provide a unity which cannot be explained away as simply the tidying up of messy events by image creators.

Both Margaret Thatcher and Ronald Reagan have been taken to embody neoconservatism. The radical shift in Britain after 1979, away from the postwar consensus that seems to have dominated political thinking of left, right, and center, means that Thatcher's brand of Conservative politics has been occasionally as much a shock (or tonic) to party members as to her (often fragmented and disarmed) opposition parties. Reagan's forthright rejection of what the Carter years were taken to represent in, for example, the evolution of Reaganomics, his slashing of public funding, his militant opposition to the air-traffic controllers' strike of 1981, represents again not simply a break from Democratic thinking but from the traditions of the American Old Right.

At least to the extent that the eighties are the years of Reagan and Thatcher in power (sometimes in power together, it seemed, as at the time of the air strike against Libya, in which Mrs. Thatcher permitted Reagan's forces to use bases situated on British soil), they are a time of distinct change and novelty. How that change and novelty may have been experienced by American and British citizens, as well as by citizens of other countries, will of course depend on such factors as social, racial, and sexual positioning, and the political bias, of the citizen concerned. Trade-union members or professionals concerned with the National Health Service or the public sector of education could be expected to have somewhat different views of Thatcherism's achievement than, for example, captains of industry or City financiers, although teachers, doctors, trade-union members may conceivably have voted Conservative in three general elections, and some stockbrokers voted for an opposition party. (Indeed, the Conservative victory in 1979 is widely interpreted as having been achieved partly by the breaking of traditional working-class voting patterns.)

Although no part of public or private life seems to be untouched by the long decade of Thatcherism in Great Britain, what is immediately recognizable in the eighties, unique to it until, that is, there are other completed decades, is AIDS. A fierce debate continues to rage around the significance of AIDS. As long as the disease is deemed to be circumscribed in its "habits," to have "chosen" to kill heroin addicts, male homosexuals, immigrant Haitians, and children of drug-dependent parents, as well as a few hemophiliacs, the media have convinced the public, by a convoluted process of thought, that it is of little consequence. (The insignificance allowed to attach to the deaths of thousands of productive citizens within a democracy ought surely to be an indelible blot on the history of the eighties.) The moment that the isolated HIV virus is thought to explain AIDS and that there is some realization of absurdity in the notion of a virus making (moral) choices, the moment that it is feared that the "general population" might be susceptible, AIDS becomes a matter of enormous consequence, ushering in the final collapse of Western civilization. And, as with plague thinking in general, those responsible for the epidemic are sought. They are found, not in the conservative politicians who jealously guarded public money, protected it from being frittered away on AIDS research, but in AIDS sufferers.

Whatever the perception of AIDS, it is new, or at least its naming and perception are new. (The disease may well have been around considerably earlier than the period of its identification would suggest.) AIDS suffering and AIDS deaths are a fact. AIDS itself is, paradoxically, not. It is a construction whose medical meaning has been determined by "experts" interpreting data in a particular, and exclusive, way. Moreover, the public and professional/medical/political attitudes to AIDS help to explain its progress, if not indeed its genesis. Those attitudes are bound up with sexual attitudes, since AIDS was first considered to be "the gay plague" and publicized as such on both sides of the Atlantic. Therefore, in order to understand the attitudes to a uniquely eighties phenomenon, the book considers sexual ideology and the eighties conceptions of sexuality. Since notions of "family-oriented" sexuality were, and still are, given such currency by politicans of the Right (who remain largely unchallenged in this by politicians of the Left), consideration of sexuality inevitably raises matters of familialism.

Thus, this book arrives at consideration of that most dreadful and most uniquely contemporary of phenomena, AIDS, by an, apparently, circuitous route; it considers Reagan-Thatcher ideology, and then considers familialism, conceptions of sexuality in general, and of homosexuality in particular, before exploring AIDS. What it explores, more accurately, is the understanding of AIDS. While medical "facts" are adduced, the aim of the relevant chapter is not to provide a handbook of information to potential persons with AIDS (everybody?). There are enough such handbooks. Some of them may represent part of the problem. The understanding of AIDS is more crucial than may seem possible at first consideration, in that there are commentators on the disease who would claim that susceptibility to it as well as recovery from it are intimately bound up with conceptions of it. To put it more simply, it may be less easy to avoid dying of AIDS complications if you believe that it represents the righteous anger of God and that you fully deserve that anger. While there is no intention—or ability—on the part of this book to valorize or to negate such claims, it is important that they be made available for the consideration of all students of the ideology of AIDS.

Since the book is about ideology, the ideology of AIDS and the ideologies involved in its understanding and treatment, it repeatedly uses popular cinema (and occasionally less popular cinema) to help to clarify the mediation of issues of familialism, sexuality, and, more problematically, AIDS to the wider public. Movies, and to an increasing extent, television "make political demonology visible in widely popular and influential forms."[1]

The interconnection of mass media practice and social perception "validated" by that practice is maintained by such investigators as Perloff, Brown, and Miller, when they conclude that, for instance, television's sex-role stereotyping proves consistent with society's pervasive stereotyping of sex roles—and that it would be politically foolish for the government, economically foolish for the networks, to reduce sex-typed portrayals substantially.[2] (Their identification of political folly could be challenged—politics can be more than a matter of staying in power by flattering the electorate's perceptions—but the suggestion of strong interconnection remains.) Caroline Sheldon goes further in her analysis of the connection. She points out that films may be considered commodities but also ideological products (determined by many historical, social, and cultural factors) often to maintain depoliticization.[3]

Two ideas of great popularity in their ambition to explain the relation of media representation and society are the reflection hypothesis and that of symbolic annihilation. The former seems too crude in practice. Happy families appear in sitcoms not necessarily because the majority of people live in similar happy families as in sitcomland. What we may discover by attention to representation could be, though, ideological wishfulness or need. One explanation is that "representation in the fictional world" should be taken to signify "social existence," and that lack of representation, or condemnation and trivialization, indicates symbolic annihilation.[4] How symbolic annihilation takes place, and why, would generate another set of debates. Stuart Hall attempts an explanation when he writes, "The area of what is considered as 'reasonable talk' about anything, as the appropriate and inappropriate registers, as the intangible boundaries which rule the inclusion or exclusion of certain things, certain points of view, is one of the most powerful of the ways the media's regimes of truth come to be established."[5]

If this explanation of media-social relations through ideology is left intact, the result may be an exaggeration of the passivity of reception, suggesting that there can be no intervention by the receiver in the decoding of the message. As Gamman and Marshment put it, popular culture is a site of struggle. It should not be dismissed as merely serving the systems of capitalism and patriarchy, feeding the masses with "false consciousness." "It can also be seen as a site where meanings are contested and where dominant ideologies can be disturbed . . . between what things mean, and how they mean, is a perpetual struggle for control."[6]

A Note on the Use of the Evidence of Movies

Critical reception of two of my previous books dealing at some level with popular, largely "Hollywood," movies is worth recalling at the outset of this book—which again deals at some level with popular movies.

Implicit in certain reviews was a feeling that a book which deals to some significant extent with movies must be a book principally "about" movies: in other words, a movie book. One reviewer, who dealt generously and enthusiastically with the first book, *Hollywood's Small Towns*,[7] seemed to review *Misogyny in the Movies*[8] largely in terms of its subtitle, *The De Palma Question*. The book was conceived, as its short title suggests, as an inquiry into (largely feminist) argument, often dense and difficult, concerning cinematic manifestations of misogyny; De Palma's films—because they are taken to be so unequivocally misogynistic—functioned in the book as a particularly succinct test case for the body of theory. If it could be shown, through attention to the corpus of De Palma's work, that the self-evident was questionable and, *along the lines of the very feminist argument marshalled against it,* open to less politically retrograde reading, there could be a reappraisal of the relationship between such work as Laura Mulvey's and dominant cinema's practices.

The book was conceived only secondarily as a book about De Palma. Reviewed in terms of admiration for De Palma, it is unsatisfactory on that subject, and may indeed appear, as the reviewer called it, tediously argumentative. The argumentation, whether or not tediously handled, was largely that of feminism, particularly of feminist appropriation of psychoanalysis. These arguments seem crucial for appreciation of the charges of misogyny. They may not be so crucial—even if they are arguably relevant—for appreciation of De Palma.

It is important, given this experience, that the present book does not pose as a movie book, or at least does not easily allow itself to be taken for one. The many films cited in the various chapters following treatments of such topics as Familialism, Sexuality, etc., are so cited to indicate the apparent range of popular interest in these areas. There is no attempt to "review" the films in terms of their success or failure by whatever criteria, though sometimes there is a passing indication of their appeal or lack of it to this writer. There is no attempt to claim that an encyclopedic list of relevant movies is being offered. They are there as proof of the importance accorded to such topics in popular entertainment and of the general slant given to that importance by popular entertainment.

The relation between media representation and what could naively be termed "reality" or even "social actuality" deserves exploration in depth. The citation of many filmic examples in the relevant chapters is not intended to answer that need. Some of the fuller consideration required is deferred until chapter 12, when a few movies are treated as "key" elements in relation to representation in the eighties. The factors that make a movie "key" are highly peculiar to the concerns of this book. Other analysts, analysing other phenomena, would quickly find a quite different set of movies as deserving of special attention. The particular movies chosen for fuller consideration are taken to be summations of certain tendencies in other movies already, in earlier chapters, reckoned to be highly relevant to the eighties phenomena under discussion elsewhere. There is no doubt that there could be some substitutions, some different choices even in terms of that summation, that there must be an element of the subjective in relation to those movies labelled "key."

Although whole chapters are devoted to movies, then, it is the relationship between eighties movies and questions of New Right thinking in general, familialism, sexuality, homosexuality, and AIDS—thus the relationship of media representation and these areas—that is being explored, not the valorization or denigration of movies in aesthetic or more ambitious socio-realist terms.

What is emphatically rejected from the outset of the discussion of movies in this book is "reflectionism," or the attitude that genre, and otherwise popular, cinema simply "mirrors"—either in terms of truth or distortion—social actuality. Rather, the attempt is to demonstrate that popular movies have a determining effect on what might be identified as social actuality, that there is a curious analogy between what might be unmasked of the horror film and what is believed to be "true," objectively, of AIDS, between what Carter-age movies have to say of sexual permissiveness and the conception of AIDS as Heaven-sent punishment lying in wait for those who have flouted social convention.

This is both to demote movies to a more marginal position than they usually occupy in books of film appreciation but, in so doing, also to give unusual recognition to their power, to their being much, much more than mere entertainment.

2

The Reagan-Thatcher Epoch

Reagan and Thatcher as the Answers to a Need

Lawrence Grossberg's explanation of the popular appeal of Reaganism includes the observation: "Feeling something, anything, is better than feeling nothing. Living some identity, however temporary, is better than living none. And the choice may have little relation to the significance of the identity itself but merely to its temporary ability to mark some affective difference and distance."[1] Grossberg stresses, in this explanation, the need to feel: to feel passionate commitment over against ideological consistency, the passion and the commitment more important than that about which passion is felt or to which commitment is made. According to him, Reaganism and the American New Right seized upon the contradiction between the emergent popular sensibility categorized by Grossberg as "postmodernity" and the identification between America's national identity and youth culture.[2] He claims that Reaganism's elevation of passionate commitment was based on an increasingly shared mistrust of common sense, that by means of this mistrust, reconstruction of "a national popular" could be undertaken.

The success of the American Right is no more marked, by his explanation, than the failure of the American Left to grasp the significance of the factors behind the rearticulation achieved by Reaganism, and thus the failure of the Left to engage in the struggle. The sites of that struggle, identified as the family, nationalism, consumerism, youth, pleasure, heroes, were not created by the Right, although they were commandeered by it, implementing its grasp of the mistrust of common sense and the widely experienced need for affect.

Real ideological battles, Grossberg accepts, are fought under Reagan's presidency. Not only does selectivity, as well as lies, in description and reporting of events occur in the eighties but large numbers of Americans actually assume that they are being lied to.

The point of his analysis is, though, to establish that hegemonic struggle in America has been dedicated to the "reconstruction of the political investment in and of the nation" by means of a redistribution of the cultural sites of Americans' affective investment.[3] In simpler terms, Reaganism has attempted to empty its construction of America in ideological terms and to provide, in lieu, potent emotional charges. Thus, for example, the president's anti-communism is taken by Grossberg to be not a political platform or an ideological interpretation but, rather, an emotionally empowering state.[4]

Viewed in this way, Reaganism's strategies for undermining resistance through use of "the very sites of everyday empowerment"[5] were peculiarly difficult for the Left to resist. The New Right did not so much capture state control as win a victory within the popular, in a way that the Left could not while it concerned itself with ideology and what traditionally passes for politics.

Reaganite entertainment, as identified by, for example, Andrew Britton, is marked by its insistence on being no more than that, "entertainment." Its reference is not outward to conceptions of sociopolitical actuality but inward or else "sideways" to other media products. "The conventions of Reaganite entertainment . . . function . . . to inhibit articulation, and the impediments to thematic development which they set up must be referred to this function."[6]

The quest for passionate commitment in the late seventies seems, however, not to be a localized phenomenon. It has been argued that, for example, the firmer moral leadership provided by Pope John Paul II and the new fundamentalism in Iran, which sanctioned the stoning of adulterers and sodomites, evidence a widely experienced desire in that period for a new moral absolutism.[7] While desire for moral absolutism is only one aspect of the craving for passionate commitment, it is an important aspect, which may help to explain, beyond the Roman Catholic and Muslim worlds, the appeal of, say, patriotism and familialism.

The British mood of intense, bellicose, patriotic fervor identified by Hall and Jacques with the early eighties is believed by them to be a matter of Thatcherite inspiration. In their view, the Falklands crisis demonstrates Thatcherism's ability to exploit the appeal of the concept of the "Nation" and to manipulate imperialistic nostalgia within a patriotism that cuts across traditional political allegiances.[8]

The historical conjuncture at which Thatcherism appeared is located as a point where three trends converged: (1) the synchronization of the British economy's long-term structural decline with the deepened recession of the capitalist economy worldwide; (2) the collapse of the Labour government and the disintegration of the social democratic consensus that underlay British politics since the end of the Second World War and (3) resumption of a new phase in the "Cold War," at an advanced stage of the stockpiling of nuclear weaponry.[9]

While Hall and Jacques view Thatcherism as novel and exceptional in political terms, it is difficult to determine from their account whether a British version of the allegedly widely experienced craving for affect helps to explain Thatcherism's appeal—whether, in other words, a novel and exceptional politics exploits a novel and exceptional popular "feeling." The Labour government did indeed come to an end as a consequence of Mrs. Thatcher's election victory in 1979, and her radical form of Conservatism certainly indicates the disintegration of the social democratic consensus. Still, it is interesting, if problematic, to speculate whether Thatcherism should be seen as a creature of a wider popular need for affect and commitment as against consensual passionlessness (in the way that Reaganism is seen by Grossberg as one possible response to that need within American experience) or whether it "causes" the demise of, for example, consensus politics. It is clear that the heartlands of traditional Labour party support were penetrated by Thatcherism's appeal in 1979, and that a significant facet of Thatcherism is its populism. Nevertheless, a question prompted by these observations is whether Thatcherism was primarily a political phenomenon, in the conventional understanding of "political," or whether the analyst has to step beyond the categories of Left and Right, be they traditional or radical, into the terrain deemed appropriate by Lawrence Grossberg for comprehension of Reaganism's appeal.[10] On the other hand, it is easily possible that the popular appeal of both Reaganism and Thatcherism might be overestimated.

The peculiarities of the British electoral system, which sets its face resolutely, thanks to the opposition of both the Conservative and Labour parties, against the more "European" practice of proportional representation, mean that a government may be elected without overwhelming positive electoral support, provided that the opposition is split by a multiplicity of parties and their candidates. It may be more interesting to ask why the opposition to the new Conservatism was so split and why the Labour party so signally lost the 1979 election than to inquire on what the Thatcher government based its ostensibly popular appeal.

The claim of a Reagan landslide in 1980 does not become true merely because it has so often been repeated. Still, the television evangelist Jerry Falwell not only made the claim but took the credit for the alleged landslide, providing himself with an excuse to press forward with "profamily" legislation.[11] Zillah Eisenstein specifically denies the veracity of the Reagan landslide, however. Reagan's victory in 1980 was, for her, a reflection of "a small, highly mobilized and organized section of the electorate alongside a much larger, disorganized, disenfranchised public which did not vote." Thus, she concludes, "although the 1980 election highlights the shifting to the right *within the state itself* (a shift which was initiated under Carter), this is different from saying that there is massive or even majority support for this shift by the public."[12] She notes that the turnout of voters represented approximately 53 percent of the electorate, and that Reagan polled 27 percent, Carter 22 percent. On her reckoning, three-quarters of the electorate did not vote for Reagan in 1980; thus, he received the lowest percentage of actual votes in recent history.[13]

It is too simplistic to conclude that because these two leaders were victorious in the elections of 1979 and 1980, they therefore enjoyed huge electoral support. Yet both were reelected, Thatcher twice. They seemed to create a popularity for themselves which, arguably, they may not have enjoyed from the outset or at all times. (Mrs. Thatcher's popularity, to judge by the polls, was significantly low before the Falklands crisis—and clearly fell significantly lower at the time of her resignation, in November 1990.) In other words, if Thatcher and Reagan did not evidently meet a need at the time of their electoral victories, their survival in the eighties is well worth scrutiny in terms of the needs which they could be thought to have been meeting during that decade. Those needs may well be summed up in the opening statement of this chapter.

The New Right

The appellation of the New Right is self-chosen. Associates of Richard A. Viguerie applied it to themselves in order to enjoy distinction from what they considered to be the effete East Coast Old Right, organized under such leaders as William F. Buckley, Jr. The latter conservative tradition in turn distanced itself from the more radical Right, described by Alan Crawford in 1980 as "anything but conservative."[14]

The politics of the New Right may be sharply distinguished from the traditional politics of both Left and Right in that it appears to be markedly less concerned with the careful working out of public policy or with programs aimed at social betterment, as variously conceived by parties of the Left or Right. True to the picture of the new politics painted by Lawrence Grossberg, the New Right would appear to be far more interested in social protest, passionate assertion, and denunciation in place of argument. Crawford describes the New Right in the seventies as drawing its considerable funds from blue-collar workers and housewives, and feeding on the anger, insecurity, and resentment experienced by such lower-middle-class supporters. Their class hostility against those above and below them on the economic ladder is expressed in the period in terms of backlash politics. While the political party deemed to be most significantly benefited by such supporters of the New Right is the Republican party, New Right activities run counter to those engaged in by political activists of whatever coloring before the late seventies, as instanced by the fact that the single issue becomes crucial to New Right politics.[15]

The attractiveness of the single issue for the New Right's supporters is evident, in that thereby passion may all the more easily be substituted for ostensibly reasoned debate, and a clear issue may be identified and decided. While the single issues could be subsumed under such larger objectives as lower taxes, a higher defense budget, or less federal regulation of small business, their apparent individuality can separately raise a single question which may be decided with a simple answer, capable of rapid and easy conceptualization in terms of moralism. The apparently discrete questions surrounding gun control, gay rights, abortion, forced busing, and equal-rights legislation are capable of being dealt with one by one. Overall attitudes emerge by implication and accretion rather than by programmatic assertion.

If the separate answers add up to a set of political attitudes, the encouragement by the New Right is for the electorate to think less of the general political posture and to "deal with" issues singly, to bypass traditional political debate in favor of "conscience" and doctrinaire, often fundamentalist, moralism. Gut reaction replaces political or intellectual sophistication. The appeal of single issues is not difficult to appreciate. "It is . . . easy issues that have given the New Right's special interest groups their appeal to large segments of the public."[16] The result of inattention to the wider consequences of single-issue concentration has been identified as inconsistency, inequity, incipient chaos, and lack of intragovernmental coordination.[17]

While it is possible to see the Nixon administration as an incubation period, it is during the period beginning in 1976 where most evidently a new sort of political activity emerges, one in which those customarily uninterested in politics hold national rallies and grow confident in their awareness of their voting power. The resentments and frustrations mobilized by the more politically astute New Right leaders are certainly not new. Nor, in their essence, are they peculiar to the United States. What focuses these resentments and frustrations is, first, the alliance of the New Christian Right with the more "political" New Right and, second, the availability of technologies and of new methodologies for the publicizing of attitudes and the unifying of disparately experienced resentments.

The religion embraced by the New Right is fundamentalist and insistent on an orthodoxy, and, though avowedly Christian and essentially Protestant, appeals to some Jews, as well as to some Roman Catholics. As Andrea Dworkin puts it, "The moral order and the social order are supposed to mirror each other: authority, hierarchy, and property are God-given values, not to be compromised by secular humanists, atheists, or liberals who have perverse ideas about equality."[18] In an intensely secularized society such as the United States, fundamentalists of the seventies were able to muster doomsday fears and to draw upon a sense of America's having "gone wrong," having strayed from the paths of righteousness, by pointing to such signs of national degeneracy as the Supreme Court's 1973 decision on abortion, the accessibility of pornography, gay activists' demands for civil rights, and the widely perceived decline of America's military prestige in relation to Soviet power.

The New Christian Right's fears, and its answers to these fears, were capable of wide dissemination through the power of television. The "electronic churches" of such "televangelists" as Jim Bakker, Jerry Falwell, and Pat Robertson could draw upon their considerable finances to organize what would otherwise have been widely scattered and inarticulate opposition to certain aspects of contemporary American life. In addition, such organizations as the Moral Majority, Christian Voice, and the Religious Roundtable used computerized direct-mail agencies to reach their hitherto disorganized and inactive supporters. Erling Jorstad reckons that between 1976 and 1980, one million dollars per week per program was elicited from television viewers for the New Christian Right of the airwaves, and that direct-mail solicitors reached twenty million voters with "moral report cards" circulated in the states of targeted senators and representatives.[19]

President Carter stayed away from the huge convention of the Christian Right at Dallas, but Ronald Reagan turned up at it in the period of his challenge to Carter. He is reported to have said, on 22 August 1980, "I know you can't endorse me, but I want you to know that I endorse you and what you are doing," and to have thus created such enthusiasm for him that his divorce and remarriage and his—in percentage terms—insignificant donations to charitable and religious organizations from his 1979 adjusted gross income were overlooked.[20]

The alliance of hitherto depoliticized malcontents with the highly organized, well-funded, and technologically reliant New Christian Right meant that a sense of moral certainty and righteousness could be developed and that there could be active proselytization of all who felt that secular developments were passing them by or leaving them bewildered. Reagan benefited the Christian Right by conferring legitimacy on them through, for example, his no fewer than five addresses to the National Religious Broadcasters.[21] He benefited by underpinning his policies and beliefs with religious conviction, whether "acted" or sincere. In Hadden and Shupe's view, "Whether or not religious principles have always undergirded Reagan's worldview is an open question. But it is clear that he sees religious significance in, and has offered religious explanations for, many of his policies in public office."[22]

One of the commonest appeals from conservative thinkers or "radical-Right" nonthinkers is to the notion of the "natural." The power of an analysis of class, race or sexual relations in terms of an assumed "Nature" is obviously augmented by the notion of the "God-given," since it is foolish to attempt to combat what is simply "human nature," but it is wicked and blasphemous to combat a human nature designed by God.

The social doctrine advanced by Hobbes, that male dominance is merely the effect of male aggression (so that biologically given sex differences account for the greater social power of men over women), is extended by the Right to explain manifold other unequal power relations. These inequalities are defended by appeals to Nature and, all the more powerfully, to God's wisdom in the creation of that Nature. As Andrea Dworkin puts it, "In the U.S., the hierarchy the Right defends is rich over poor, white over black, man over woman. There is a frequently articulated belief that social inequality simply expresses natural or God-given differences; that hierarchy is unchangeable. It is frequently argued that those who want equality want to change 'the nature of man.' "[23]

In contrast with the situation in the United States, where Reaganism formed something of a public alliance with the New Christian Right, Thatcherism—in the sense of the public posture of Thatcher's party and of her cabinet—disavowed such embroilment with analogous interest groups. Officially, there was a "neutral" policy on abortion, divorce, and gay rights, although such a claim must be weighed against, for example, the reality of Section 28 of the British Local Government Act, 1988 (which seems far from neutral on gay rights), voted in during a period of an unassailable Conservative majority in Thatcher's third term of prime ministerial office.

Grossberg sees an absence of explicitness about the American New Right's project, the only pronounced objective seeming to be the return of America to its former (date unspecified) glory and strength, and detects a great degree of importance attaching to the popular in American New Right politics.[24] By contrast, he believes that "Thatcher does not so much attack popular culture as ignore it in an attempt to re-install an imaginary vision of British culture."[25] Thatcherism's concentration appears to be less on a sustained moralism than on a construction of "Britain" centering on an imaginary past, together with a construction of the enemy within.[26]

Reagan/Thatcher: Hobbyhorses and Bugbears

The passionate commitment of these leaders on behalf of or against certain ideas, people, and elements may find its roots in their individual psyches, or in their relation with the New Right and therefore, necessarily, with its attitudes, or, again, in a combination of these factors. Whatever the explanation, it is easily possible to detect certain recurrent attitudes in their discourse, as well as in their actions and declared policies.

Lloyd deMause, in his study of the first term of Reaganism, is fascinated with Ronald Reagan's personality. He detects in him castration anxiety, manifesting itself during his acting career via, for example, the panic he felt about playing a man whose legs are amputated at the climax of *Kings Row* (Sam Wood, 1942),[27] and later, in his presidential discourse.[28]

Michael Paul Rogin detects a demonologist in him. In broad terms, Rogin characterizes a demonologist as one who splits the world in two, attributing magical, pervasive potency to the bad half, a center of evil which emits its malign influence by conspiracy, so that the demonologist's mission is one of countersubversion. The American brand of countersubversion takes its shape, he argues, from the pervasiveness of propertied individualism in American political culture, from the expansionist character of American history, and from the definition of American identity, against what are determined to be aliens, on lines of race, ethnicity, class, and gender.[29]

In the latter regard (demonological detection and countersubversion of the un-American alien), the peculiar attractiveness of cancer in its metaphorical aspect as "alien invasion" becomes obvious. As Susan Sontag has observed, "Cancer is a demonic pregnancy. . . . The patient is 'invaded' by alien cells which multiply, causing an atrophy or blockage of bodily functions."[30] Rogin believes that, uniquely among presidents since the Second World War, Reagan has separated benignity from malignity in terms of national boundaries. He has been the benign center of America, keeping malignancies outside America, and thereby directing popular attention to the high priority of keeping American borders impenetrable by these alien forces of malignancy.[31] "Even the bodily well-being of the leader was equated with the health of the body politic (for the cancer that had been cut out of the president's body must now, before he left office, be excised from 'the American mainland' [in reference to Nicaragua] as well."[32]

DeMause, having argued that Ronald Reagan's phobic obsession with illness was evident even to Hollywood film directors, who usually cast him as sick, notes that in his presidential utterances the metaphors of health and disease keep recurring. Thus, the problems of the economy are likened to a disease out of control.[33] With the recovery of the economy in late 1982, deMause argues that Reagan's morbid fascination with ill health is redirected, that what he calls the Great Reagan Poison Alert (a period of six months in 1983 when there was domination of the media "by fears of disease and poisons of all sorts, real and imaginary, usually connected with fantasies of punishment for sexuality") must be so explained.[34]

Given the claimed hypochondriacal obsessions of the American president, his insistence on presenting himself as the source of health who kept alien ill health at bay by keeping it beyond the national borders, and given the long-standing metaphorical connection between the human body and the body politic, taken to new extremes in Reagan's discourse, the terror inspired by AIDS is readily comprehensible. The perception of a need to police the body, to defend its health by protecting its borders from alien invasion, is evident enough. What renders AIDS peculiarly terrifying under the influence of a demonologist whose unique achievement was to dissociate himself from the sickly alien by keeping that alien beyond his (and America's) borders is that HIV is seen as the first human retrovirus. In other words, it is an invader that may already have penetrated the body and that hides within the body's borders, an alien that seems like part of ourselves.[35] Arthur and Marilouise Kroker write in 1988 of the politics of Body McCarthyism in the United States, again making an overt connection between the human body's immune system and the immunological order of the body politic. "The politics of Body McCarthyism, which is motivated by panic fear of viral contamination, . . . responds to a double crisis moment (the *external* crisis as the breakdown of the immunological order in economy [panic money], culture [panic media], and politics [panic Constitution]; and the *internal* crisis as the existential breakdown of the American mind into a panic zone) . . . It focusses on the illusory search for the perfect immunity system; and it calls up for its solution a whole strategical language of cellular genetics, from AIDS research to star wars."[36]

The fuller discussion of AIDS is reserved for chapter 10 of this book. For the present, it may be relevant to note that the understanding of a disease may be far more crucial than was hitherto realized and that a country's understanding of a new disease may be vitally affected by the metaphors habitually employed by that country's leader, that an individual leader's obsessions can vitally augment the horror and "other-ness" of AIDS within a culture conditioned to consider itself protected inside a benign center's sphere of benign influence, relegating disease to the alien who is seen as literally outside that sphere.

The alien brought into existence by Reaganite discourse has as a counterpart the welfare state's public sector, the social workers, educators, city planners, and so on, who are discerned to have been picked out for attack by means of Reagan's 1981 budget cuts.[37] The New Right's ideology has the ring of liberalism, since it ostensibly supports equality of opportunity and individualism, but the results of New Right hostility to the welfare state may work in quite different ways. Both Reagan and Phyllis Schlafly would claim to be in support of equal rights for women. Yet, they did not support the Equal Rights Amendment, on the grounds that ERA encouraged state intervention in the private lives of individuals. Again, while Carter and Reagan seem united in their profamily stance, there is a world of difference between belief under the Carter administration that the family's welfare requires upgrading of social services and belief under Reagan that family welfare demands noninterference by the state. (Interestingly, there is no adverse commentary under the same administration on increased state spending in the military area.)[38] Thatcher's government appeared to find the welfare state and state "interference" no more supportable than the Reagan administration did, and pursued an economic policy dedicated to discouraging or to preventing welfarism and to promoting privatization strategies within the spheres of education and, most controversially of all, medicine.

One of her most noticeable bugbears, to judge by Mrs. Thatcher's speeches, was all that she summed up under the names of "the sixties" or—so closely allied as sometimes to be indistinguishable in import—"permissiveness." On 27 March 1982, she said, "We are reaping what was sown in the sixties. The fashioniable theories and permissive claptrap set the scene for a society in which the old virtues of discipline and self-restraint were denigrated."[39] At the end of the decade, she was still explaining what to her was unattractive in British life through the errors of the sixties. The decade, and particularly the sexual revolution associated with it, has been singled out for castigation by radical feminists also, who feel that women were duped by the male-centered claims of sexual liberation made during that period. In this way, the decade has united unlikely partners who otherwise have little in common—radical feminists and such right-wing moralists as Mary Whitehouse—in what has been labeled the "new puritanism."[40]

Even if the sixties can fairly be associated with a noteworthy liberalization of sexual attitudes—not, though, a sexual revolution in any sustainable sense of the latter word—it is possible to explain the claimed moral declension in other terms. Jeffrey Weeks, for example, offers the interpretation that the traditional bourgeois virtues of self-denial and of saving had to give way to the need to spend, in order for the postwar boom to continue—thus, the "liberalization" of the decade is, in effect, demanded by the requirements of capitalism.[41]

In both Reagan's America and Thatcher's Britain, consensus politics is viewed with strong suspicion and undisguised hostility. It is possible to see interest group liberalism as the principal system of government from the time of Roosevelt's New Deal up to the 1980 election. Not thereafter. From the time of Reagan's victory, the trade unions and the liberal base associated above all with the Democratic party are given little place in government.[42]

Equally, under Thatcherism, self-help and individualism are encouraged and lauded, while "socialism" and "the welfare state," along with "the sixties" and "permissiveness," become terms of bitter opprobrium. "Thatcherism has successfully attempted to organise the diverse forces of the 'backlash'—reacting against trade union militancy, national aspirations, permissiveness, women's liberation—in favour of an essentially regressive and conservative solution embracing such themes as authority, law and order, patriotism, national unity, the family and individual freedom."[43] The mobilization of popular feeling against consensus politics was achieved by emphasizing big (and therefore impersonal) government and linking that big, antipersonal government with previously obtaining social democracy, characterized in terms of its "statism."[44] Thus, the nonpolitical "little person" is made to feel that his or her best interests are denied by the huge, complex welfare state, while any anarchistic appeal in the philosophy of individualism is contained by fear—the orchestrated popular cry for law and order enabling authority to be imposed without resistance from those on whom it has been imposed.

It is by reason of this process that Hall and Jacques term Thatcher's brand of Toryism "an authoritarian populism."[45] For Hall, the understanding of her "hegemonic project" is crucial. This project is explained by him in terms of "Thatcherism's search for 'the enemies within'; its operations across the different lines of division and identification in social life; its construction of the respectable, patriarchal, entrepreneurial subject with 'his' orthodox tastes, inclinations, preferences, opinions and prejudices as the stable subjective bedrock and guarantee of its purchase on our subjective worlds; its rooting of itself inside a particularly narrow, ethnocentric and exclusivist conception of 'national identity'; and its constant attempts to expel symbolically one sector of society after another from the imaginary community of the nation."[46]

The exclusivity of Thatcherite thinking on the individual on the one hand and group impersonality on the other, whereby she denies the reality of society while asserting that of individuals and their families, is crystallized by her "Sermon on the Mound." In May 1988, she preached to twelve hundred ministers and elders of the Church of Scotland at its General Assembly, avoiding the term "community" and choosing instead "the collective."[47] Criticizing her overestimate of the importance of the individual in society, the Church of Scotland moderator, the Right Reverend Professor James White, said of that speech that he had heard "much about the importance of the individual, a little about the family, but nothing at all about these other communities which give us our sense of where we belong. . . . Instead, the individual is contrasted with a dread concept called 'the collective,' as if we lived either as isolated individuals or in the stifling anonymity of a collective."[48]

Concomitant with the hostility to the consensual and the promotion of the individual and the family (unsupported by social services) on both sides of the Atlantic, a revival of positive valuation of machismo is discernible. Whether or not the value placed on "masculinity" and self-seeking aggression finds its illustration, as has been claimed, in the American public's fascination with and identification with rapists,[49] whether or not the need to rediscover the frontier[50] revivifies the hardy independence of pioneering men and dependable womenfolk, after the manner of the John Ford western, monetarism seems undeniably to involve the elevation of traditional masculinity. "In the popularization of a monetarist economic policy on both sides of the Atlantic, care has been taken to present these strategies as being proper to the competitive instincts of red-blooded American and British males. The call goes out to kill off lame ducks, to forswear compassion. It is asserted that in the market place only the fittest should survive, and that a hard, lean industrial sector is necessary."[51] Mrs. Thatcher, with her militaristic posture, her opposition to the women of Greenham Common, her expulsion of "wets" from her cabinet, made herself the near-embodiment of machismo.[52]

Alongside the emergence of machismo appears the extolling of sacrifice, the eschewing of the "good life" in favor of the greater austerity of asceticism. Casper G. Schmidt thinks of the introduction of Reaganomics in 1981, with its emphasis on pruning and slimming and sacrifice, as a manifestation of the belief that things have been "too good" in terms of "permissiveness" and that a period of withdrawal and self-castigation is inaugurated thereby.[53] It has been argued that the "brink of disaster" from which Reagan claims to have pulled America back by Reaganomics was a collective fantasy. "Never before in our history had a nation so strong and wealthy felt so weak and impoverished."[54] Reagan's success, by this explanation, was partly built on the fantasy need for a hero who would purge a degenerate nation of its sinful pleasures and make people pay—financially, too—for their backsliding.

National sacrifice seemed to be the watchwords for both Great Britain and Argentina in 1982 during the period of the Falklands invasion, which was, according to one interpretation at least, the culmination of the nation's need for self-immolation. Again according to that interpretation, during her first three years as prime minister, Mrs. Thatcher had almost doubled the British rate of unemployment, but that was insufficient purgation for the anxiety that seemed to follow on the prosperity of both the sixties and seventies, and, interestingly, on the upturn of British economic indicators after the summer of 1981.[55]

Reagan, Thatcher, and the Eighties

The two leaders were remarkably alike—in their commitment to capitalism, to a service economy in place of a manufacturing economy, in their hostility to compromise and social-democratic consensus, to civil liberties, and in their dedication to fashioning themselves into national leaders, unafraid of demanding sacrifice and of portraying themselves as possessed of the virtues of machismo. Together, they provided Americans and Britons with a sense of "the meaning of the eighties." One British commentator sees the decade as not only dominated by a single political party but "by the personality, politics and grand obsessions of a single political leader."[56]

Yet, dominant and dominating as they have been, champion capitalism as they might, these leaders were controlled by forces beyond themselves, since capitalism does not obey the dictates of even the most monetarist of Western leaders. Society in America and Britain is both patriarchal and capitalist, and "would return individuals to self-reliance while maintaining structural barriers related to economic, racial and sexual class that limit and curtail the individual."[57] Crucially, for such interest groups within American and British society as women and gay men, capitalism and patriarchy are not equatable, even if they are mutually dependent. Sexuality and economics may be closely related, but that relation is best described as dialectical.

It is perhaps in the interstices of Reagan's United States and Thatcher's Britain, where the "philosophies" associated with their names penetrate but cannot maintain absolute sway, that entertainment movies are most worthy of examination for what they tell us—not just of the new sorts of official ideology but of the sites of conflict, where that ideology encounters difficulty or resistance.

3

Movies and the Reagan-Thatcher Epoch

American Nationalism . . .

The blatancy of John Milius's *Red Dawn* (1984) makes it not only less interesting but less typical of American movies' embodiment of the spirit of Reaganite nationalism than, say, Taylor Hackford's *White Nights* (1985). Milius's film harks back to the sort of Cold War entertainment in which an invasion of an unremarkable area of the subcontinent is recognized for what it is and then repelled by a hitherto less unified, aware, or single-minded group recognizing the common bonds created by their civilization, which is more humane than that represented by the invaders. The explicit redness of Milius's dawn is noteworthy, since it is only by implication that Don Siegel's body snatchers and other fifties invaders from outer space have some relationship with Communism or Moscow.

The whiteness of Hackford's nights is not difficult to place in terms of a Soviet spectrum of colors. In addition, the movie is largely set in the Soviet Union. The most interesting inflection of a familiar anticommunism is, however, that the principal characters are a Russian ballet dancer (who formerly defected from the Soviet Union) and an American tap dancer. The threatened clash and actual coalition of high- and popular-culture dancing styles, revived by Mikhail Baryshnikov and Gregory Hines respectively, is not new. Similar feats of productive coexistence are achieved in, for example, Minnelli's 1953 musical, *The Band Wagon,* where it is Cyd Charisse as ballet dancer and Fred Astaire as "hoofer" who ally their talents in the cause of a musical show's success, after forming misleading prejudgments of each other's attitudes. What is new in this distant relation to the generically traditional tale, centering on movie-musical synthesis of high and popular culture in the interests of showbiz, is that these two dancers are, in context, testimony not only to freedom but to the freedom believed to be discoverable only in individualism—which is discoverable only in the West. It is not so much the teaming of two great talents from different dance traditions that is celebrated as the appearance of two great, but quite different, individual talents performing side by side, as it were, but in retention of their "uniqueness."

A factor which gives further "credibility" to the Reaganite picture of the United States as a haven of individual freedom as against the impoverishment of a state-controlled "official" culture is the casting of Baryshnikov, his biography readable as the flight of individual genius from constricting artistic bondage to welcoming liberation of his talent.

The movie appears to be—paradoxically, despite the political nature of the ballet dancer's choice to defect and the surprising overtness of the setting—principally an entertainment, in that the Baryshnikov character involves himself in politics only to fulfill himself in dance terms and to provide the extradiegetic as well as the diegetic audience with the pleasure of his virtuosity. The tactics of *White Nights* seem to suggest not exactly that it is only an entertainment, which is Andrew Britton's summary of the posture of Reaganite entertainment movies (see chapter 2), but that the precise point of politics is to release oneself from the hold of politics in order to get on with the real business of dazzling an audience, providing emotional charges rather than political messages. That this is in itself a political message is, obviously, concealed. Here, the state is what obstructs audience affect. Flight to the United States is to be understood as involving a recognition of American culture's superiority as evidenced in leaving highly talented individuals alone, in being, in that sense, "nonpolitical."

. . . and Militarism

The proximity of nationalism and militarism as issues makes the appearance of Harold Becker's *Taps* (1981) and the surprising, even to the industry, commercial success of Taylor Hackford's *An Officer and a Gentleman* (also 1981) more comprehensible so soon after Reagan's election. It is not difficult to discover New Right elements in both movies, but the temptation to categorize them as unproblematically rightist entertainment should be resisted, since attentive reading of the movies throws up areas of conflict which are resolved only with difficulty in the narratives concerned. The difficulties may be as revealing of irresoluble tensions within New Right ideology as of the nature of genre movies, which, arguably, always center on but never "satisfactorily" resolve ideological conflict—since the conflict is fundamental to American society throughout its history and cannot finally be resolved within it.

The crisis of *Taps* is brought about when Bunker Hill Military Academy is to be shut down and sold off for development as real estate. The cadets organize resistance under one of their number, Cadet Major Brian Moreland (Timothy Hutton). Their occupation of the building escalates into a siege, involving equipment from the military academy's armory. Division among the cadets begins to appear when they are confronted with the state police, with their own parents, and, ultimately, with National Guardsmen. A parley between Moreland and Colonel Kerby (Ronny Cox) fails to offer a solution, so that the siege is continued until Moreland, recognizing the hopelessness of the cadets' position, decides on honorable surrender. Gunfire is exchanged between the cadets and the troops, leading to the injury of several and the deaths of Moreland and Shawn (Tom Cruise).

Taps, in an obvious sense, is a film centering on what are traditionally right-wing values, above all those of militarism. Because, however, it dramatizes the split between two kinds of Right (the younger men being, paradoxically, the champions of an older, militaristic tradition embodied earlier in the film by George G. Scott's General character), its interest may be in its commentary on the New Right's conflict with the Old. Although the National Guard's caution as well as efficiency is depicted, the stars—Scott, Cruise, Hutton—play the parts of cadets or of those who inspire the cadets, and the Academy in this context attempts to preserve Old Right values (and property) against the depredations of capitalism in the particular sphere of the property market.

If *Taps* sets forth, but does not solve, questions concerning honor and tradition versus pragmatism and the demands of the market, the military education of *An Officer and a Gentleman* seems to center more on models of masculinity and femininity. The casting of Richard Gere is worthy of consideration, in that he, along with John Travolta and Robert Redford, for instance, is one of the few male objects of the erotic gaze in seventies movies. At the beginning of this movie, his retention of that objectified position through such devices as the Brandoesque motorcycle fetish appears to be, in this context, "problematic" in that he has to be rescued and reeducated by an induction into militarism.

The chief spokesperson for that system is played by Louis Gossett, Jr., whose opening speech to the new recruits sets out the basic opposition within the military's conception of maleness—

"steers and queers." Steve Jenkins's reading of Foley, the character played by Gossett, is that he is, as the dialogue indicates, "Mom and Dad" to the recruits, and that he sets the hero on the correct oedipal path by a castrating kick to the genitals when there is threatened diversion from it by his embracing the dead body of his fellow trainee.[1] The overt project of the movie, then, seems to be to teach masculinity by militaristic substitution in the absence of parental guidance. While that aim is indicated to be achieved in the confidence and gratitude finally expressed by Gere to Foley, the mise-en-scène suggests that it is less simple than that: rather, the physical appeal of Richard Gere is provided with a new setting, military props replacing the earlier motorcycle. He remains an object of the gaze in this setting—a possibility that, as Jenkins emphasizes, is hardly ruled out by the frequent repetition of the military command "Don't eyeball me."[2]

A similar uncertainty hovers over the female characters' induction into "correct" femininity. The severity and universality of the disapproval felt for the use of a fake pregnancy by Lynette (Lisa Blount) to trap her man into marriage is only uneasily incorporated into this movie. It has, after all, earlier presented with sympathy Lynette's more active role in the bedding down of her chosen man and has permitted Paula (Debra Winger) to remark on the gulf between what is permitted to a woman and what *Cosmopolitan* advises women to do.

British Nationalism

There is little need for demonstration that Ian Sharp's *Who Dares Wins* (1982) is intended precisely to celebrate the kind of military efficiency believed to have been responsible for the ending of the siege of the Iranian embassy in London, since the film's producer, Euan Lloyd, is known to have been, immediately after the event, trying to choose among various titles for a film of it. One of the most obviously Thatcherite elements in the script is the manner in which the kind of dissent in British society represented by the Campaign for Nuclear Disarmament, to the nuclear-deterrent militarism associated with Margaret Thatcher, is branded here as providing a front for terrorism.

Few eighties movies are as unsubtle as *Who Dares Wins* in their lionizing of Thatcherite values. Hugh Hudson's *Chariots of Fire* (1981), a surprise Academy Award winner for best picture, offers its nationalism in terms of the past and through unlikely representatives. Its dream of "Englishness" and of tradition is complicated by the oddity that its heroes are "outsiders" to that dream and experience rejection by the Establishment. Abrahams (Ben Cross) is a Jew, Liddell (Ian Charleson) a Scot (and therefore not, despite American imprecision in the use of the term, English) and also a Presbyterian at odds with the widespread secularity of British life in his determination not to compete on the Sabbath. Their athletic success does not simply redound to their own fame but to that of the country which they represent at the Olympics. Although Liddell rejects a particular brand of patriotism which would put appeal to "king and country" before his Presbyterian conscience, the country is somehow enriched, patriotism restored, by his victory.

The location of national glory in individuals who have suffered marginalization by that very nation's Establishment is curiously analogous to *An Officer and a Gentleman*'s choice of a black actor to play Foley, the instrument through which Richard Gere's education into becoming an American gentleman is achieved. Once again, as in *Taps,* a battle is fought out between one kind of—here discredited—conservative, traditionalist nationalism and a more youthful, upstart nationalism. Elements (standing for the unaristocratic bourgeoisie? the lower middle class?) heretofore undervalued by the Establishment revitalize and enrich the nation. These movies seems to suggest that there is nothing wrong, per se, with blacks, Scotsmen, or Jews, even when they assert their cultural difference, provided that ultimately they are working for the greater glory of the nation. The nation, in turn, needs to reexamine its attitudes to those deemed marginal to it so that their difference can be recuperated and glossed over in the interests of more important, national ideals.

Richard Eyre's *The Ploughman's Lunch* (1983) addresses itself to the issue of the rewriting of the past for the greater glory of the dominant politics of the present. It also concerns the means by which the hero, who deems himself in some respects inappropriately equipped, in terms of class and family, for the task, edits out the inconvenient to allow him to join the "right set." The title brings into prominence admen's successful imposition within British pubs of the lunchtime meal referred to as a "ploughman's lunch," creating connotations of rurality and tradition in place of its actual modernity and the artificiality of its creation.

The central character, James Penfield (Jonathan Pryce), a radio news editor for the British Broadcasting Corporation, believes that greater upward mobility in both professional and social terms will be secured for him by his writing of popular books on recent British history. The popularity of a particular kind of nationalism and militarism in the wake of the Falklands war suggests to him the good sense in producing a book on Suez, with the topic viewed in a way designed to ingratiate himself with those embracing current Tory thinking. In the interests of the new kind of Conservatism, Penfield abandons his political convictions. In order to pursue his affair with a television researcher, Susan Barrington (Charlie Dore), he conceals the fact of his working-class background in suburbia, where his mother is dying.

The price to pay for inclusion among the politically powerful seems, on this evidence, to be the falsification of personal past and present, together with a rewriting of history, so that, for example, it becomes conceivable to write a book on Suez to fit contemporary Thatcherite policy on the Falklands. The film pinpoints its action precisely in time by reference to the then-recent Falklands campaign and by the inclusion of its climactic scenes during an address by Margaret Thatcher to the Conservative Party Conference in Brighton. The inauthenticity of early eighties Britishness and the creation of nationalism by collective amnesia provide a bitter commentary on those films celebrating nationhood where a marginalized social group takes its place proudly in the nation by the very expedient of renouncing the history by which it has in the past been marginalized.

The "Spirit of the Eighties"

The principal sociopolitical function of Reaganite entertainment is taken by Robin Wood to be a discouragement to political activity through twinned strategies, one designed to persuade audiences that all is already well—reassurance—and another that all is so hopelessly wrong that resistance is useless. (Interestingly, Reaganite entertainment is not taken, by Andrew Britton at least,[3] to be necessarily entertainment appearing in the eighties [after Reagan's election], since one of the named "Reaganite" entertainments is *Star Wars* [George Lucas, 1977].)

Wood detects value in what he terms the "incoherence" of such key "Carter" movies as *Taxi Driver* (Martin Scorsese, 1976), *Looking for Mr. Goodbar* (Richard Brooks, 1977), and *Cruising* (William Friedkin, 1980) on the ground that these films' inability to provide solutions within the dominant ideology implicitly call out for social and sexual revolution. For Wood, their incoherence, "the proof that the issues and conflicts they [these movies] dramatize can no longer even appear to be resolvable within the system, within the dominant ideology," is eloquent proof of "the logical necessity for radicalism."[4] He draws a clear line between the seventies, the period when the dominant ideology came close to disintegration, and the eighties, a period dedicated to reaction, recuperation, and reassurance. The latter period does not attempt to provide the solution which the "incoherent texts" of the late seventies could not, but rather encourages a forgetting of the need for solutions.

Noticing that films he finds unreassuring do badly at the box office in the period, Wood offers an analysis of the elements within the "box office smash" movies of Steven Spielberg and George Lucas, drawing attention to what follows from his conclusions, that they offer:

1. Childishness—their success implies the populace's desire for infantilism, to evade responsibility

2. Special effects—dazzling, luxuriously unnecessary

3. Imagination/originality—the audience, though it wishes to be constructed as children, also wants to be sophisticated and "modern"

4. Nuclear anxiety—a widespread sense of helplessness encourages the sentiment that audiences should not worry since there is nothing they can do

5. Fear of Fascism—how are individualist hero and Fascist hero to be distinguished (a problem consequent on the prominence of the Right and its promotion of individualism, with its potential for Fascism)?

6. Restoration of the Father—concomitant restoration of women to subordination (together with restoration of blacks and gays) and promotion of the virtues of family life[5]

Some questions could be asked concerning this analysis. There seems, for example, to be an implicit belief that reading is unified and predetermined, or that audience reception exactly corresponds to what is taken to be producers' intentions. Yet, Wood himself reads the most commercially successful movies of the period in ways that must clearly go beyond the intentions imputed to the producers by his own analysis. (This is particularly true of his observations on nuclear anxiety and the fear of Fascism.) Broadly, it could be asked whether the refusal of many Reaganite films to confront their own contradictions does not speak eloquently of the ultimate failure of the political system in which the entertainment is produced to provide answers. There may be observable differences between key movies of the seventies and key movie entertainments deemed "Reaganite," but active reading of eighties movies may yield insights into the failure of dominant ideology as effectively as less "against-the-grain" analyses of their predecessors. In the course of this chapter, the "incoherences" in the sexual politics of *An Officer and a Gentleman,* the contradictions involved in popular-movie notions of nationalism, have already been observed. The movies may not foreground or encourage these observations, but that is different from concluding that the encouragement to forgetfulness must be obeyed.

That said, Wood's analyses are remarkably cogent. So is his interpretation of the star persona of Debra Winger. "What is at issue," he remarks after consideration of her character as an anti-feminist force in both *An Officer and a Gentleman* and *Terms of Endearment* (James L. Brooks, 1983) "is . . . the star image that has been constructed around her. Winger-as-star has become the indispensable 80s woman, a major focus for the return of the good old values of patriarchal capitalism and the restoration of women to their rightful place."[6]

His point about the restoration of gays to their appointed place (wherever that might be, other than in a convenient closet) is supported elsewhere. Dennis Altman notices, for example, that 1982 is a year when a number of movies with homosexual themes appear, but that the central viewpoint tends to be that of heterosexual male fantasy, as in *Personal Best* (Robert Towne), while he dismisses *Partners* (James Burrows) as another *Cage aux Folles.*[7] These viewpoints are echoed by Vito Russo's complaint that, for example, *Making Love* (Arthur Hiller, 1982 again) is a gay film for straight people.[8] Whether these films do or do not represent this particular kind of "restoration" of gay themes and characters— since that judgment would require demonstration that Hollywood movies had allowed them some autonomy previously—what is at the very least the retention of gay elements in their "proper," heterosexually determined place is worth remarking.

Andrew Britton makes a point relevant to the last observation when he states that Reaganite entertainment does not so much create as "consummate" preexisting social tendencies.[9] That Reaganite movies cannot address the problems that they themselves throw up is attributed by him to their mobilization of "the utopian imagination." Failure to address problems is both inevitable, since utopia is, by definition, unrealizable, but also explicable in terms of

Right social policy, which is surprisingly inimical in its effects to such elements of the Reaganite utopia as the late-nineteenth-century bourgeois family.[10]

Optimism about the Decade

Nancy Walker's *Can't Stop the Music* (1980) seems in retrospect a singularly ill-timed film, in that it is permeated with euphoria about the newly arriving eighties. This in itself seems unremarkable, since Reaganite entertainment has been identified with the celebration of utopia. In more generic terms, it could be argued that musicals embody the kind of euphoria and high energy that Steve Guttenberg attempts to embody when, during the titles sequence, he roller-skates through New York City streets singing the number "The Sound of the City." What suggests a seriously misconceived entertainment is that, while none of the characters is overtly gay, there is a discernible gay subtext to the movie. And the eighties does not, with a hindsight unavailable to the movie, seem utopian, to put the point very mildly, when studied from the viewpoint of American gay experience.

The movie centers upon the appeal of the Village People—a group associated originally, in the seventies, with a gay-disco ambience, although this "image" was subsequently explicitly rejected by the group.[11] One of its more ambitious musical numbers involves near-naked and, fleetingly, fully naked young men in a YMCA changing room, then in the swimming pool—as clearly objects of the erotic gaze as the young women forming Busy Berkeley's choruses.

The knowingness of the movie need not, of course, be assimilated by an audience interested exclusively in the screen romance between Guttenberg and Valerie Perrine or their efforts to promote a promising new singing-dancing group (one of whom happens to be dressed as a construction worker, another as a loinclothed Red Indian). The detail that the Guttenberg character's doting mother (June Havoc) holds her grand charity party in San Francisco may be of no particular consequence. It is difficult, though, to believe that a disco musical with the Village People at its center and a YMCA as the subject of one song would be received as just another uncomplicatedly heterosexual musical by urban Americans—and it is urban life that is celebrated in the lyrics of the opening number.

If it is not absurd to see in *Can't Stop the Music* a musical whose closet door is at least half-open, there could scarcely be a more inappropriate enthusiasm for the new decade, since the eighties is the time of AIDS, which has devastated gay communities, particularly in New York City and San Francisco; it is also the decade when that devastation in those places is taken by commentators on the phenomenon to have been long ignored or little acknowledged by the administration with which the eighties is most associated.

"Making It"

If optimism is tragically inappropriate for sexual minorities at the outset of the eighties, the utopianism which suggests ease of socio-economic mobility and which makes individualism charismatic may explain some of the altered emphasis to the Malamud novel on which Barry Levinson's film of *The Natural* (1984) is based. Skin diseases are likely to be seen as obstacles to charisma. Malamud's linking of the Fisher King's obsessional pursuit of the baseball pennant with a skin ailment is excised from the film, presumably to stifle any suggestion of the association of frenetic aspiration with sickness.

Charlie (Tom Cruise), the character who has, to some extent, made it in another, later, Levinson movie, *Rain Man* (1988), is not entirely happy, but the character who is in an obvious sense "sick" is his long-lost brother, Raymond (Dustin Hoffman)—and yet it is Raymond who comes into money, by inheriting three million dollars from their father, while Charlie is left only a convertible and rose-bushes. *Rain Man* constantly suggests that there are severe penalties to be paid for the pursuit of the dollar. The impatience that Charlie manifests with the environmental safety checks which threaten his financial stability at the opening of the movie is a clue to the attitude that the audience is encouraged to take to his dubious business ethics. This is made more explicit when Charlie's girlfriend walks out on him only because it is clear to her that he has removed Raymond from the institution in which he has been housed for years and is trying to take him back to Los Angeles as a means to his securing half of the inheritance for himself.

By the end of the narrative, Charlie discovers that the protective rain man whom he remembers from infancy is Raymond, and that this autistic savant's phenomenal memory and skill at numbers have been able to save him from financial ruin when they are, willingly, put to use by Raymond to win in the casinos of Las Vegas. Raymond's autism cannot be cured, even by Charlie's love; at the end of the movie, he has to see Raymond on to the train that will carry him back to institutionalization. By this point, it has become clear that it is Charlie, rather, who has been cured of the sickness identified with his alienation from family relationships—past (his unloving father, his unknown brother) and future (his on-again, off-again liaison with his girlfriend). In context, Charlie's need to succeed in financial terms is a morbid substitute for the truer happiness of familial integration; by implication, his ruthlessness and egotism are aspects of his sick personality, his tenderness and concern a mark of wholeness. *Rain Main* seems no longer to celebrate the attractions of go-getting individualism but to be wary of it, since it must damage, or it is in turn a manifestation of damage by, family relations.

Working Girl (Mike Nichols, 1988), on the other hand, appears for most of its narrative to celebrate the possibility and attractions of social mobility, success, and go-getting in the character of Tess McGill (Melanie Griffith), who moves upward to the world of Sigourney Weaver, a parodically ambitious and insincere businesswoman. For much of its running time, the movie seems—in its celebration of a nice, honest, working-class woman's triumph over a selfish, unscrupulous aristocrat—to be another Reaganite fairy tale of a movie. At the very end, however, when Tess has achieved all that she could wish, having acquired the love of the hero (Harrison Ford) as well as power and financial independence, the final image leaves the audience with a quite different impression of her success. An office of her own, which looks so attractive from the inside, with its own window and its sharp contrast with the markedly unprivate, workaday inner office of her secretary, is shown as part of a rabbit warren of similar offices, by a shot from the outside. As Richard Combs observes, "What Tess will become, real person or New Woman, is left open by a final helicopter shot of the New York skyline, losing the office in which she has just been installed, only with great trepidation persuaded to abandon her secretarial post in the outer office, in the anonymous façade of the tower block."[12]

Commercialization

It is difficult to find from popular movies, in a period where monetarism and the free play of market forces are encouraged at the highest levels of government, an unqualified eulogy for these factors, in terms of their effect on social and even commercial life. The emptiness and valuelessness of the pursuit of wealth, strongly suggested in *Rain Man,* the sting in the tail of Working Girl success are present again in many other major films of the eighties, whether through comedy treatment, nostalgia for a less commercialized period, or from the safer distance of a Dickensian perspective.

When, in *My Beautiful Laundrette* (Stephen Frears, 1985), Omar's (Gordon Warnecke) hardheaded, pragmatic Asian family turns the Thatcherite economic free-for-all to its advantage, his estranged father can offer a scarcely competing role model to him. The father, with his socialist commitment and his belief in the liberating powers of education, cannot hope to persuade Omar to follow his principles in a country where the rewards and penalties for their respective attitudes are so clearly marked out in the gulf between the father's impoverishment and the less scrupulous family members' affluence. Omar grasps the nature of power in Thatcher's Britain and proves that he can come out on top despite the racial harassment that he suffered at school from National Front sympathizers by giving employment to a schoolmate (Daniel Day Lewis) who was once one of his tormentors. Omar, like his upwardly mobile relations and the movie itself, never attempts to argue that these choices are morally right. Survival in a racist area of London demands that the opportunities presented be grabbed with both hands. Opportunism works in a society where traditional power is destabilized.

So does greed. "Greed works, it clarifies, it cuts through and captures the evolutionary spirit, the upward surge of mankind," Gekko (Michael Douglas) announces in Oliver Stone's *Wall Street* (1987), to explain the sources of his energy and success as discoverable in a kind of economic Darwinism. This speech encapsulates the movie's demonstration of the free market's seductiveness. Drive, the rush of adrenalin, are experienced as exciting.

Both the British and American film highlights the appeal of coming out on top in economic power terms, which are the only meaningful ones in the societies depicted, at the same time as they highlight, by their absence of reference to morality and by their characters' absence of interest in it, universal bankruptcy in all other terms but the economic.

Empire State (Ron Peck, 1987) adopts a more straightforwardly critical approach to its theme of corruption in the development of London's docklands area. American influence in the power games that culminate here in physical violence is symbolized by the spatially imposing nightclub, with its Manhattan decor, from which the film is named.

The comedy generated from the acquisitiveness and dishonesty of a more blatant form of commercialism in both American and British society is the more customary avenue into social criticism. John Schlesinger's *Honky Tonk Freeway* (1981) has every person and every thing in Ticlaw, Florida, including the customarily sacred (and soon to be Reaganite) small-town ethos of pride in democracy and independence, dedicated to one objective only—economic survival in an otherwise economically buoyant nation. That objective, being threatened by the new highway's routing past the town, means that all ways, regardless of their tackiness or immorality, must be used to bring customers back into the township. The moral authority of the town, usually located in the doctor or preacher in the small-town movie, is here invested in the most entrepreneurial spirit from among the burghers.

When Pat Kramer (Lily Tomlin) begins to shrink, in *The Incredible Shrinking Woman* (Joel Schumacher), a comedy of the same year (1981), it is evident that she is a victim of the accidental spillage of a new perfume on her. Her husband, Vance (Charles Grodin), is able to be persuaded by his boss that the danger to users of the perfume, which he himself is in charge of marketing, need not be publicized until Dr. Nortz (Henry Gibson) has discovered an antidote. Even at the height of a mere three feet, and as a national celebrity for her shrinking, Pat concurs that she should not blame the product when she appears on national television. When she does decide to expose what she knows, it is only because of the World Shrink plan devised by Nortz and his colleague to develop a serum that will shrink everybody else in the world but themselves, giving them unrivaled power. The narrative demonstrates the ease with which the desire for commercial viability and business success permeates private life, so that family members recognize that only by applying business ethics to their relations with each other can their family, the showcase for their economic success, survive. Similar points are made in *Down and Out in Beverly Hills* (Paul Mazursky, 1986), that only those marginal enough to be of doubtful sanity could want to do anything else than support the bourgeois consumerist family, though here that attitude is less guyed and may be read with less irony.

Lindsay Anderson's *Britannia Hospital* (1982) centers not on family life in its relation to market forces but on Britain's health service. It demonstrates the social divide and inequities between sectors of the British population, and the corruption of medical research by profit motives.

The sharp and evident criticism of increasing commercialism in *Wall Street* and *Britannia Hospital* has a gentler counterpart in nostalgia for less pressurized times and more humane environments, in *Atlantic City* (Louis Malle, 1980) and *Blade Runner* (Ridley Scott, 1982).

Malle's film centers as much upon the physical changes being wrought upon the eponymous city as upon the transitions forced on its older inhabitants. The past of Atlantic City, garish as it may be taken to be on the film's evidence, is making way for a grimmer present, with gambling casinos the most visible sign of the new, more hardheaded outlook on the city's function. Youth (Susan Sarandon) fascinates old age (Burt Lancaster), but neither side of the age divide could be identified as a "winner." The principal characters are united in their frailty but also in their dogged survival. The human beings of the movie seem to be stranded in an environment which cannot value the very qualities which make them human and vulnerable.

It may seem, at first glance, surprising that *Blade Runner* comments on the present by nostalgia for the past, since its narrative is set in the future. Against the advanced technocracy of the commercial world, epitomized here by the giant image of an Asian face apparently addressing the antlike beings on the rainswept pavements of Los Angeles, are the ants themselves, the human beings who turn their coat collars up against the incessant rain. Intermingled with the human beings are the replicants, who look and, more importantly, feel human, because they have been programmed with a life history. The poignancy of nostalgia is, paradoxically, rendered the greater by the revelation that their familial memories are artificially created. The present is soulless, inhumane. What makes the replicants more appealing than most of the human beings ranged against them is their possession of emotions and memories that explain their present rebellion. The most resonant architecture in the movie is that which looks the most old-fashioned, out-of-date, even in terms of the eighties, more *film noir* than futuristic or even "realistic," as in the final roof-high confrontation between Rutger Hauer and Harrison Ford.

The technique of commenting obliquely on the present by narratives set in other times but in the same places is discoverable in the use of the past, specifically the Dickensian version of the past, in two eighties movies. Clive Donner's *A Christmas Carol* (1984) has at its center one of the most famous, and caricaturable, of monetarists, Scrooge (George C. Scott). Inevitably, Christmas is baffling and meaningless to him, since it is an interruption to the process of wealth accumulation. It does, admittedly, encourage consumption but also encourages unbridled spending in place of obsessional saving. The ghosts offer a nightmarish picture of unfettered capitalism's terrifying social results. Capitalism's unacceptable face becomes more acceptable only when Scrooge learns to be charitable, to dispense amounts of his riches on what would have been to him, before the visions, the undeserving poor. Both Dickens's fable and Donner's film set up their problems and their solutions within capitalism. The notion of private charity lending virtue to private accumulation of wealth is one that was frequently mobilized by Margaret Thatcher and that has been given practical demonstration in the range of charitable telethons run on national television in Britain.

Little Dorrit (Christine Edzard, 1987) is an altogether more critical tale of the extremes of luxury and privation existing within a monetarist British society. The absence of any effective amelioration thanks to the bureaucracy and self-importance of the Circumlocution Office; the wretchedness of the life of incarceration in the Marshalsea, the debtors' prison; the suddenness with which a debtor is propelled into wealth and high society, or with which a comfortably off capitalist may be hurtled into the Marshalsea by events or forces that seem to be out of the control, and beyond the interest, of himself or of London society; all combine to portray monetarism as a heady dream whose converse is terrifying nightmare. The downfall of the hero Clennam (Derek Jacobi) under pressure of the paramount need for material acquisition provides an object lesson in the perils of upward mobility in an age of inadequate or nonexistent social relief. It seems impossible to seal off the lessons of Dickens at his most socially critical on the pretext that he is writing of an England that has gone.

Consumerism

Chris Auty sees in *Poltergeist* (Tobe Hooper, 1982) two different visions of America which are impossible to coalesce in one horror film. While, Auty argues, Steven Spielberg sees suburbia as "like the libido—a lake of contradictory wishes and impulses which can be expressed in forms either beatific or horrific," the director, Tobe Hooper, sees it, according to Auty, as the graveyard of American consumerism.[13] One aspect of that consumerism is the bloating of the family on television images, so that the child's quite literal absorption into the television set is part of the revenge of Nature and the Past (also symbolized by the ghosts from the ignored graveyard, redeveloped as a housing estate) upon it.

The consumption of the child by the television set whose images have been consumed by the suburban family is upstaged by the several movies, mostly British, which deal with the most drastic form of consumers' consumption, cannibalism. Peter Greenaway's British-French coproduction, *The Cook, the Thief, His Wife and*

Her Lover is treated elsewhere, in chapter 12. *Eating Raoul* (Paul Bartel, 1982) is American. It not only extends *Poltergeist*'s principal joke, of the consumer consumed, but draws into its satirical sights the moralism that characterizes New Right thinking on sex. Bland by surname, Paul (Paul Bartel) and Mary (Mary Woronov) dream of moving their monogamous marriage to the country and of opening a restaurant. They are able to strike a blow against the degeneracy on every hand in their city by killing lecherous hedonists, lured into their power by tabloid advertisements, and by collecting the five-hundred-dollar fee so that they can build up sufficient funds to leave the Sodom and Gomorrah that is Hollywood. Raoul Mendoza (Robert Beltran) temporarily muscles in on their scheme, offering to dispose of the dead bodies and their belongings and to split the money raised from them. Raoul shows his enterpreneurial talents by selling bodies to be made into dog food. Paul and Mary demonstrate their concern with chastity by killing the lecherous Raoul, who has designs on Mary, and by literally making a meal of him. The "happy ending," in which the Blands fulfill their plan of opening a restaurant in the country, testifies, as do *Wall Street, My Beautiful Laundrette,* and *The Incredible Shrinking Woman,* to the current prioritization of consumerism and commerce as the chief values by which life should be led.

Bruce Robinson's punningly titled *How to Get Ahead in Advertising* (1989) centers on an advertising executive who, after developing a hideous boil on his neck, has his head removed by mistake in the operation intended to rid him of the boil. The boil, which has without difficulty taken over in place of his head, masterminds the advertising campaign to sell antipimple cream, which had earlier driven the hero Dennis (Richard E. Grant) to despair. The free-market philosophy by which he has tried to live is represented for the middle section of the film by the boil, when it is not pouring forth obscenities and lecherous sexism. That Thatcherism should be given its most ardent mouthpiece in a boil rather than in the advertising man says much about the satirical aspirations of Robinson's film. The attack on Thatcherism seems diffuse and somehow unfocused, however.

A similar sense that Thatcherism is being held up to scorn but that the nature of the attack is nebulous is discernible in Mike Leigh's *High Hopes* (1988), where the most sympathetic characters are the socialists, Cyril (Philip Davis) and Shirley (Ruth Scheen), and the most dislikable are the exploitative yuppies, Laetitia Boothe-Braine (Lesley Manville) and her wine-merchant husband, Rupert (David Bamber). Cyril and Shirley apparently possess no

Thatcherite aspirations, and their values are manifestly different, but their assault on Thatcherism seems to be by example (their concern and care for Cyril's old mother in marked contrast to the Boothe-Braines' condescension and moralism about individual responsibility when confronted with the same lady, their next-door neighbor) and in their distaste for the avaricious and vulgar Martin Burke [Philip Jackson]) rather than by commentary. The nearest they come to direct criticism is the christening of a cactus plant in Shirley's keeping as "Mrs. Thatcher" because it pricks those going out the door.

None of these movies seems able to treat the world of commerce and go-getting with a straight face, let alone sympathetically. Atypically, Colin Bucksey's *Dealers* (1989) does attempt to tackle big-business melodrama, pitting the clever young Daniel Pascoe (Paul McGann) against a director's mistress, Anna Schumann (Rebecca De Mornay), to recover a dealer's vast trading loss at the bank of Whitney Paine. The qualities which are heroized in this unusual venture are the very ones held up to ridicule or disgust in the bulk of eighties movies taking the world of commerce as their chief subject.

Unemployment

Although the affluent, those who have most evidently profited most from Reaganomics and Thatcherism, are attacked in some movies through trenchant satire, and although unemployment became a far commoner feature of British life in the earlier years of the decade than at any time since the Second World War, few mainstream entertainments seem to render unemployment visible.

Maxim Ford's *Live a Life* (1982) is hardly a mainstream entertainment. It is partly a record of the November 1981 Concert for the Unemployed at London's Rainbow Theatre, which becomes a study of the subject of unemployment. The concert having been sponsored by the Trades Union Congress, the inclusion of a film of Margaret Thatcher waxing eloquent about the nation's love of freedom suggests a critical distance from her message, the new context of the speech offering a different insight into it than the prime minister intended when she thus addressed stalwarts of the British Establishment.

Looks and Smiles (Kenneth Loach, 1981) centers on growing up in a town (Sheffield) where the choice facing working-class teenagers—male teenagers, in any case—appears to be between going on the dole or signing up for the army. Mick (Graham Green) chooses the former, Alan (Tony Pitts) the latter. When Mick is offered a job interview, he fails it because of the black eye he has sustained during fisticuffs with Alan, at home on leave from the army, and then turns to stealing cigarettes from a pub to finance improvements to his bicycle. A desultory relationship develops between Mick and Karen (Carolyn Nicholson), who does have employment, in a shoe shop. She leaves Sheffield to make her way, driven by Mick, to her father in Bristol. (The nature of the father's job—long-distance lorry driving—seems related to the transience of his relationship with Karen's mother.) There, the young couple are turned away and have to rely on each other—and Mick's dole— for what is suggested will be their life together.

The film essays comment on Thatcherite ideology. This is not so much in its depiction of desperate choices, between dole and the danger of the army or the boredom of the shoe shop, as in its illustration of the breakdown of family support systems because of privation at the very time when the family is being publicly admonished for failing to perform its duties and overdepending on the welfare state for solutions to its problems. It is by reason of their lack of space that Karen's father has to turn the couple away. It is for similar reasons that Karen and Mick cannot maintain any privacy in her mother's council house and that Mick is ordered out.

Decay

Overtly oppositional films of the *Looks and Smiles* variety tend to be made in Britain rather than in the United States and to be financed and exhibited in unusual ways. Derek Jarman's *The Last of England* (1987) announces its difference by largely abandoning recognizable narrative for painterliness and, occasionally, abstraction. The relevance of his imagery to contemporary England is made clear by using commentary on the Royal Wedding on the soundtrack to accompany a quite other, sexually ambiguous, event, or using the British flag as a background to lovemaking between two men. The nation in its present state is seen as desolate and in a terminal state of decay, through Jarman's footage of un-cared-for housing estates and unswept, filthy city streets. Beyond that, he uses footage from his grandfather's and father's home movies so that he can reenter England's past through film shot, for example, in fifties Pakistan and suggest links between the colonial past and the shabby present.

The use of colonial past to comment on present-day England is discoverable again in the Channel 4–sponsored *Playing Away*

(Horace Ové, 1986). Some of the most prominent among the Suffolk villagers residing in Sneddington are able to recapture their connections with Africa by, for example, offering a slide show of their Kenyan experiences in the village hall. The cricket match is the climax of a week of fund-raising for the benefit of the Third World. Ranged against the charity-minded villagers is to be a West Indian team culled from Brixton, under Willie Boy (Norman Beaton). In the event, the expected superiority of the West Indian side is not realized within this film. What scuppers the ostensibly friendly relations between host and guest sides is the lack of British temperamental control, the loss of stereotypical sangfroid, so that even though the visiting team is soon struggling against an English side that, against expectations, proves superior, the English side loses when key players storm off in protest. The traditional pride in civilized behavior maintained by the vicar, for example, is here swept away in less sporting times by the histrionics of some of the cricketers as they express their resentments in bad sportsmanship. The comment on the decline in Englishness's former quintessence is unmistakable, in that cricket has so often in films signaled Englishness, as has green and pleasant village life. Nothing is as it once was, not even West Indians' legendary superiority in this game.

Repression: Blankness, Deceit, Depoliticization

The themes of present-day squalor in Britain coupled with confusion about the meaning of the past and of "Englishness" surface again in Stephen Frears's *Sammy and Rosie Get Laid* (1987). The film's opening uses a voice-over from Margaret Thatcher exhorting inner cities to renew themselves by industriousness and hope. As in *The Last of England,* official cheerfulness about the possibility of miracles being wrought without governmental economic intervention is sharply contrasted with the visuals of urban decay. Into this grim setting, London as he never wished to envisage it, comes Rafi (Shashi Kapoor) to take up residence with his son, Sammy (Ayub Khan Dim) and Sammy's social-worker wife, Rosie (Frances Barber). He is appalled by the near-riots against what is taken by the neighborhood to be police racism, as well as by the "openness" of his son's marriage (Sammy fails to pick Rafi up at the airport because he is in bed with an American photographer [Wendy Gazelle].) Rafi himself had once been a freedom fighter, but his reputation as an anticolonialist is now seriously tarnished by reports of his torture of political opponents. Part of his return trip to England is explained by his desire to resume a relationship with Alice (Claire Bloom), who represents an ideal of English womanhood to him, but she recognizes its impossibility and rejects him.

The movie focuses on a well-meaning, leftish couple who have stepped back from the social chaos of their environment in order to concentrate on conceptions of freedom within personal relations. The expansion of notions of the family to include lesbians and communes, the expansion of notions of "Britishness" to create alternative multiracial communities are of uneasy and temporary achievement at this time in this society. The waste site where Rosie gets laid and where different models of community begin to assert themselves is finally bulldozed by property developers. Rafi, recognizing that the past has gone, to be replaced with what is to him a bewildering chaos, hangs himself. The movie offers almost idyllic possibilities of personal happiness, but all of them are finally rendered unrealizable under the pressures exerted by the injustice of the social system tyrannizing them even when it is apparently forgotten.

The deep pessimism of a film such as *Sammy and Rosie* is more regularly to be found in British movies of the eighties than in those from North America. One notable exception is the Canadian *Decline of the American Empire* (Denys Arcand, 1986), whose history-professor characters' expressed concerns center obsessively on sexual adventure—but no more than do the female characters when they are separate from the men and free to discuss the relation of sex and power in their lives. Then, too, Claude (Yves Jacques) is homosexual, and confesses that he would cruise every night if only it did not affect his ability to work the next day.

These characters are like those in the Frears film, in their removal from the less private world of American—or, for that matter, Canadian—politics, their dedicated self-enclosure within the field of the search for sexual fulfillment. Both works suggest that on either side of the Atlantic, there are intellectuals and leftists who in their despair about the "system" have tried to make sense of an area which remains apparently available, that of sexual politics—and sexual enjoyment.

In British movies, the principal accuser of Thatcherism must be David Hare, who has stripped away masks to show the blank faces of the depoliticized and amoral, especially in his two films *Wetherby* (1985) and *Paris By Night* (1988). At the center of the earlier film is repression and—one result of repression—mendacity. Once again, as in *Playing Away,* a British director chooses rural English life as the milieu. *Wetherby* is Hare's "privet hedge" movie, one in which the invasion of the safe, forever-English village is evidenced. Blankness (John [Tim McInnery] is described as "a blankness, a central disfiguring blankness"), facelessness, emptiness, are the creations of that invasion. Of what does the invasion consist? Of repression, Thatcherism's punitive repressiveness. Thatcher's activity is described during a dinner party in these words: "It's as if she's taking some terrible revenge for some deep damage, for crimes behind the privet hedge."

Hare comes as close as a director would dare to direct comment on the woman, as well as her politics, in *Paris by Night.* At the center of the 1988 film is Clara Paige (Charlotte Rampling), an ascending Conservative star of the European parliament (which, admittedly, Mrs. Thatcher would never wish to be). Her alcoholic Westminster-MP husband Gerald (Michael Gambon) is no match for her, and she cares little about her son. The film gains its un-illuminating title from her pushing of Michael (Andrew Ray), a businessman ruined by Gerald, into the river Seine; edgy because of the anonymous phone calls she has been receiving, she believes Michael has been shadowing her around Paris one night. The film ends with Gerald shooting her as she is selected to be the Conservative candidate for Birmingham South West and after she determines to continue her affair with the designer, Wallace Sharp (Iain Glen).

The director comments on the relevance of the film to Thatcherism: "Thatcher is a moralist, and the tone of her regime is moralistic, with much emphasis on Victorian values. Yet whenever one of her own number has been caught out transgressing, either in their private lives or in their public standards of honesty, Mrs. Thatcher's first instinct has been to let them get away with it on the grounds that they're 'one of us', and that when 'we' do it, the rules don't apply."[14] The narrative charts the deceit and amorality of his heroine, so much a model of Thatcherite womanhood that she is at times inseparable from the earlier image of the Thatcher woman. More than this, the narrative, by demonstrating that the failed business handed on by herself and Gerald to Michael was so handed on deceitfully, indicates that the ethos of self-reliance and sheer industriousness as virtues which will bring their own reward, material success, is a sham.

Hare's sense of repression and sham moralism as a crucial part of Thatcherism is shared by Derek Jarman, who seems to believe that repression is not only Thatcher's gift to the nation but that it "cut[s] across normal politics."[15] He considers the repressiveness of Mary Whitehouse and Winston Churchill—the latter's Obscenity Bill was aimed particularly at the broadcasting of Jarman's films *Jubilee* (1978) and *Sebastiane* (1976)—a politically useful smokescreen for economic mismanagement. Jarman states: "Of course, the real causes of violence set out in that film [*Jubilee*] are never tackled by an establishment which seems to have lost any form of relationship with people, which seems to dislike people. Even Edward Heath came out with the true causes of violence last night—economic ones."[16] Derek Jarman's reaction to the Winston Churchill Obscenity Bill is, interestingly, reminiscent of *Wetherby*—he claims to feel "a strange blankness" to it.[17]

The repression regarding expression of sexuality which Hare and Jarman claim to be a necessary part of Thatcherism is addressed in a British short of 1985, Ron Peck's *What Can I Do with a Male Nude?* Claimed to be a direct response to the Bright Video Recordings Bill and to the incursions of Customs and Excise officers in pursuit of "doubtful" works by Jean Genet and Oscar Wilde,[18] the film involves a direct address to the audience by an unseen photographer who is exploring the possibilities of enjoyment of the male body through his camera lens at a time when the authorities are making such enjoyment reprehensible and dangerous.

That falsification through repression can lead to nightmarish violence is demonstrated by an American film of 1987, Kathryn Bigelow's *Near Dark*. Pam Cook notices how the small-town movie, which she surprisingly refers to as "a minor sub-genre," is enjoying arthouse success in the eighties through such works as *Blue Velvet* (David Lynch, 1986). While it is difficult to think of *Kings Row* (Sam Wood, 1942) or *The Deer Hunter* (Michael Cimino, 1978) as minor movies, her basic point that small-town movies in the eighties may be evidence of "rumblings of discontent . . . with Reaganite America's nostalgic celebration of home town values"[19] seems entirely apposite. Underneath the folksy surface of Fix, Arizona, a world of sadomasochistic eroticism—as in *Blue Velvet*— and of vampirism lies hidden. The horror genre often explores that which is repressed under the surface of "normality." Indeed, one explanation of horror is that it represents the return of the Repressed. That Repressed has particular inflections in the eighties, and its return is appropriately achieved in the wholesome, complacent atmosphere of small-town ideology as this is filtered through Reaganite rhetoric.

Attitudes to the Sixties

The Impracticality of Politics

Two 1986 films, *Down and Out in Beverly Hills* and *The Decline of the American Empire*, cast a jaundiced eye back at the sixties, in contrast to Bruce Robinson's *Withnail and I* (1987), which is set in the final days of the sixties and celebrates what is most remarkable about the decade, at least from the point of view of one of its youth.

Those who are down and out in the Mazursky movie hang out pointlessly on the beach. Unemployed, they lack all the bourgeois accoutrements—some of them such "necessities" as a fixed home, though everything, including his home, that the Richard Dreyfuss character possesses looks like a luxury rather than a necessity. In the movie, the present-day "losers" are the hippies of the sixties, adrift in a consumer society that they expected to destroy by turning their backs on consumables. Withnail already looks like a down-and-out, living in inner-city squalor, lacking the commitment to achieve success even within the art world, let alone within the kind of middle-class society represented by his comfortably off uncle. The major difference is that *Withnail and I,* taking its social perspective from the sixties, regards the successful with as satirical an eye as its dropout heroes, whereas *Beverly Hills* seems to suggest in its finale, without irony, that nobody in his right mind would choose the dropout life when he can reside in a swanky home with its own swimming pool.

American Empire suggests that it is not simply that affluence is preferable to material privation, but that the politics of the sixties cannot hope to match up to the depoliticized hardheadedness of present times. Perhaps it must, since it is set in an academic ambience among history professors who are just old enough to have had personal experience of the sixties. One particularly Canadian inflection of the sixties is the Quebec separatist movement, a movement which failed and which helps to explain the principal characters' absence of commitment, except to sexual adventure. Their former militancy is channeled now into meditation upon the differential power relations between male and female and into consumption—of superior food, of superior female company.

As early as 1979, John Sayles's *Return of the Secaucus Seven* deals with similar disillusionment among those who were young and militant in the previous decade. They are so named because they were arrested in Secaucus on their way to an anti–Vietnam War demonstration. Their present incessant talk, circling around

their awareness of compromise and inability to resolve contradictions, highlights the nature of what could be deemed wrong with
their sixties politics—that it was unanalyzed, unfocused. Their
present nostalgia is not only a testament to the fleeting sense of
purpose lent to them by the sixties but indicates the fragility of that
reality and the lack of grasp that their commitment had upon power
structures—always reducible, then and now, to "the system."

Bogus "Liberation"

Anna (Jamie Lee Curtis), the heroine of Amy Jones's *Love Letters* (1983), urges herself on into a love affair with an older married
man, Oliver (James Keach), partly because, on her mother's death,
she has discovered poignant love letters to her from a man with
whom her mother did not have the courage to live. These letters,
written during the sixties, when Anna was a child, represent to her
a vision of personal liberation that she may now act upon. Her
burning of the letters, once she has discovered the pain that she
has brought on Oliver's family and the humiliation she has thus
inflicted upon herself, may well suggest a discarding of false hopes
of sexual liberation, which must, as conceived in sixties terms,
always work to the detriment of the woman in an extramarital affair.

The lives of Joe Orton and Kenneth Halliwell, as mediated in
Stephen Frears's *Prick Up Your Ears* (1987), are less concerned
with questions of homosexual "liberation" in the years before homosexual relations between consenting adults were legalized by
British law than understood within the context of what is conceived
as its opposite—the marriage. While Orton is depicted as "masculine" in his promiscuity, his amoral hedonism, Halliwell becomes
here the "feminine" partner, more domesticated, more "neurotic"
in his sense of betrayal. The exploration of a conventionally conceived marital union, albeit between men, could be considered to
take conventional heterosexuality as the norm against which the
partners' lives and values are measured, and the film could thus be
dismissed as wasting its potential as an investigation of representations of permissive gay attitudes in a repressive society. On the
other hand, the fact that these characters conceive of their relationship as a version of conventional marriage, that conventional
notions of masculininity and femininity surface in a gay relationship, surely reveals more about the sixties than that heterosexuality was conceived to be the norm. The apparent impossibility of
escape by even subversive artists (as here depicted, that is) from
the narrowly circumscribed sexual roles available to them in pre-

legalization London, their self-oppression in competing terms of the masculine and feminine, says a great deal about not only the confinement of "liberation" to the dominant male in the sexuality of the sixties but about self-recuperation in a hostile environment.

The fascination as well as the absurdity of aspects of popular culture and of popular political and sexual thinking in the sixties is best epitomized in the eighties by John Waters's *Hairspray* (1988), which testifies, by its fetishization of what are now pop memorabilia, to the present decade's nostalgia as well as its sense of embarrassment about that nostalgia.

Together, these movies' abandonment of the sixties seems at some remove from the Thatcherite castigation of the sixties for all the evils that existed during her own period of power. They repeatedly indicate that American and British life has moved on, with no regrets for the damage done to women and gays in the name of a sexual revolution that was but another manifestation of patriarchal values. Yet they remain somewhat shamefaced about the loss of (albeit unfocused) idealism, together with optimism, in the pursuit of material success and a "realism" that can be equated with unfettered acquisitiveness.

4

Familialism

The Battle over the Signification of "Family"

The issue of the contested meanings of the term "family" was brought into sharp focus in Great Britain in 1988, thanks to the British Local Government Act of that year, which prohibited the "promotion" of homosexuality in terms of its conception as a "pretended family relationship."[1] Obviously, over against the notion of pseudo-family—believed by the act's supporters to be created and encouraged within the context of equal opportunities and positive images espoused by certain local councils, particularly in London—must be the ideal of the "real" family.

At the very time in which British confidence in the reality and falsity of family relationships is being given public expression in lawmaking, investigators of the family phenomenon seem to be advocating a move away from, or beyond, simple assumptions about the nuclear family, on the grounds that if it represents reality, it is odd that the model of that reality is based on minority experience. Four investigators of the American family note how striking it is "that the conventional form [of family] that so narrowly sets the parameters of scientific inquiry in this field represents a shrinking minority of households." In addition, they remark, "Equally important is that this form was never fully realized until the post-World War II period, and then prevailed only for a short period of time."[2] Their uncertainty about the advisability of continuing to think of "close relationships" in terms of a model of family that is more "real" than other versions of such relationships is clearly signaled by the subtitle of their work, *Rethinking Families and Close Relationships.* Early in their study, they suggest that professionals and students will profit more from thinking in terms of close or primary relationships, while recognizing that terms such as "families" or "single parents" are helpful, even inevitable, ways of communicating about relationships at a lay level.[3] Contrary to the 1988 legislation, these authors claim that "alternative life-styles" are of no less significance than that of the traditionally claimed "benchmark" nuclear family—"nor are they Qualitatively Other."[4] While the family form sets the parameters for scientific inquiry, and for comparative judgment of all other types of relationships, that form "represents a steadily shrinking minority of households."[5]

Eli Zaretsky says of the family: "Increasingly cut off from production, the contemporary family threatens to become a well of subjectivity divorced from any social meaning."[6] Not only, therefore, is the dominant sense of "family" countered by experience of social actuality, so that a minority version of it becomes normative, but the family, being a "well of subjectivity," is made available as a vacuum to be filled by the passionate convictions and prejudices of dominant groups in the late eighties, expressing their will through, for instance, the British parliament. That this will coincides with popular sentiment, as Jeffrey Weeks has demonstrated,[7] is not the point. (Popular sentiment may be molded, as well as expressed, by interest groups, after all.) Precisely when experts in the field counsel the abandonment of a single model of the "familial," new legislation demands that a wishful version of it become "real," so real that other versions are marginalized out of existence as "pretended."

Familialism and the Right

Available as actualizations of the wishful ideal of the "family" are the presidential family and the particular organisation of the British monarchy into its most customary appellation, "the royal family." Thus, while Reagan represented a particularly strong arm of government for American citizens by being president, at the same time he humanized his presidential role by appearing in public with his First Lady. Ronald and Nancy Reagan did not simply happen to be a married couple. They constantly stressed the interrelation of governmental and marital roles by Reagan's frequent pronouncement on television of presidential opinion while his wife stood silent but approving at his side. A particular model of marital relationship, with Nancy Reagan apparently proud to bend to her husband's will, was suggested, even though the model tended to strain credibility when she, as has happened on television, had to prompt her husband on the wording of matters of policy, and when their offspring were more notably absent from the public scene than, say, Carter's were during his term of office. The role of the royal family is more complicated in relation to British subjects' perception of it, in that the monarchy is in most senses titular and known not to be in command of government, despite the ceremonial insistence that the elected government is Her Majesty's. Moreover, there is an important difference in British experience of "first families" in that Mrs. Thatcher is perceived to signify more than Mr. Thatcher, just as the queen is that bit more "royal" than Prince Philip. Yet the same basic service is fulfilled for British citizens, as for American citizens by courtesy of the presidential family—namely, that an abstract national identity is given a glamorous "human" face.[8]

The symbolization of "family" through presidential and royal families is but one means to fix the signification of the term. There are two crucial points for understanding familialism. One is the profound importance of the sentiments that can be mobilized around the term "family." The other, even more crucial, is that the term, being fluid and capable of multiple interpretations (just as the actuality may theoretically and practically take many forms with many different distributions of power and authority), is a site of passionate contestation. Political interest groups may seek to outlaw rival meanings of the term in order to insist on the "naturalness" of their version of the family, and thus to use "commonsense" understandings of the family to suggest that any other version is fake, and therefore inferior.[9] Still, it is important to bear in mind that whatever sense is implicitly given to the word by particular users of it, "family" does not have a unified, self-evident meaning. That it appears to have is testimony to the skill with which it has been deployed by the Right in the United States and Britain. Not only are the passions stimulated into life by the term "family" a crucial part of the Right's "hegemonic project." So is the achievement of a self-evident version of it, whereby its meaning, and therefore its friends and foes, can instantly be grasped without ratiocination.

To be "profamily" was in the eighties profoundly important to political parties of different persuasions. The very militancy of the Right's profamily stance calls into being a version of profamily politics from the Left. (It would be a form of political suicide for an interest group with aspirations to power to call itself "antifamily." The term "family" may well be challenged, its strands of meaning teased out, but otherwise there is nothing else for a political party to be at present but "profamily," given the Right's apparently successful rhetoric.)

In the United States, Reagan did not initiate political use of a profamily stance. It was President Carter who organized a nationwide White House Conference on Families. But as Levitan and Belous observe, "Not to be outdone, Ronald Reagan proclaimed, upon accepting the Republican nomination, that his administration would be a crusade to revitalize American institutions. The first institution on his list was the family."[10]

What version of the family, though? The only family tolerable to a New Right ideologue seems to be a thoroughly patriarchal version, with no blurring of the demarcation between, for example, paternal rights and maternal duties. New Right thinking appears to have accepted a causal link between what it detects as the breakdown of that model of the family and the encroachment of the welfare state, so that the ills of the nuclear family are traced to the alleged evils of "welfarism." Therefore, in the name of the family, public sentiment has been mobilized against the encroachment of the state. The antifamily aspect of the state is deemed to be its taking over of functions more "properly" undertaken by the patriarchal family— such functions as care for the sick or education of the young. Once this distribution of duties is accepted as proper ordering, then the Reagan administration's clear duty is surely to halt the tide of "individualistic," antifamily legislation believed to have reached new limits under Carter (although some would argue that the Supreme Court's lessening in support for such legislation by the midseventies makes the anti-Carter stand less timely than it may have at the time appeared).[11]

In historical terms, it is doubtful if the welfare state, as it seems to have grown up in the United States, could be held responsible for the alterations in family models and life-styles. Levitan and Belous believe, for example, that the breakdown of the extended family precedes the establishment in the 1930s of a social security system. They go so far as to suggest, indeed, that the welfare state, far from weakening family bonds, permitted many families to remain together.[12]

A similar, allegedly profamily voice has been heard in Britain. As Weeks puts it, "With a developing reaction to the 'socialism' and 'welfarism' that were seen as the roots of social decay, the restoration of moral standards and the stability of the family became one of the catchwords of the conservative repertoire, alongside law and order, and self-help."[13]

Within this conception of the family and of its relation to wider political activity, women are the proper guardians of hearth and home. Alan Crawford sees the women of the New Right family as behaving like the women of the Old West, working alongside the school and church to safeguard the home and its neighborhood. While the men are exercising their frontier spirit on such macho issues as gun ownership, law and order, "free market" economics, women are concentrating their energies on the struggle over textbook selection, busing, abortion, gay rights, and—a potent symbol of all that New Right family women are against, particularly since it affects women's social status—the Equal Rights Amendment.[14] For Jerry Falwell and his Moral Majority, Inc., followers, homosexuality explains the deterioration of the home and family.[15] (In this connection, it is interesting that the anti-gay-rights movement springing from Anita Bryant's 1977 campaign in Dade County, Florida, chose to call itself Save Our Children.) By an appeal to a natural "femininity" against which women seeking outlets beyond hearth and home may be taken to be rebeling, it is possible for the New Right to take an anti-ERA stance, on the grounds that it is antifamily and, remarkably, antiwomen. Women may be the chief scapegoat for all the ills reckoned to be brought into being by the supposed deterioration of family life. For example, "women's abdication of their age-old responsibility for the family is . . . being blamed for the apathy and moral delinquency of the 'me generation,'" Betty Friedan writes in 1982.[16]

Thatcher's profamily posture in Britain embraced similar notions of antiwelfarism as are to be found in American New Right thinking. Her public emphasis on family morality and greater discipline led easily into a demand for greater and wider family responsibility, particularly with regard to the care of sick or elderly family members. Given the traditionalist understanding of women's family roles, this in effect is a demand of women that they devote themselves to nurturing, caring roles within the family and forget their demand for experience beyond the home. The effect of such familialism is to prepare the country for swingeing attacks on social services and welfare benefits. These areas, of particular relevance to the survival of women and children, may be attacked by this means in the name of women and children. The more that the family looks after its own, the fewer the economic demands on the state. Through its manipulation of the meaning of "family" and thus of morality and sexuality, the Conservative government was able to cloak its highly ideological interventions in the organization of British social life in invisibility by means of appeal to "common sense." Its highly artificial conception of the family might pass itself off as "natural" and thus beyond argument. Where Nature fails, there may be appeal to religion, as in the United States. Mary

Whitehouse's affirmation of sexual anarchy as the precursor of political anarchy assumes itself to constitute a "defence of the family."[17]

In both American New Right and Thatcherite thinking, the family has become a metaphor, a highly evocative and useful metaphor for that which is stable and right beyond question and from which all that is deviant (from a middle-class, white, patriarchal viewpoint) may be denigrated and devalued.

Given the extraordinary political mileage that a particular version of the family has won for the Right, and the damage done through vaunted profamilialism to groups deemed subversive of the family's interests, an important lesson for feminists and others opposed to the Right emerges. It may not be nearly enough to analyze the Reagan victory of 1980, as Zillah Eisenstein has done, to show that the majority of the electorate who did vote did not vote on antifeminist, profamily issues.[18] For too long, the New Right conception of "family" has been unquestioned by those with competing conceptions. This apathy or despair has meant that those women, for example, who place themselves outside the traditionalist notion of family have automatically been easy targets. Betty Friedan, on the other hand, declares that the family must be taken as the new feminist frontier.[19] Fighting on that frontier must surely entail a reassessment of the uses of the term.

What has been achieved through a profamily stance and a "commonsense" implicit understanding of the sense of the term "family" is not only a promotion of a particular model of family over other competing models. It is also a dangerously antidemocratic demotion of the interests of those who seem to be living outside the only acceptable model of the "true" family. The considerable achievement of that profamilialism espoused by New Right ideology in America and by Thatcherism in Great Britain is a division into sheep and goats, those with rights and those lucky to have any, those who belong and those who manifestly do not. Thatcherism's zeal for hunting down "the enemy within" (to borrow Stuart Hall's formula), for example, is much facilitated by that formidable combination of religion and Nature and common sense which enables actual attacks on the family to be undertaken by those whose public pose is as advocates of family values.

Some of the claims made by the Right on behalf of the family (as it conceives of it) are as follows:

IT IS NATURAL (AND THUS MORAL). The consequences of this belief are well adumbrated by Barrett and McIntosh: "The prevailing form of family is seen as inevitable, as naturally given and biologically determined. As such, however, it is imbued with a unique social and moral force, since it is seen as the embodiment of general human values rather than the conventions of a particular society. The image of the family in contemporary society relies heavily on this combination of the natural and the moral."[20] As long as this image of the family as a biological necessity, probably God-given, holds sway, there can be no serious gaining of ground for issues of women's rights, but instead a reinforcement of the rightness of male supremacy. Moreover, since crimes against nature may well lead to sickness, according to, for instance, late-nineteenth-century medicine, those social ills believed by the Right to be plaguing contemporary society may not unreasonably be diagnosed with reference to the crime against nature which abandonment of the traditional family seems to it to be.

IT IS A MEANS OF SEXUAL CONTROL. Michel Foucault claims that, from the eighteenth century onward, the family "conveys the law and the juridical dimension in the deployment of sexuality" and also "conveys the economy of pleasure and the intensity of sensations in the regime of alliance," so that it has become "an obligatory locus of affects, feelings, love."[21] Historically, according to Foucault, sexuality is understood, organized, promoted, or penalized in its various forms and manifestations along the axes of husband-wife and parent-child.

Anita Bryant cites with uncritical approval a book by George F. Gilder, intriguingly entitled *Sexual Suicide,* which claims that the principal cause of America's problems in what were to her (in the seventies) recent years is family breakdown, and that family ties were weakened, thus "problems" worsened, by feminism, fostered in many cases, Bryant assures her reader, by "women with lesbian tendencies."[22] She is equally trusting of Gilder's statistics and his interpretation of them. These prove, she avers, that the chief source of crime and social disruption is single men. Thus, she concludes, "He argues convincingly that marriage is essential to male socialization in the modern world."[23] (Evidently, nothing needs to be said by him concerning female socialization. Otherwise, to argue in this way about socialization, where the prevailing societal sexual norm is the familial, seems unremarkable. The sleight of hand whereby "single men" become implicitly homosexual and, therefore, ipso facto antimarriage may be more interesting.)

In Britain, Mary Whitehouse's musings on sex also centered on the need for marriage, less as a focus for pleasure than as a bulwark against "cheap-imitation" sexuality, which she believed to have been engendered by the dethronement and secularization of sex, concomitant with what she took to be the undermining of the family, as traditionally conceived.[24]

In the eighties, the connotations of "family" were vigorously reassembled and mobilized against those held to be chiefly at risk from HIV infection by reason of their deviant sexuality (deviant by virtue of being held to be at variance with the conception of familial sexuality). Homosexual men were stereotyped in terms of sexual promiscuity, and therefore inevitably enemies of "the family"— whose actual sexuality could through another kind of stereotyping remain sanctified and unexamined at a time when knowledge of sexual abuse within the family had become widespread in Britain and the United States. Thus, those most at risk from infection, who were enduring a new health scourge in disproportionate numbers, were converted from victims into predators.[25]

Given the longevity of familial mythology and the power with which it proved its effectiveness in, for example, the shaping of hostile public attitudes to people with AIDS in the last decade, it is not surprising that the family—as it is understood even more importantly than as it is experienced—is of such fascination to feminist analyses of the construction of female sexuality. As Sonja Ruehl puts it, "Families are seen as a structure basic to society and the way that sexuality is *socially,* rather than biologically, linked to reproduction within families is of paramount importance here."[26]

IT OFFERS RESISTANCE TO THE STATE. Very early in his extraordinary book, *The Subversive Family: An Alternative History of Love and Marriage,* Ferdinand Mount fairly points out that all politicians claim to be on the side of the family.[27] He immediately goes on to declare that the family is the last ditch from which to resist the state. In order to revitalize the already prevailing, and (in his thinking) linked, notions of "family" and "the natural," he argues that deviance from a claimed nature by no means disproves that that nature is illusory. "Not all males in any species are sexually attracted to females," he concedes, but all that this proves, according to him, is that a person can be "denatured" by physical or psychological pressures. "Whatever the language we use to explain natural behaviour—we may talk of instinctual drives or biological programming—the purpose of invoking the idea of nature is to contrast it with unnatural behavior resulting from untoward or abnormal outside forces."[28] Mount may well be right in his description of the way that the discourse of the natural is used, to invoke the idea of nature in order to segregate a certain kind of conduct from a certain other kind. "If we *always* behaved naturally, and could behave in no other way, the idea would be much less useful."[29] Again, and always given the use of the term "natural," a fair point. Nevertheless, there is a slippage between recognizing the usefulness of a nature discourse and the position where such discursive practices become, simply, truth. What Mount offers, without benefit of data, as evidence of nature (that males are attracted to females) could be as well interpreted as statistically significant in ways that do not invoke notions of the natural—in terms of socialization rather than "biological programming," for example. His attack on "the Marxist trick" of dethroning "nature" by pointing to unmotherly behavior among mothers, for example, could be easily turned round against the writer. Because most mothers, according to his assumptions, do behave "maternally," is it not a "trick" to suggest that putative majority behavior may be equated with "natural" behavior?

Having attempted to reinvest the relatively modern phenomenon of the nuclear family with natural qualities, Mount tries to persuade his reader that its very naturalness fortifies the family against the artificial nature of the state, so that it becomes a site for resistance to it. The point of this resistance is less clear, except in terms of "the family" winning back the rewards of care for the sick and elderly, for example, privileges wrested from it (or, more accurately, from its "natural nurturers," mothers) by the welfare state. It may not be surprising to learn that Ferdinand Mount has been one of Margaret Thatcher's speechwriters.

IT CAN SAVE SOCIETY. Perhaps this claim could be subsumed under the previous two. Certainly, the reasoning behind the claim can easily be anticipated after a reading of these earlier claims.

The fundamentalist televangelists find themselves with, apparently, an unusual ally in Sigmund Freud, who saw (bourgeois) families as the "germ cells" of civilization.[30] Describing differs from promoting, nevertheless. Freud would have parted company with the New Christian Right's conception of the family as "a means to recover a lost meaning as well as a lost past" and, through its profamily stance, a means to intervene moralistically in "the teaching of evolution, prayer in schools, abortion, traditional roles for women, sex and drugs, pornography, and so forth."[31]

* * *

The immediate results of such beliefs about the family are evident in recent American history. During the 1980 election, Reagan's profamily policies included an anti-ERA stance and opposition to abortion. Because of the (highly selective) "prolife" and "pro-family" sentiments of the American Right, not only have abortion rights been attacked but so, physically, have abortion clinics. Because of the dominance of perception of the "naturalness" of caring, nurturing, subordinate roles for women in the nuclear family of patriarchy, Phyllis Schlafly was able to muster significant anti-ERA support among women by dubbing feminists as traitors and dupes. The defeat of the ERA is described by Barbara Ehrenreich, for example, as being celebrated by its opponents in the grand ballroom of the Shoreham Hotel in Washington, D.C., as a "great victory for women" and a "great achievement by women."[32] The particular women's right threatened by the ERA must surely, by this reasoning, be the right to be housewives. The ERA, according to Reagan and Schlafly, deserved to be combated because it encouraged state intervention in individuals' private lives.[33] Thus, such anti-ERA spokespersons can in the same breath as they attack them in one form claim to be in support of women's rights (. . . as long as those rights are grasped as lying within the ambience of the nuclear family).

The reason suspected by Zillah R. Eisenstein for anti-ERA zealousaness on the part of Reagan, at least, is the wish to keep married women out of the labor force.[34] If so, a norm of family life that happens not to be majority practice was insisted on to validate anti-ERA hostility. According to her, the most common form of family in society is the two-wage-earner family, since 57 percent of two-parent families have two wage earners in them. (As if that were not striking enough, she points out in addition that the "single-parent woman-headed family is now as common as the traditional patriarchal form.")[35]

In Britain in the eighties, Conservative rhetoric may have been more subtle than the American New Right version, but most of the underlying sentiments are again discoverable. Mrs. Thatcher stated significantly in 1979: "Every housewife with a weekly budget to balance knows that nothing is impossible, given the will, the character and the strength of purpose."[36] The emphasis in this statement is on the essentially self-sacrificial role of the housewife, her ability to take on economic burdens by dint of her strength of character. That strength is particularly likely to be tested under a government which shifts responsibility for care of the chronically sick and elderly on to the family, and thus on to the nurturing mother. In the world of Victorian family values so dear to the then prime minister's heart, a world which presumably found its expression in Victorian times, the economic burdens imposed upon women were so over-powering as to force tens of thousands of them into prostitution in London.[37]

It is evident that feminism has largely found the version of sexual liberation offered in the sixties to have been a trick created for the benefit of men, designed to reduce women to objects of sexual pleasure. Thatcher picked up women's discontent with that period's trends in order to attack sexual reforms of the 1960s as detrimental to women, on the grounds that they undermined "the family." According to this kind of thinking, the expansion of welfare ser-vices invades the sanctity and privacy of this same "family." Yet the British ideological picture of the family is markedly wishful, corre-sponding little to the statistically "normal" forms of family. Lynne Segal, for example, points out in 1983 that 56 percent of married women work outside the home today, while only 20 percent did in the 1920s.[38] In addition, she produces the more remarkable statistic that over 70 percent of all households live outside the traditional family structure.[39] Her consequent suggestion is that the "ideal family" functions as a myth, so that family ideology blinkers itself against social actuality to inflict damage on those deemed not "normal," thus not desirable, in the name of a norm that exists less in fact than in right-wing fancy. She asks, "With friends like Mrs Thatcher, who needs to 'smash the family'? Tory pro-family senti-ments relate to pro-family policies (ones which might assist those caring for dependants) like the expression of love relates to the act of murder."[40]

The Family Demythicized

Michele Barrett and Mary McIntosh usefully epitomize a pri-mary effect of the mythologization of the family when they write, "The world around the family is not a pre-existing harsh climate against which the family offers protection and warmth. It is as if the family had drawn comfort and security into itself and left the outside world bereft. As a bastion against a bleak society it has made that society bleak."[41]

It is naive to believe that a myth can be automatically deponten-tized by a challenge to it as "truth," since myths serve psycho-social purposes. The statistical data, as must already be evident, cannot support the publicly disseminated image of the family, how-ever. Politicians ought surely, since they are ever ready to harness myths for their own parties' ideological ends, to be constantly confronted with such statistics as are available. Electors in a democracy ought surely to attempt to measure the force of the ideal family's image against data of how people in that democracy actually live and how they organize themselves in terms of family or "pseudofamily" relationships.

The American New Right's confidence in the natural and God-given form of the patriarchal nuclear family might be tested against the statement that, at the end of the seventies, more than eight million American families were headed by "divorced, separated, widowed, and never-married women," that the living arrangements of over 75 percent of the population differed from those regarded as "normal."[42]

Mrs. Thatcher's peculiar notion of profamily attitudes even when she took office deserves to be contrasted with the sort of information provided by the General Household Survey of 1979. This appears to indicate that only 16 percent of British households consisted of one-wage-earner couples with dependent children. "A further 16 per cent consist of couples with dependent children who are both wage-earners, and 3½ per cent consist of single-parent families. The remaining percentage is made up of combinations of adults without children and people living alone."[43] By 1987, Barrie Gunter and Michael Svennevig write of Britain, "Of all homes, 23 percent are one-person households, a further 46 percent contain two or more people but no child under school leaving age; which leaves less than one in three homes as family households in the traditional senses."[44]

The tendencies outlined by these statements are clear. On the one hand, the image of normality appealed to and ever reinforced by moralizing politicians is an image of a distinctly minority phenomenon in social terms. Yet the myth is so powerful that it cannot, apparently, be dismantled by an appeal to such data, since politicians over the spectrum of party politics seem reluctant to undermine the version of family so passionately espoused by the Right. While the effectiveness of a myth can never be comprehended purely in traditional political terms, the exploitability of the myth, suitably augmented and slanted, by political parties is obvious. Thus, the profamily ideology of the Thatcher government is explicable in economic terms. "Were it not generally accepted that 'the family', and the family alone, is the only proper place for loving, caring and sharing, the barbarism of the Tory attack on welfare would surely seem unthinkable."[45]

The fear of feminism mobilized and organized against the ERA bears little relation to what seems actually to have been achieved in such matters as women's pay within workplaces at the very time of that mobilization. Profamily moralists seem anxious to return women to total economic dependency on wage-earning husbands, when statistics would suggest that, in order to explain women's relative economic exploitation in work beyond the domestic sphere, there has to be explanatory appeal to the neediness of even those women within traditionally understood families. In the United States in 1982, it was claimed that three out of every five persons with incomes below the poverty line were women.[46] In the same year, it was claimed in Britain that while women constituted 43 percent of the work force (60 percent of these women being married), they were employed largely as servants, not leaders, that on average only about 5 percent within the professions were female, that Britain had the lowest number of women Members of Parliament since the Second World War.[47]

It is possible, nonetheless, in the teeth of the statistics and their obvious interpretation, for the New Right and like-minded thinkers to claim that while the "true" family is in the statistical minority, it is in that position only because of the American (or British) nation's departure from natural, and therefore right, paths of behavior. In other words, "nature" is calling back those who have turned their backs upon it before it is too late, before the nation is destroyed. According to this scenario, the family was healthy and normal until such plagues as feminism, the demand for gay rights, or the greater availability of pornography infected it. Some thinkers are unimpressed with this account. Dennis Altman, for example, believes that the explanation for changed family life-styles and family organization is discoverable in a combination of: decreased demand for reproduction; the decline of kinship as a form of social organization; the decreasing importance of gender roles in the determination of the division of labor; the relocation of courtship into specialized commercial establishments.[48] One could quarrel with such detail as the little-argued identification as effect of what one group might take to be cause, or, in the light of evidence cited earlier, with the notion that gender has lost importance in the division of labor. Nevertheless, the relocation of family-change debate in socioeconomic factors, in the advance of capitalism, rather than sin, seems helpful. Altman underlines, for instance, the inclusion of sexuality in the mechanisms of consumption rather than of production, seeing this new placement as a product of shifts in the nature of modern capitalism.[49]

The Family and the Left

Several commentators on the mythical support for profamily rhetoric, while not blind to the nature of the myth or to its uses, express their dismay at the cul-de-sac which publicly stated opposition to the family seems to have become in practice. Their assertion of the mistake that feminists and leftists of different persuasions have made may be the more confident because of their observation of the distrust which a declared antifamily policy engenders in potential, but unpoliticized, supporters. Familialism has a long history which it is rash to ignore.

The more advanced forms of capitalism ushered in by the nineteenth century in, for example, Europe and the United States acted at one level to undermine the family significantly. The basic processes of commodity production were socialized, labor removed from the private efforts of families or villages and centralized in corporate units on a larger scale. Thus, the factory system took over the family's functions in terms of production.[50] Yet while what was in the nineteenth century taken to be the traditional form of family life suffered change under capitalism, the violence of the change did not mean the end of family life. Rather, there was a split between material production in its specialized forms and "private labor" performed in the home, predominantly by women.[51] The family retained much of the importance attached to it by the early bourgeoisie (when it was a basic unit of production) by the link between bourgeois individualism and the transmission of private property.

So tenacious is the family in the last two centuries, adapting itself against the incursions of capitalism, that Freudian psychoanalysis appears to regard the individual in isolation as unintelligible, and to be forced to have recourse to the family to furnish an explanation of the individual, as commonly apprehended. So crucial is the bourgeois family as a means of enlightening the analyst in regard to his (only apparently) individual object of inquiry that Freud may be taken to regard the bourgeois family as universal and necessary.[52]

While a grasp of the historical cruciality of the bourgeois family at the period and place of Freud's investigations would suggest that he made an unwarranted leap to the claim of universality, his recognition of the family's significance ought not to be set aside lightly. Whether socialists should go in the direction of the "Friends of the Family" movement in the United States,[53] they ought at least to desist from underestimating the powerful place of familialist discourse in British and American thinking. The Russian Bolsheviks began by introducing policies demonstrating their distrust of and hostility to conventional marriage and the family, yet in time the party line changed to characterize a stable family structure as an essential feature of the progress toward socialism. To put the matter more pessimistically, a socialist revolution does not by any means guarantee in practice an emancipation of women. Accordingly, such change as there is in family structure is not regularly traceable to changes in the ownership of the means of production.

That socialist regimes in theory should show some awareness of the need to address the organization of the family within socialism, but also that they should in practice prove largely incapable of following through to a new position on the family, is predictable. If Marx and Engels are taken as starting points for socialists concerned with the family, their criticisms of existing familial institutions seem sharp enough. Marx claims that capitalist industrialization has destroyed or tainted family bonds in the working class so that the family unit's function is only to produce workers, leaving the family with a further function only in terms of the bourgeoisie, that function being the retention and transmission of private property. Engels follows this up by predicting that under socialism the patriarchal family will be destroyed and that "pairing relationships" will take its place, that the abolition of private property necessitates the abolition of the patriarchal family.[54] Yet while Engels grasped that the existing form of family was not immutable, he appears to have made assumptions about the naturalness of the social division of labor (whereby, for example, women are biologically designed to be primarily responsible for child care). The attack on the family is worth mounting, according to Engels, only with the development of private property. His vision of the transformed socialist family still continues to incorporate a traditional division of labor.

If the family is not immutable, the "personal" does seem to remain so in Engels by virtue of its "naturalness."[55] The division of labor being validated by reference to biology, heterosexuality is automatically given normative power. An analysis of the family in the historical moment of capitalism which refuses to dismantle the claims for a biological basis for the traditionally different rights and duties of men and women within it and which continues to split sexualities into natural and deviant has little hope of revolutionizing it. The apparent promise of Marxist analysis of the family, together with its failure to tackle the problems remaining within that analysis, helps to explain socialist regimes' interest in, but apparent inability to cope with, change in traditional family structures.

Feminist analysis of the family was obviously unlikely to stay content with the modest undermining of biology and of the natural achieved by Engels. The issue of women's equality could not emerge while male supremacy within the organization of even the socialist family, however that was envisaged, remained intact. A more credible analysis was offered by Althusser, who argued that the family was one of the ideological state apparatuses with the particular task not only of providing, as in Marxist analysis, labor power but of creating in its members submission to the rules of the established order.[56]

Feminists have identified the family as "the core institution of the oppression of women,"[57] particularly in its veiling, and consequent underrewarding, of women's domestic labor as production essential to capitalism and in its treatment under capitalism of married women as a reserve army of labor.[58] Feminist analysis must move beyond Engels's partial dismantling of oppressive family institutions. It has "come to see the private rearing of children in the heterosexual, monogamous nuclear-family household as inseparable from male dominance" so that "jettisoning the bad bits and preserving the good bits" is unimaginable.[59]

What is observable here is not so much an antifamily attitude per se as opposition to the sort of family structure which is unthinkingly equated with the traditionally conceived nuclear family's. This possibly obvious point needs constant restatement, since the simplest antifeminist tactic appears to be the representation of critics of the traditional form of family as violently opposed to "family" of any description. While the New Right tends to think of crises within the patriarchal family as being the fault of leftist analysis, the Left would argue that capitalism is responsible. Feminists might be more interested in observing the "dialectical" relations of capitalism and patriarchy, whereby these systems seem mutually dependent but may be conflictual, such that "family and personal instability is a weak spot in capitalism."[60]

When Betty Friedan writes, "To the degree that feminists collude in assuming an inevitable, unbridgeable antagonism between women's equality and the family, they make it a self-fulfilling prophecy,"[61] she is not being entirely fair to feminists. The antagonism between women's equality and the family may indeed be unbridgeable if the family in question follows the patriarchal model. Women might find equality in some other form of family. The absence of an explicit definition for the particular model of family about which feminists have expressed doubts should not preclude its implicit presence. What is contested between the Right and feminism is surely the conception of "family." Every time the Right uses the term, its denotation but also its connotation must be borne in mind. Every time feminism expresses its opposition to family, it must be realized that it is not every model of family that is being condemned. Within the patriarchal family, nevertheless, even the most politicized member of it must be aware of contradictory loyalties and affections which are so easily exploited by conservative politics. As Gordon and Hunter put it, "without condemning many people's love and need for their families we can fight against the romantic, reactionary, reassertion of family as an ideal model of authority and community."[62] It may not be enough to agree with Friedan that feminism's opposition to the family weakens the likely appeal of the movement, since there is a constant danger of the valorization of family, any kind of family, however demonstrably certain models damage women's interests. Rather, the academic-seeming definition of family must constantly be on the agenda, so that every time the Right purports to speak in the name of all families, the veiled power relations of very particular conceptions of family are exposed to scrutiny and criticism. Lawrence Grossberg believes that, "Insofar as the Left ignores this increasing investment [of the family in the construction of a conservative cultural hegemony], it has given up the struggle to find another discourse of the family."[63] It is the discourse of the family around which feminism certainly, if not the entire Left, must organize its struggle.

5

Movies and Familialism

The Family of Reaganite Entertainment

When Andrew Britton attempts to characterize the shift in filmic representations of the family within the eighties, he notices a significant trend in contemporary melodrama, concerning the father-son cycle: the objective aimed at within such melodramas' narratives is the establishment or securing of the patrilineal bond. These films divide on the question of the source of the obstruction to that bond, whether it be from the mother or the father. Britton claims that the essence of the project is always the exclusion of the mother. He believes that such movies articulate a conservative riposte to the Women's Movement's critique of patriarchy within the nuclear family.[1]

The credibility of Britton's claims, at least in the sense that America was ready by the late seventies for the return of the patriarch in restored form, is suggested by Lewis John Carlino's *The Great Santini* (1979). In this film, the militaristic, bullying martinet of a father played by Robert Duvall, who seems to be unbearably oppressive to his wife (Blythe Danner) and sensitive, adolescent son for much of the film's action, turns out at the film's closure to be not only the military hero that was seldom in doubt but also, astoundingly, a model parent. His sacrifice of his life on behalf of the community may be taken to indicate his well-earned military status but, despite every appearance of persecuting his son, he vindicates his conduct toward him by steering him through the oedipal crisis to "manhood." (His achievement in this respect is notably similar to that of Richard Gere's drill instructor and surrogate father in *An Officer and a Gentleman*.) Thus, it is suggested that it is his family's perception, and by implication the audience's perception, of the disciplinarian father that is at fault. The adjustment required is not of the father in the interests of the family but of the family—and of the audience—in respect to the ultimate achievements of the patriarch. Liberal concern with the rights of a son experiencing a father's bullying behavior is shown to be misplaced, when against expectations (though surely not generic expectations?) the son pulls through successfully into manhood. The father, by his sacrifice of his life, demonstrates the "true" reading of his familial conduct.

Reinstatement of the father after, in this next case, an absence of four years appears to be the subject of Robert Lieberman's *Table for Five* (1983), where the essence of the narrative is the need for the vacant chair at the dinner table to be filled by the hitherto unconfident, but now restored, father, so that by this means the nuclear family may be most closely approximated. Although the film initially suggests that the hero's lack of confidence in the paternal role may not simply be a matter of individual psychology but may find its roots in the uneasy fit between family life and an increasingly competitive society, it soon jettisons this articulation of familial role conflict for a study of the father's personal growth.

In both of these films, the reputation of the father is being dusted off and restored, the family being "his" to make or break simply by the strength or weakness of his personality. Machismo, which for the bulk of the movie is apparently overbearing machismo, is proved to be only a misleading disguise for strength in one film. In the other, former weakness becomes quiet strength.

In certain other eighties films, women, particularly when politicized or organized in feminist terms, prove to be a threat to the family. Thus, as its title—*Independence Day*—gives promise, Robert Mandel's 1982 movie foregrounds the accepted and celebrated American way of life, in relation to the tensions created by it for those who favor different values. As in women's or family melodrama of the fifties, the choice of family or career is set out—as a choice, which only certain conceptions of the family make it—with a final weighting against the "independent" career woman.

George Roy Hill's *The World According to Garp* (1982) makes the most potent threats to the bliss promised to the hero (Robin Williams) from his nuclear family those that come either from female deviation from the patriarchal norm (his wife's adultery) or from the organization of women into separatist and silent communes (recognizably—but only just so through the parodic treatment of them—feminist in sympathies). While the women of the movie rebel against the strictures placed upon them by masculine values or expectations, as well as against male violence, there is little attempt to analyze the sources of their rebellion. Attention is focused instead upon the harms experienced by the family through misfit women, rather than upon explanations from within the family as to the women's feelings of being misfits.

In all the movies mentioned so far, paternal virtues are emphasized, largely in terms of fatherly strength preserving the family. Women in these movies tend to be potentially or actually obstructive to the family, misreading male strength as brutal aggression or else overreacting to what is correctly construed by them as brutal aggression. The absence of the mother is already a central feature of *Table for Five*. In Leonard Nimoy's *Three Men and a Baby* (1987), the actual mother is of almost no consequence, attention being directed to the maternal potential within three bachelors who must learn to change dirty nappies, choose baby foods, and deploy their worktime around the need for baby care.

The horror that is taken broadly by Robin Wood to emanate from within the nuclear family in "progressive" horror films of the seventies and eighties could be thought to lose its critical edge in certain eighties dramas. In these, horror finds its source within nuclear-family relations not in their "ideal" organization, but in a breach of that organization through, for example, adultery. *Fatal Attraction* will be discussed at fuller length in chapter 12. For the moment, the point may be made with reference to Lewis Teague's *Cujo* (1983).

The Saint Bernard dog named in the title becomes rabid and monstrous because of a bite from a rabies-carrying bat. In the meantime, the Trenton family is being threatened by the wife's adulterous relationship. That the entry of disease into the blood-stream of a hitherto lovable animal to produce hideous change should not be a metaphor in this movie for the poison of adultery seeping into the hitherto charming family's vitals would seem unlikely. The lengthy confrontation between rabid animal and trapped mother and child makes the connection specific, though less overt than in the Stephen King original.

Someone to Watch Over Me (1987) is noticeably less reminiscent of the horror genre than *Fatal Attraction,* but the Ridley Scott movie shares with it the basic structure of familial relations versus extrafamilial attractions. In each, an apparently super-straight married man is tempted by the world that the single woman inhabits. At the end of each, the threatened wife kills the source of violent threat. However, in *Fatal Attraction* the single woman combines, in her early manifestations, the allure of erotic excitement and, later, violence toward the nuclear family, while in the Scott movie the single woman's threat to the family is purely from the attraction that the hero feels for her, while the violence that is directed toward the family is the killer's means of getting at his real target, the single woman.

It could be argued, reductively, that the estrangement of the hero (Tom Berenger) from his wife (Lorraine Bracco) and family renders them more vulnerable to attack from the outside so that adultery "causes" a violent threat to the family. This argument would be less persuasive in relation to familialism in the eighties than another observation: the family represents a haven of security against the coldness and impersonality of the jungle beyond the family.

While the neighborhood in which the family lives is one that it wishes to leave because of its high crime rate, there is also a suggestion that the uptown, classier world of Claire Gregory (Mimi Rogers) is at heart colder, less "real" than the family environment. This is offered partly through the use of music, particularly opera, that is alien but seductive to the Berenger character, undermining his former values, but also partly through decor and architecture (areas to which Scott had already demonstrated his sensitivity in *Blade Runner*). Claire's apartment, from which the downtown cops must mount constant surveillance, is characterized by its size, its spaciousness (which has, as its converse meaning, emptiness— particularly emptiness of children, since it is the child-rearing aspects of married life which "fill" the more cramped living quarters of Berenger's family home). It is also characterized by not just the elegance of its marble columns but the coldness of the surface of marble.

While the *appearance* of Claire's life-style attracts the cop hero, much of the movie involves a gradual stripping away of appearance not only for him but for the audience, which is invited to enter the affair sympathetically with him. (After all, the obvious sense of the words sung by Sting behind the credits is that the person who needs to be watched over is the woman being protected by the cops and then, more personally and lovingly, by the hero.) By the end of the movie, the audience, along with the Berenger character, is reminded that the society in which Claire moves is one in which a psychotic killer also moves easily and which can bring its threat to the very doorstep of the more proletarian wife. Claire is not the psychotic killer, which is why this movie differs markedly from *Fatal Attraction,* but they come from the same sort of world. The family draws together against threats both specific and diffuse from the outside world, which is at once both disordered and highly ordered. While the family's own warm and "meaningful" disorder suggests no clear solution to crime, it confirms the essential sanity and benignity of the nuclear family as the single bastion of decency in an indifferent world.

The kind of recuperative version of family horror suggested by *Cujo,* where completion of family bonds provides cathartic closure rather than a springboard for the narrative, is exemplified again in Fritz Kiersch's *Children of the Corn* (1984). A ready-made potential-parent couple, played by Peter Horton and Linda Hamilton, finds itself threatened by a bloodthirsty religious community of adolescents and children. During their struggle for survival, the hero is helped by those two children from the community who seem most likely to defect from it. The film ends with a number of promises of normality. The as-yet-unmarried hero and heroine escape, departing from a rural hinterland to a nearby town, accompanied by the boy and girl who seemed most willing to help them to survive. The appeal of the family is heightened here by the promise of its perfection, by its delayed fruition (delayed beyond the narrative's close), as something yet to be achieved by the bringing together of the potential family elements into a "normal" pattern of life in a normal setting.

A different strategy suggests the longing for that normality represented by the nuclear family, even in imperfect form, in Matthew Patrick's *Hider in the House* (1989). Here, the psychotic character looks in upon the family and is maddened by his desire to be part of it, so that his threat to it is motivated as a form of destructive jealousy for that which is so precious that he feels threatened by his inability to achieve it.

Critiques of the Family

Possibly the most unremitting criticism of family life in an eighties film is to be found in the British director Terence Davies's *Distant Voices, Still Lives* (1988). As an art-house movie, it can perhaps take greater risks, not only questioning but denying family mythology. Sequence after sequence centers on the violent degradation of women in the working-class family of at least the forties and fifties. Some women resist, sometimes husband and fathers do not get their way forever. All the same, the freedoms that women members of the family secure for themselves are hard won and relatively meager. Male dominance relies on brute force whenever it is resisted. The characters' loyalties, often to the mother figure regardless of the gender of the child, count little against the realities of economic and physical power. Justification for the unequal power division in families (largely deprived of economic power in the world beyond them, severely deprived when male physical power is lost) is seldom attempted by those wielding or experiencing power within the family. This is how things are, the characters seem to feel, at the same time that nobody feels that this is how things ought to be.

It is interesting to examine a possible relation with family politics in the Australian *An Indecent Obsession* (1985), since Lex Marinos's film does not center on a nuclear family at all but concerns itself with an army hospital at the end of the Second World War. Most of the characters are male. The psychiatric ward sister Honour Langtry (Wendy Hughes), however, relates to her disturbed charges in some measure as a substitute mother. "All the comforts of home and a Mum too!" one character notices, while Honour describes herself as a mother trying to hold the family together when it has lost its reasons to exist. The familial subtext is further opened up, but also complicated, by the presence of Michael Wilson (Gary Sweet) in the psychiatric ward, since he also adopts a nurturing, caring role in relation to the men, and it is to him that Honour transmits her responsibilities for tending these men, her "children." The oedipal nature of some of the narrative—Honour makes love with Michael when another, malevolent patient makes homosexual advances to him and is nearly strangled for his assault upon Michael's self-image—reinforces the notion that the film is really centered on family relations. On the other hand, its intimations about the family institution and the painful prices it exacts from its members may be lost on those who shout the loudest about the virtues of family life, precisely because we are dealing here with "pretended family relationships."

A less oblique undermining of the family takes place in Joseph Ruben's *The Stepfather* (1986), which follows *Hider in the House* in aligning an obsessional maintenance of the familial ideal with psychosis. (This alignment is a tactic that has notable predecessors in, for example, Alfred Hitchcock's *Psycho* [1960] or, within the eighties, De Palma's *Dressed to Kill* [1980].) One distinct achievement of such movies as *The Stepfather* is that they underline the separability of family as ideal and family in practice, making a point that the previous chapter argues is of fundamental importance if questioning of New Right familialism is not to alienate those with profound sentimental attachment to particular families. The central notion of the narrative is that the film's "hero" will eliminate any family member whose attitude or behavior threatens to obstruct his utopian notion of family life.

Balancing of Familialism and Critique

A less schematic contrasting of image with actuality takes place in Charles Shyer's *Baby Boom* (1987). Here, the careerist heroine, J. C. Wiatt (Diane Keaton), on the brink of achieving a partnership in her management consultancy firm, living an uncomplicated private existence with her boyfriend Steven (Harold Ramis), has her life style disrupted, her values held up to question, by the arrival of her late cousin's baby daughter into her home (and work). Unable emotionally to proceed with her plan to have the baby adopted, and abandoned by Steven, she finds that she cannot combine child care with success in her citified career. When she retires to the country, into the recognizably Sirkian-inspired town of Hadleyville, she quickly becomes bored with her domesticated rural existence and moves with spectacular success into another branch of business by making and marketing her own baby-food recipe, "Country Baby." At the end of the film, she has it all; she is a model of business success, but she is also still living away from New York City, caring for Elizabeth, about to complete her family via union with the local animal vet, played by Sam Shepard.

On a superficial reading of the movie, it would be reasonable to think that the heroine's progress from hardheaded careerist through a period of relatively self-sacrificial single parenthood to happily partnered mother represents a Reaganite dream of feminine fulfillment. The movie, both in its narrative development and its construction, suggests that its apparent tale of antifeminist recuperation may not be quite so simple. The naming of J.C.'s small town as Hadleyville, with its near-unavoidable allusion to the town of *Written on the Wind* (1956), makes at least the cine-literate member of the audience consider the possibility that the comfortable closure has the "forced" and therefore incredible quality discerned for the closure of many key fifties melodramas, whereby the very ideology which has proved inadequate to the task of providing answers for the protagonists' problems is reasserted, more nostalgically than believably. While business success in the city is deemed unlikely for the single parent, so that the old career versus motherhood choice reappears, J. C. does finally combine business success and motherhood, albeit in the "less real" and wishful environment of Hadleyville. If the family of the closure is difficult to distinguish from conventional pictures of the conventionally conceived nuclear family, it is a family chosen and in a sense created by the heroine. Moreover, it is a sort of private reward for public success, not the result of the more traditional maternal self-sacrifice lionized in melodrama.

Eugene Corr's *Desert Bloom* (1985) performs a similar feat of suggesting the impossibility and fragility of the American dream of family against its actualization while at the same time allowing the poignancy of the wishful dream to valorize the imperfect achievement of it. It is not so simple as allowing the brutalities of patriarchalism (the patriarch being Jon Voight) to be explained and softened by the exposure of the pressures exerted by culturally dominant notions of masculinity and by the unrelenting economics of the world beyond the family home, though those elements are there. Rather, by setting the action of the film in early fifties Las Vegas and portraying the family in a period of little-understood atomic-bomb testing, the particular conception of the family is historicized. Nuclear family and pre-nuclear atomic testing are linked in time. The lack of fear and the delight and pride shown by some in the nuclear test has to be read today as misguided, but, in the circumstances, beyond harsh, superior judgment. A similar reading of the movie's familialism might also be suggested.

An apparently more trenchant account of the family, Danny DeVito's *War of the Roses* (1988), manages also to overlay its more overt criticism with the comforting suggestions of atypicality. While the Roses (Kathleen Turner and Michael Douglas) illustrate the dangers that go-getting, or at least go-getting on the part of both marriage partners, can generate for a marrige's stability, the movie's critical edge is blunted in a number of ways. The husband's pet dog is not, after all, killed, disguised as haute cuisine, and fed to him by his wife. The lawyer telling their story appears to have learned from this sorry example of modern marriage and is about to embark on an altogether happier version. The story itself is framed as a moral tale. It is a tale both universal in its implications of the potential destructiveness of ambitiousness in both marriage partners and highly particular by virtue of being couched as a morality, unusual enough to be told to a potential divorcé.

Perhaps the most striking example of the critical-sentimental vision of family is discoverable in *Parenthood,* which will be discussed at greater length in chapter 12.

Destruction of the Family

Philip Brophy, in 1986, identifies a growing trend in contemporary horror films, the destruction of the family. He argues that *Amityville 2: The Possession* (1982) marks the commercial peak in this trend.[2] Suspense, he declares, is no longer a matter of individual identification but has "now shifted onto not a family identification, but a pleasure in witnessing the Family being destroyed—it being the object of the horror and us being the subject of their demise."[3] *The Hills Have Eyes* (1977) is described by Brophy as positing two totally opposite families in a fight for survival. On the one side, there is an all-white, all-blond middle-class American family, what the director Wes Craven calls the "white-bread" family. On the other is an inbred family of cannibals dedicated to killing the all-American family as gruesomely as possible, one by one. While Brophy thinks of *Hills* as horror comedy, he takes *Amityville 2* as social-realist. In it, the family is reinforced through pictorial framing as "a pathetic polaroid of complacency, ripe for the total destruction that eventually befalls it."[4] This total destruction is provided by the son who, in his state of possession, shoots all the other members of his family.

Damiano Damiani's family horror movie is reminiscent in this respect (family destruction) of Tobe Hooper's work. In Hooper's *The Funhouse* (1981), as in his celebrated *Texas Chainsaw Massacre* of 1974, he concentrates primarily on the family and, by means of that concentration, on the "permissive" society. Notably, in both movies, the members of the exterminating family are exclusively male. The two families involved are parallels, Cynthia Rose argues. The family portraits build, she claims, "towards a Dorian Gray-style scream of Freudian recognition as the permissive society confronts its true self."[5]

The pleasure invited by the Wes Craven and Damiani movies, pleasure in watching family destruction, seems to suggest at the least the possibility of a distanced, critical perspective on the American nuclear family. Yet that family-destruction movies cannot be taken on the ground of content analysis alone to place their audiences in a once-for-all defined political position vis-à-vis familialism is strongly suggested by Cynthia Rose's conclusion that it may be a particular sort of family which is eliminated. When that family is a product of a society deemed "permissive," then its destruction appears to represent an assault less on the nuclear family than on the less certainly familial values of that sort of society.

Re-creation of the Family

That the family is multifaceted and capable of multiple identifications is suggested not merely by the different sorts of family which populate the family-destruction horror movies but by a recent Australian film—Ann Turner's *Celia* (1988). The family of *Celia* becomes a site of resistance for a rebellious child's need to organize revolt against the more conformist wider society beyond that family. The claim that the family may be subversive, a focus of resistance, has become familiar as an element within the Right's familialism. Ferdinand Mount, as was seen in chapter 4, affirms resistance to the depredations of the state as a particular privilege of the family. While that attribution seems to lead in practice to the granting of such further, and dubious, privileges as familial caring for the chronically sick, there is a lesson of sorts for the Left in the notion that the family can organize with more cohesion and effectiveness than can members of the Communist party, for example, and that the personal can be recognizably political, as feminists have for so many years argued.

This would suggest afresh the importance of one conclusion of the previous chapter for "progressive" sexual politics, that it is not the family per se which is oppressive to its members and which is a force for conformity, but a particular version of it.

6
Sexuality

Sex and Nature

Those who believe in the naturalness of sexuality generally assume that it is a particular form of sexuality which is natural, other forms being perversions or constituting an interference with the God-given form. That form—conceived by, for instance, the American Right to be in accordance with nature—involves the superiority of male over female in the hierarchy. This particular hierarchy in turn is rationalized on the basis of biologically given differences in aggression between the sexes. In turn, again, superior value is accorded to "natural" male aggressiveness because of a particular, Hobbesian, social doctrine that individual success is explained by competition, the male being the better equipped to achieve that success (which is positively valued). Thus, through, for example, prioritization of a social system which is highly artifactual at the same time as it validates itself in terms of natural drives, a particular form of heterosexuality, involving a particular power distribution between the sexes, is exclusively valued, on the grounds that it is the only form which is in accordance with Nature's design.

The problem in this set of beliefs is obvious. Wide varieties of heterosexual behavior as well as frequent incidences of homosexuality are easily discoverable within human societies, as well as within the animal kingdom, and would therefore appear, in that sense, natural. Ferdinand Mount exemplifies the problem and the Rightist thinking that discards the evidence of problem when he writes, "The knowledge of . . . deviations from natural behaviour does not prevent us from saying that 'it is natural for rats to do such-and-such' or that 'it is natural for males to be sexually attracted to females.' "[1] Mount is right. Knowledge of even widespread and statistically significant deviations from what is *deemed* natural does not prevent thinkers of his sort ("us") from continuing to say that it is natural. By setting up a norm of naturalness from which natural events differ at the cost of being termed unnatural events, Mount demonstrates the logic by which a particular model of sexuality becomes the only one that may be given positive value, with the imprimatur of naturalness. It is a very short step from this kind of argumentation to Anita Bryant's confident proclamation that "God has ordained sexual identities innate in male and female: so homosexuality is a twisting of divine order"[2] or to her curious notion that the body parts appropriate to sodomy do not "fit." (The way that body parts are made to serve a prevailing sexual ideology is, incidentally, well illustrated by Pat Caplan's observation: "Sex-change operations, . . . while they arouse enormous public interest, do not appear to be condemned; it is as though surgery removes not only organs but also anomalies, making a correct fit between sex, gender, and sexuality."[4]

The sexual essentialism illustrated by Mount, Bryant, and many other spokespersons of the Right has been significantly challenged from a number of directions. Jeffrey Weeks summarizes the different theoretical approaches relevant to this challenge as (1) interactionist, (2) psychoanalytical, and (3) discursive.[5]

Theoreticians of the first sort argue that nothing is intrinsically sexual, that anything can be sexualized. Psychoanalysts, reinterpreting Freud after the pattern of Jacques Lacan and Juliet Mitchell, can—as with Lacan—deduce that sexuality is constituted in language, that it is vitally connected with the child's entry into the Symbolic Order and thus the child's acquisition of language. The relationship between the second and third of Weeks's categories is clearest through the link between sexuality and language suggested by Lacan. Michel Foucault is today reckoned to be the foremost investigator of the way that sexuality is constructed through discourse. "Sexuality" is employed as a term descriptive of a historical construct. Foucault's conception of sexuality as a historical apparatus interestingly suggests how mistaken it may be to use the singular noun and that it might be more illuminating to investigate sexualities in terms of the apparatuses (medical, psychiatric, etc.) which engendered them. "What is ultimately of most significance in Foucault's work," Weeks concludes, "is [his] . . . recognition of the constant struggle within the definitions of sexuality. . . . It is not the release of a hidden or blocked essence that should be the target of sexual radicalism, he suggests, but conscious intervention at the level of definition of appropriate sexual behaviour."[6] From his study of Foucault, Weeks draws the lesson in his investigations of sex and sexuality that sex is relational, shaped in social interaction, to be understood only in a historical context in terms of the cultural meanings ascribed to it.[7]

This understanding of the meaning of sexuality is all the more vital in a culture which suggests that at the very core of personal identity is sexuality, and that sexuality has a vital connection not with discourse but with nature. If people within the dominant culture are encouraged to see their selfhood in terms of their sexuality, the illumination that an experience is sexualized only by the application of socially learned meanings is profoundly significant for sexual politics, as well as for such politically relevant "personal" processes as self-appraisal. Freud, at least prior to re-reading by Mitchell, is understandably taken to be "oppressive" by feminists by reason of such concepts of his as penis envy. Even Freud, though, attempts to demonstrate that identity is not a matter of destiny achieved through inevitable progression from innate instincts. Rather, identity in Freud is a struggle, through which there is tentative and precarious accommodation of drives with structures of language and structures of reality.

The various theoretical positions adumbrated in the preceding three paragraphs combine to suggest strongly that sexuality is not a manifestation of immanent truth, but rather that what our sex expresses is "a complexity of biological, psychic and social influences, all of which are deeply embodied in relations of domination and subordination."[8]

Sexual Mythology and "Permissiveness"

"Few political metaphors in recent times have been as powerful as that of 'permissiveness.'"[9] Part of its power may derive from the term's apparent clarity, which masks, at deeper consideration, opacity. Weeks defines "the permissive moment" not as coterminous with the sixties but as a period from the midfifties to midseventies wherein there was no single social imperative, no inherent tendency within capitalism, no single political strategy organizing and underpinning the political and legal reorganizations of the period.[10] He further describes the changes under four headings, which may be summarized in the following terms:

1. The intensification of the commercialization and commodification of sex
2. Shifts in male/female relations
3. Changes in the mode of regulation of sexuality
4. New or reordered social conflicts and new political movements[11]

Such description refuses to discover commonalities where these seem not to exist, and extends and diffuses by widening the time span well beyond the sixties and by identifying the causes of change as multifarious and lacking unified organization. Almost inevitably, this kind of description has less popular appeal than, say, Mary Whitehouse's or Margaret Thatcher's deployment of terms such as "permissiveness," "sexual revolution," "the sixties" and "social breakdown" to suggest conspiracy—a sinister trend which can be powerfully and virtuously resisted before it is "too late." The political appeal of characterizing complex social change in an easily comprehensible, unified and—importantly—moralistic way, as evidence of looser moral standards and of disrespect for tradition, needs little establishment. The effect in the seventies and later was obviously to generate a sense of crisis and thus to mute opposition to authoritarian "solutions" to the artificially stimulated sense of crisis.

Even in the sixties themselves, there were moral panics over the "new morality," a morality which impinged on prostitution, abortion, homosexuality, and drugs, these panics manifesting themselves in the uproar surrounding the Profumo affair and in the arrest of Mick Jagger, for example.[12]

By 1980, Alan Crawford found one explanation for the rise in the United States of such charismatic political leaders and cult figures as Phyllis Schlafly, Anita Bryant, and Jerry Falwell in the engendering of belief that American society was severely shaken by waves of "permissiveness." Such concerns as those inspired by a rising divorce rate, an "epidemic" of sexually transmitted diseases, increases in teenage pregnancies, in abortion, in births of illegitimate children, in homosexuality, in drug abuse and alcoholism among teenagers, in violence and crime, were linked at the end of the seventies. They were all taken as examples of the sorry results of liberal "permissiveness." Some of the claimed increases make no sense even in themselves. (How, for example, is an increase in homosexuality measured, since the incidence of homosexual acts must be difficult to monitor. By self-identification? By attendance of the self-identifying at clinics or at rallies?) Some may make a sense opposite to that required (a rise in divorce statistics *could* paradoxically suggest greater value attached to the concept of marriage). Nevertheless, the increases and the claimed causes are all instantly capable of exploitation by such activists as Phyllis Schlafly and Anita Bryant or by such organizations as Moral Majority, Inc.

Casper G. Schmidt identifies the midseventies as a period of clampdown on sexuality and drugs: Bryant attacked "runaway gay liberation," and various states passed a series of "Anita Bryant Laws"; the Moral Majority, Inc., was formed in 1978, followed by the Religious Roundtable in 1979; Richard Viguerie instituted his direct-mail missives on behalf of conservative causes; and Ronald Reagan, that apotheosis of conservatism, was elected president in 1980.[13] Occasionally, Schmidt's listing may read like another grouping of only loosely connected phenomena after the manner of the Right's uncritical grouping of "permissive" events and legislation. There is a vital difference, all the same. The way that conservatives grouped controversial matters and used their influence to pick out "single issues" for the concerned electorate, in terms of their exemplification of attacks on the fabric of American society, makes sense of the linking of apparently different phenomena.

In relation to sexuality singular (as the very title of this chapter has it, in recognition of the power of dominant ideology to deny the existence of sexualities), the important point is that the eighties is a period of conservative consolidation; the intermittent conservative moral panics of the sixties were mobilized and organized in the latter seventies into political groupings. These groupings had high on their agenda the need to legitimize one form of sexuality in order to marginalize and delegitimize other forms, and to burden such sexuality as they termed "deviant" and "unnatural" with blame for a huge variety of what they discerned to be social evils, leading to the possible destruction of the nation itself.

Capitalism and Sexuality

If growing fear of and hostility to any sexuality other than that of the heterosexual family model has become a tradition of the Right, the traditional Left comprehension of the relation of capitalism to sexuality has been largely in terms of repression. Caroline Sheldon takes the function of the heterosexual family unit within modern capitalism as the production of workers "already alienated by the experience of lack of power (in childhood) and by a strictly defined sexuality."[14] In so doing, she offers a classic Left analysis of the nature of, and constraints placed on, sexuality within a developed capitalist system. Weeks notices how sex outside procreation is condemned in the Judeo-Christian tradition.[15] However, he helps to corroborate Sheldon's formulation when he notes that while there has been a long tradition of the persecution of "deviant" sex, this persecution intensified in the nineteenth and twentieth centuries and orthodoxy and deviance crystallized in sexual terms. He believes that it is the capitalist family that provides a specific context for "acceptable" relations of men to women and for labelling certain forms of sexuality as deviant, even if "much of the language and terminology may have derived from pre-capitalist cultures."[16]

Michel Foucault, however, questions the classic account. (His study of the history of sexuality is, in large part, a study of how sexuality has been conceived of and described through history but also a study of the understanding of certain historical stages' relations to what was then or is now deemed to be sexuality.) He notes how the advent of the age of repression is traditionally placed in the seventeenth century and thus permitted to coincide with the development of capitalism.[17] He highlights the explanatory value accorded to the general and intensive work imperative in the traditional account of repression. In this way, he concludes, demands for sexual freedom gain the respectability of a political cause. "A suspicious mind might wonder if taking so many precautions in order to give the history of sex such an impressive filiation does not bear traces of the same old prudishness: as if those valorizing correlations were necessary before such a discourse could be formulated or accepted."[18] Foucault has just such a suspicious mind. A measure of the grounds for suspicion of the classic Left account of capitalism's relations with sexual repression might be that such an account leaves sex and sexuality as things-in-themselves outside discourse. In other words, the underlying argument is that capitalism has "interfered with" what must be taken to be a force in its own right, that could flourish and produce happiness were it not for repression. This implication sounds remarkably like an extension of the notion that sex is an instinct, and that sexuality is naturally, presocially engendered.

A feminist account of sexuality would have to bring into play, within the boundaries of capitalism, the significant role of the patriarchal, and would have to attempt an analysis of the relations of patriarchy and modern capitalism. While these may be seen to constitute what is ultimately a mutually dependent totality, patriarchy and capitalism can be discerned to be differentiated and conflictual systems. Their relationship has been deemed by more than one analyst to be dialectical.[19] For example, industrialism proved detrimental to the home-as-workshop and introduced individual wage labor, thus weakening family bonds; this has proved damaging to patriarchal forms, for which Right-inspired legislation has recently attempted to provide protection. Within this tension of the depredations of capitalism and the needs of patriarchy there lie both profit and loss, depending on one's politics. The greater emphasis on the individual released by a more assertive capitalism does weaken the family and the wider community and can produce loneliness, anomie, a damaged social order. On the other hand, it can also grant greater autonomy to women and single persons.[20] The tension and the contradictions recognizable within the sometimes competing claims of patriarchy and capitalism mean that the instability of the family and of individuals encouraged by capitalism may be explored profitably by those with no automatic allegiance to that system or to the patriarchal.[21]

During the period of capitalism's development that could be characterized as production-oriented, there is a point to restraint and repression. Dennis Altman claims that Third World countries frequently impose a rigid morality, but that when production orientation gives way in a successful capitalist economy to consumption orientation, the point of that rigid morality becomes obscure. "The collapse of traditional values, whether in regard to sex, work, or authority, are in a sense the result of the very success of the capitalist societies these value systems had helped engender."[22] Thus, he argues, Reagan could not lead America back to traditional values because there is a basic conflict between such values and those of consumer capitalism, which Reagan himself eulogizes.

Consumer capitalism makes a very poor bedfellow with a fundamentalist, essentialist, moralistic sexuality. And yet in the very societies where traditional, familial values are attempting a highly publicized comeback, consumerism reigns. As Zaretsky puts it (writing about Americans), "Working people now see consumption as an end in itself, rather than as an adjunct to production, and as a primary source of both personal and social (i.e., 'status') identity. This is often expressed within the 'middle class' as 'lifestyle', a word that is used to defend one's prerogatives regardless of the demands of 'society'."[23]

It is interesting, in this regard, to see how an expansionist capitalism has affected sex and to look at the surprisingly close relations that business has developed with the commoditized sex which capitalism has developed. The potential for the buying of sex through prostitution was vastly increased by the fifties, in the sense that fantasy was packaged and sold; by the midseventies and eighties pornography had become, first through magazines and films but increasingly through videocassettes, a huge industry, especially in the United States. The pursuit of pleasure was vitally aided by capitalism, which colonized desire and also encouraged proliferation of desires, incidentally revolutionizing social attitudes to masturbation.

Altman draws special attention to the alliance of the business world with the demand for homosexual gratification. He particularly cites the growth in gay bathhouses, which he characterizes as a product of the union of sexuality and consumerism, and links the specific needs which brought bathhouses into public visibility with the generalized expression of consumers' needs in the seventies, dubbed the "me decade" by Tom Wolfe. The reliance of what he thinks of as a freer sexuality upon business institutions to provide the means of expression of this freedom strikes him as an irony.[24] Yet, he concludes, "As the emphasis in capitalism moves more and more toward consumption, sex inevitably becomes big business."[25]

His analysis of the relations between sex and consumer capitalism leads Altman to deduce that social change, so passionately resisted by the Right from the middle seventies onwards, is explicable in no other terms than shifts in the nature of modern capitalism. He believes that changes in seventies life-styles in the United States are based on three factors: (1) the divorce of sexuality from reproduction; (2) the changing role of women; and (3) sexuality as one of the mechanisms of consumerist capitalism.[26] (Jeffrey Weeks's analysis of homosexual attitudes to sexual pleasure in the seventies bears out Altman's broad conclusions about the vital interrelation of consumer capitalism and conceptions of sexuality, although Weeks is aware of what might be termed the political dangers of activists' celebration of sexual pleasure for its own sake—that it suggests a narrow focusing on sex as the essence of the [male] gay life-style and a devaluation of the importance assigned to sex by the culture.)[27]

Sexual "Prudery"

Gregg Blachford takes up head-on the issue of the devaluation of sex implied by, for example, "promiscuous" sexual encounters between men. He argues that such encounters do indeed devalue sex, and threaten its centrality, in a society which gives gay people meaning as primarily sexual beings. He suggests also that to characterize a casual sexual encounter as necessarily involving the "use" of people is to take the dominant culture's viewpoint, whereby only sex within a long-term monogamous relationship, occurring within a context of love and possible reproduction, is positively valued.[28]

Blachford, in taking up the issue within gay politics of moralistic distaste for the pursuit of sexual pleasure as an end in itself, seems to be combating a more diffused set of attitudes distrustful of sexual pleasure. It may seem needlessly provocative to label such distrust as "prudery," but it is exactly in these terms that Gordon and Hunter attack it, seeing contemporary sexual prudery as a tool of domination, of men over women, of old over young, of class over class.[29] Mariana Valverde uses a different term, "sexual pessimism," in relation to a similar sort of attitude within feminism. She recognizes the inevitability of such response to "the newly discovered reality of the *massive* abuse of women and children by men who are otherwise 'good citizens and fathers,' and who often sincerely believe that they are within their rights in beating or raping women and children."[30] She concedes that if a factor inherent within men's physiology or psychology makes them sexually violent, then pessimism is rational, as is defeatism in relation to heterosexuality. However, she argues, sexuality is a process, not a thing, and that process is shaped by societal relations. She believes that the notion of sex as something we privately own is a myth promoted by an individualistic consumer society.[31]

All of these writers feel concern about sexual prudery. They believe that it is a political loser, being yet another example of the repressiveness which finds its clearest expression in the most entrenched opponents of women's and gay rights, and being hardly less dispiriting if it comes from a "progressive" instead of a "regressive" position. They feel, with more alarm, that prudery is as much an instrument of domination as some feminists have argued that heterosexual relations themselves are.

George L. Mosse finds that prudery is pressed into the service of "respectability," which in turn finds one expression, through virility and manly bearing, in nationalism. He cites Richard von Kraft-Ebbing to illustrate the late-nineteenth-century belief in the interconnection of a "respectable" sexuality and "civilization": "If the normally constituted civilized being was not capable of mastering his sexual urges as soon as they came into conflict with the demands of society, then family and state, the foundations of the legal and moral order, would cease to exist."[32] Such beliefs about the relation of controlled sexuality to civilization and of unrestrained sexuality to aliens, those who manifestly do not belong within a particular civilization, strengthen racism. Mosse, in reference to racism, writes: "All those who stood outside the respectable norms of bourgeois society were thus blended—the 'accursed race,' as Marcel Proust called Jews and homosexuals."[33]

Precisely on these lines, that the price for bourgeois civilization is respectability and control of sexuality, opposition to this respectability is given a political, leftish edge by Reich and Herbert Marcuse. Both of them stood the Kraft-Ebbing line on its head, claiming that opposition to the authoritarian state requires sexual liberation—that social revolution itself is impossible without personal (and, thus, sexual) liberation. Much of the "permissiveness" claimed for the sixties grounds itself in the philosophy of Reich and Marcuse. Their followers had to embrace a form of essentialism as regards sexuality, whereby capitalism has not so much shaped sexuality as repressed and thus distorted it. (An analogous belief in an essentially female sexuality which has been repressed in men's interests obtains among some feminist writers.) Marcusian conceptions of the antithesis between "respectable," societally encouraged sexuality and a precapitalist sexuality "untampered with" by that system permit the valuing of, for example, regressive fantasies because they have a progressive side, namely the imagining of a utopia. Marcuse writes, "Against a society which employs sexuality as means for a useful end, the perversions uphold sexuality as an end in itself; they thus place themselves outside the domination of the performance principle and challenge its very foundation."[34]

The central problem of the Reichian and Marcusian harnessing of unrestrained sexual expression with social revolution is the assumption that sexuality can be presocietal, individualistic, and "truthful." It is against the sexual essentialism that characterizes Marcuse that Foucault mounts a particular attack in his explanation of the vital role of discourse in sexuality and in his insistence that sexuality is a historical apparatus, not a thing-in-itself.

While sexual pessimism has been saddled with part of the responsibility for loss of certain minority political groupings' appeal, and while the sexual optimism of Reich and Marcuse has foundered, no less, on its uncertain intellectual foundations, "official" sexuality remains deeply problematic. The price paid by women and gays for macho masculinity is particularly high. In Victor Seidler's words: "As long as a sense of masculinity is built upon the systematic denial of 'feminine' qualities, men are left in a continuous and endless struggle with themselves, in constant anxiety and fear of the revelations of their natures. They think they can control these fears within themselves, but they do so by projecting them . . . on to women, homosexuals, Jews, and blacks."[35]

A particular example of the manifestation of male sexual anxiety of this sort in ways that directly damage the interests of women is provided by Metcalf and Humphries. They discuss the threat of rejection that his partner's pregnancy can activate within a man, since an association can be set up between the rejecting mother of oedipal conflict and the pregnant partner. The memory of rejection can result in the rejection of "not only the sexuality of our partner and her potential motherhood, but her being, herself as a person."[36] They also discuss the usual pattern which the original rejection generates—a turning to somebody else, this new relationship re-affirming threatened maleness, which involves the capacity to separate sex from its emotional and social contexts.[37]

Since "maleness" is so esteemed within male sexuality, the threat which the male homosexual poses to the conception of active virility as male is easily comprehensible—at least in a society which defines the male homosexual in "female" terms. It has been credibly claimed that the gay man's crime is betrayal of the myth of the "real man," so that it is heterosexism which is crucially oppressive to him.[38]

Curiously, perhaps one of the most powerful encouragements to at least a questioning of sex's crucial placement is the profound significance within contemporary culture accorded to one's sexuality in terms of one's identity. Sexuality, since the nineteenth century, as Weeks points out, is taken as the very kernel, the cause and "truth," of the individual's being.[39] It is the unquestioning centralization of what is taken to be a thing-in-itself, sexuality, which Foucault most effectively combats in his insistence on discourse as a vital step toward understanding of the meaning of various sexualities.

Sexuality's Relation to Power

Foucault's primary interest in the study of sexuality appears to be in its intimate connection with power: "Never have the agencies of power taken such care to feign ignorance of the thing they prohibited, as if they were determined to have nothing to do with it. But it is the opposite that has become apparent. . . . Never have there existed more centers of power; never more attention manifested and verbalized."[40] In this connection, sexuality is seen as an apparatus of unsurpassed importance in contemporary power relations. The power of which Foucault writes is not state power, or that of class relations. Rather, it is ubiquitous in social relations, an "intangible but forceful reality," as Weeks terms it.[41] It is also "not a single thing," but "relational, . . . created in the relationships which sustain it."[42] Thus, far from seeing sexuality as a drive alien to power, Foucault defines sexuality as an "especially dense transfer point for relations of power."[43]

Weeks discerns problems in Foucault's account. He recognizes the usefulness of Foucault's notion of power as exceeding class reductionism for an explanation of women's subordination or of the regulation of unorthodox sexualities, but he wonders how, if power is everywhere, it may be broken out of or resisted.[44] Again, he feels that Foucault underestimates the role of the state, as expressed in its legal apparatus.[45] Nevertheless, in his investigation of the close relation of power and sexuality, Foucault is able to see beyond, for example, Sigmund Freud, who fails to notice that in the Little Hans case, "sexuality is defined for the child through his interactions with his parents," so that the focus is wrongly placed on the child rather than on his parents.[46]

Feminists have for longer than most investigators into sexuality been aware of the proximity of sexual and power relations, in that the differential access of men and women to social, economic, and political power must mean that the apparent alignment of their interests in the sexual sphere is illusory. Rape may be interpreted as a particularly graphic example of social control on women's lives through male sexuality. Women's frigidity, as well as the concept of the prude, may be seen as an invention to scare women into willing participation in a form of sexuality designed to keep them in their subordinate place. "It is clear," Sheila Jeffreys writes, "that we must look at the area of sexuality, not as merely a sphere of personal fulfillment, but as a battleground; an arena of struggle and power relationships between the sexes."[47]

A key method of the exercise of power, of control, within the sexual field is, for Foucault, categorization. He recognizes in the setting apart of "the unnatural," and in the creation of the homosexual as a species, an exercise of power through specification. Instead of seeing in division and description an attempt to exclude aberrant sexualities, he discerns "the specification, the regional solidification of each one of them."[48]

One of the principal steps in the categorization of unorthodox sexualities was through their medicalization. "The medical examination, the psychiatric investigation, the pedagogical report, and family controls may have the over-all and apparent objective of saying no to all wayward or unproductive sexualities, but the fact is that they function as mechanisms with a double impetus: pleasure and power."[49] Foucault takes particular interest in the way that homosexuality became a form of sexuality from the moment that it was so characterized by psychological, psychiatric, and medical categorization from 1870 onward. In order to become that particular form of sexuality, "it was transposed from the practice of sodomy into a kind of interior androgyny, a hermaphroditism of the soul."[50]

Thanks to medical zeal in categorization of a particular unorthodox sexuality, a species was brought into being. The "medical model" of the homosexual thenceforth creates a set of images for those identifying as homosexual. "To classify a social phenomenon as a disease is immediately to put validation into the hands of doctors, and here their class role, their relationship to their patients and their middle-class assumptions become central."[51] Interestingly, while medicalization of homosexuality (a sexuality that had no independent life until it was deemed to have one by medical "experts") instilled a sense of inferiority in those characterized as homosexuals, close attention to Freud and his preoedipal ascription of bisexuality would suggest that heterosexuality is no more or less remarkable an "achievement" than homosexuality, and that this state is arrived at by the suppression of homosexuality within the subject. To understand the sexuality labeled as homosexuality, however, attention has to be directed not just to information from those identifying as homosexual but far more significantly to the work done by the medical, psychiatric, and legal agencies who shaped this sexuality at the moment of defining it.

Richard Dyer shows that historical categories are far from negligible, that they have real-life results: "Because a category is historically and socially constructed, it is not any less real."[52] The category of the homosexual—as, incidentally, the category of women—requires defense because of the fact of oppression. Understanding the history of categorization and the profound importance of a category's genesis for those so categorized does not, to follow Dyer, result in the dissolution of the category as "merely" of historical interest. Tangible results follow from the invention of the category, for the way people live their lives and understand "their" sexuality. Foucault enables those living up to, down to, or closeted away from what the medical and legal professions assert is their sexuality to recognize and use the information that a sexuality does not "exist" prior to categorization. His work does not, however, permit the dissolution of that sexuality, since the sexuality in question has not only come into being but become part of social and therefore, inevitably, personal history.

7

Movies and Sexuality

The Backlash against Feminism

Even before the eighties began, Richard Brooks's *Looking for Mr. Goodbar* could be read, on the basis of a number of points from the narrative, as both an antifeminist and antigay statement. This 1977 film, like Brian De Palma's *Dressed To Kill* of 1980, seems to some commentators a significant element in a cycle of movies designed to scare women back to conventional, monogamous relationships by suggesting that the wages of sin is death and, less dramatically but probably of equal significance, that infidelity to a marriage partner, or refusal to accept a marriage partner, is indeed sin.

David Shipman takes the Brooks movie to be as moralistic as any Production Code movie.[1] Sexuality, he claims, is shown to be bad and wrong, and yet Shipman does notice that the heroine, Teresa (Diane Keaton), "is not depicted as abnormal," that she is not portrayed as a nymphomaniac.[2] This observation is allowed to count for little, though. He comes to the odd conclusion about the heroine's "trouble" (she is raped while being stabbed to death!) that she confused straight with gay. The corollary could be extrapolated from this that she would not have been raped and stabbed to death if only she had had the talent to pick straight men for her bed. This is a nonsensical moral for this movie, as is shown by Robin Wood, who points out in his cogent analysis that Teresa's murder is anticipated in two key sequences, where both of her principal suitors, "straight" in the simple terms that Shipman uses, are potential killers.[3] Tony (Richard Gere) performs a wild, threatening, half-naked dance with a luminous switchblade in Teresa's bedroom when she inadvertently chances on the weapon. That he treats the danced menace to her as a joke does not mean that his aggression to her, his enjoyment of her fear, is easily explicable for the audience in terms of a joke. James (William Atherton) tells Teresa a tale of his childhood, in which his father beat his mother half to death when she ridiculed his impotence. This story, which James later claims to be a fiction, is only a slightly less terrible version of Teresa's own death at the hands of a homosexual who believes that Teresa is laughing at him because he cannot "perform" after she has picked him up.

Throughout his analysis of the movie, Wood demonstrates his ability, rarely demonstrated in other commentators on *Goodbar*, to use inconvenient, contradictory evidence. He too recognizes that Teresa is not portrayed as sick or "abnormal." Diane Keaton, he claims, brings zest and vitality to her role, so that her sexual experiences, while unsatisfactory, are also a matter of fun. (A particularly useful piece of evidence to corroborate this interpretation is Teresa's amused recollection of the time that she was mistaken for a hooker and then of how her immediately subsequent lover stole her "immoral earnings" from that occasion.) He also notices how the action unfolds from Teresa's viewpoint. We see with her and, largely, judge with her. Thus, we are able to see behind the traditional moralisms spouted by her father and embodied by the social worker, James. For this reason, the voice of patriarchy speaks with much-compromised authority in the film. As E. Ann Kaplan puts it, "The spectator experiences the uncontrolled rages that men exhibit, and cannot help but be aware of their excess. To this small extent, then, the patriarchal need to possess and dominate women is exposed."[4] The extent of the effect of spectator positioning must be less "small" than Kaplan suggests, since, by means of it, Wood shows that the film denies any concept of the "normal" as yardstick.

Inattention to or underplaying of this element in the film results in the judgment that Brooks's film is ultra-right-wing and reactionary, that it encourages violence against women. (A similar negative judgment of *Dressed to Kill* was made more strongly and more publicly in the early eighties. The De Palma film is one which can be taken as an endorsement of patriarchy and of the violent denial of women's sexual desire only by a somewhat partial reading of it.)[5]

Wood is by no means declaring the film to be unproblematically "progressive" in terms of its sexual politics. He notices, for example, that Teresa is made into a special case in her stepping outside the stable social/moral structure, by reason of her inability to procreate for fear of passing on her hereditary disease to children. "Her sexual freedom can now be explained, implicitly, as the result of her being excluded from a normal life."[6] In this sense, he finds the movie confused, if not evasive, and discovers parallels to this in the treatment of the gay murderer. (The movie was seen by gay activists as validating the popular myth whereby homosexuality is

associated with neurosis.) He points out that the murder is ultimately occasioned by self-oppression, since it is his inability to
accept his sexuality that generates the killer's neurosis. "Like
Teresa, he is the victim of a society that assigns people fixed roles,
imposing on them notions of what a real man or real woman should
be."[7] In this measure, the movie is of interest within the context of
feminism and gay liberation, since it demonstrates the connections
between two kinds of oppression under patriarchy. Still, the stereotyping of the murderer's lover as hysterical, and the treatment of
the gay bar as a stage in Teresa's descent, could increase suspicion
of the movie's messages. "It's as if the film wants to say both that
homosexuals would be all right if society let them accept themselves and that homosexuals are inherently sick and degenerate."[8]

Because of the splits and contradictions in its treatment of the
actively desiring woman and of the gay world, Wood characterizes
Looking for Mr. Goodbar finally as "unreadable," meaning that it
cannot resolve, perhaps cannot recognize, its contradictions, and
thus cannot organize them into a "significant dialectic."[9] This
verdict of unreadability, based on the film's ideological failure, is
remarkably reminiscent of Geoffrey Nowell-Smith's conclusions
about Hollywood melodrama, that it raises questions that it cannot
resolve within the prevailing ideology.[10] Inevitably, the questions
about current ideology raised but not answered deflect attention on
to ideology itself, away from the apparently simpler issues of deciding whether a film is feminist or antifeminist, whether it is interested in promoting or damaging gay rights.

Graphic and prolonged violence often occurs in those films,
particularly of the late seventies and early eighties, which address
such topics as female sexuality and the active desire of a central
female character in a society which relegates the heroine's active
gazing to the field of the "abnormal." This is partly explained by
Barbara Creed. Creed argues that essential for the construction of
the monstrous in the horror film is the concept of a border. That
which threatens to cross, or which does cross, that border becomes
the monstrous. The function of the monstrous, in Creed, is to
eventuate an encounter between the Symbolic Order and whatever
may undermine its stability. One of the examples of the monstrous
which she offers is at the border separating those who take up
proper gender roles from those who do not. One of the films cited
by Creed as exemplifying this border is Dressed To Kill.[11]

Another example from 1980 might be Kenneth Hughes's Terror
Eyes. Here, the murderer turns out to be a woman. Eleanor Adjai
(Rachel Ward), a research assistant living with an anthropology

professor who has been enjoying affairs "on the side" with some of his female students, explains her decapitation of these women by claiming the wish "to cleanse him of the corruption of their sexual attraction."[12] Thus, the sexually active woman is once again deemed monstrous and violently reduced, this time by a sexually "normal" woman who wants only marriage and children. Possibly the most subversive feature in all three movies (*Looking for Mr. Goodbar, Dressed To Kill,* and *Terror Eyes*) is that sexual normality and the nuclear family's traditional demands on women are represented by a character who is at least neurotic, if not more accurately described as psychopathic. In all three movies, the figure of terror lives on at the film's close: the rapist murderer, not to mention Teresa's father, lives on after her protracted death in *Goodbar;* the murderous "Bobbi" survives in Liz's nightmares; while in *Terror Eyes* the professor is gunned down in mistake for his murderous assistant.

The notion of the traditional family as under threat motivates the action of many key movies particularly of the early eighties. Titled with unusual significance, *The Last Married Couple in America* (1979) helpfully lists the trials through which a marriage has to fight in the seventies, as "police strikes and Women's Lib and condominiums." The emphasis is presumably on the second of these three, in that it is infidelity which is particularly considered in the movie, and feminism which is simplistically linked with the breakdown of the family and its declared codes. The risks incurred by infidelity are again helpfully outlined: impotence, venereal disease, emotional trauma, and so on. While this Gilbert Cates movie is an altogether cozier vehicle for Natalie Wood and George Segal than, say, *Goodbar* was for Diane Keaton, its diagnosis of danger in marital infidelity is noticeably similar. (Venereal disease crops up as an immediate penalty for the unfaithful heroine of *Dressed To Kill,* also.)

The heroine of Douglas Day Stewart's *Thief of Hearts* (1984) suffers for her ambitions beyond the family when her fantasies are alarmingly realized. The actively desiring female once again brings violence into being, the better to justify her being returned across Barbara Creed's sort of border and restored to traditional familial femininity. The idea of the family as under threat—sometimes specifically from feminism, as in *The World According to Garp* (1982), sometimes from elements fairly or otherwise associated with feminism by New Right thinking—keeps recurring in the eighties. Perhaps the most emotionally charged version of the single-woman/family conflict is in Adrian Lyne's *Fatal Attraction* (1987), but similar sentiment is created for the familial and against feminists (who are by virtue of being careerist automatically enemies of the family), in James L Brooks's *Terms of Endearment* (1983). The stereotyping of East Coast, citified, "uncaring" career women serves the purpose in the film's narrative of gaining more sympathy for the Debra Winger character's maternalism. The political damage this sort of tactic does beyond the movie's world, by reason of that sympathy, is worth considering. Robert Mandel's *Independence Day,* of similar vintage (1982), offers a subtler variant of family versus feminine independence, but once again sympathy is weighted against "independence."

Part of the proof of the reprehensibility of the protagonist in *The Ploughman's Lunch* (1983) is that, in his unscrupulous am-bitiousness, he turns away—Joe Lampton-like—from his real fam-ily to ingratiate himself with another, "superior" version from another stratum. The film also includes topical denigration of the women of Greenham Common as part of its contemporary "feel." While *Love Letters* (1983) is praised by Pam Cook for its fashioning of "a romance for the post-feminist 80s,"[13] the romance still in-volves the heroine's learning self-restraint, then holding back her desire so that the family of that desire's object does not suffer more harm through her selfishness.

The Ascendancy of Men

Betty Friedan notices in the early eighties a tendency for such male novelists as Saul Bellow, John Updike, Norman Mailer, Thomas Pynchon, and Philip Roth to create principal male charac-ters who go to desperate lengths of violent, or covert, aggression against women because they fear such "female" qualities within themselves as vulnerability and passivity.[14] She sees this tendency as part of a "revolt against masculinity" within fiction, whereby such heroes as Garp seek a woman who will thrive on his pas-sivity.[15]

This revolt is not confined to the world of novels, but appears in popular (narrative-based) media, too. She discovers a new interpre-tation of masculinity in, for example, the hero of *Kramer vs. Kramer,* with "short, sensitive, nervous loser Dustin Hoffman" replacing "tall, strong, silent, winner John Wayne" as American hero because of his prowess as a parent, and she takes this as "a feminist triumph."[16] She also notes the surprising success of *The Great Santini.*[17] Yet she knows that may be too simplistic a reading of the emergence of the sensitive male parent as hero in terms of feminist triumph. The new heroism of the male Kramer seems, in the film's terms, to mean a downgrading of the female. More noticeably, for father to affirm his latent, nurturing side in *Ordinary People,* the mother is made into an unloving, all-controlling bitch caricature, to use some of Friedan's terms.[18]

She concludes that male heroes' disengagement from the old patterns of American masculinity and success leaves men as short of role models as women. Thus, while there is a movement beyond traditional notions of virility, there is an attendant nostalgia for male heroism to fill the void left by the creation of the "new man." (This nostalgia is evidenced, for Friedan, in the popularity of *The Right Stuff* and in Mailer's quest for a final heroism in the death chamber in *The Executioner's Song.*)[19]

Barbara Ehrenreich suggests another, less politically "progressive" twist to men's departure from the old, tired models of male chauvinism. One of the most telling of Friedan's points is that men's emergence as sensitive and fundamentally tender and nurturing beneath the layers of machismo is at the expense of women, who become uncaring bitches in many "new man" vehicles. Yet, she does not discuss class and social mobility, or the relation of class to the old and new styles of masculinity. Ehrenreich, however, notices that in seventies movies, machismo is associated with working-class life-styles. Both in *Bloodbrothers* and *Saturday Night Fever,* the audience is offered "didactic condemnations of traditional masculinity," and she finds the self-improvement of the young heroes to be remarkably like middle-class men's liberation.[20] The choice for the hero of *Bloodbrothers* is to be a construction worker like his father, to join the working-class world of the union and the family, or to be a children's recreation assistant in a hospital and thus graduate to a middle-class world of social service. In *Saturday Night Fever,* Tony (John Travolta) is persuaded by his girlfriend to transform himself so that he can leave the sleazy (and dull) working-class world of Brooklyn to cross the bridge into glamorous Manhattan.[21] However unclear the movie is in its suggestions about the "classlessness" of Manhattan, it is fairly unequivocal in its linking of machismo with working-class culture and in its suggestion that the posture, like Brooklyn the place, has to be abandoned in the interests of upward mobility.

Both of these commentators on the shifting nature of masculinity in the seventies usefully draw attention to the way that the kind of critique of traditional machismo which feminism necessarily embodies does have visible results in media representations of male heroes. Even more usefully, they begin to demonstrate how the "new man" emerges only at the expense of women's rights, and particularly (and paradoxically) at the expense of feminism. This is achieved by "redressing the balance" within depicted male/female relations: the more caring and nurturing the male is allowed to become, the sharper somehow the critique of the less caring, less "natural" mother/wife. It is as if the movies are suggesting two things: (1) that the regular criticisms of the damage inflicted by traditional maleness on females within the family are accepted and to some extent met; and (2) that therefore surely it might be expected in those circumstances that women would want to stay within the family and behave like good family members instead of filling their heads with careerist notions or trying to dominate in the place of the newly tender men.

Kramer vs. Kramer (1979), while it does not launch a traditionalist attack on the mother as neglectful and selfish, still does heroize the child-oriented parent played by Hoffman and makes an implicit commentary on the sort of woman that Meryl Streep represents, thus on the kind of woman that feminism encourages. The attack on the mother in Robert Redford's *Ordinary People* (1980) is less guarded. The father's (Donald Sutherland) ineffectuality is rendered more sympathetic when it is in part explained by the mother's ball-breaking will to dominate instead of to express tenderness or need, even at a time of bereavement. The stress placed on psychiatry, the insistence on relating problems to family, help to render femininity incomprehensible here in any terms other than the familial. The Mary Tyler Moore character is permitted no dimensions other than those of wife and mother. She manifestly fails in these roles, since she alone of the three family survivors refuses to acknowledge need and therefore denies herself psychiatric help. Failing in these roles, she fails as a woman, since, in this film, a woman is no more than these roles.

The notion that crops up at the closure of both *Kramer vs. Kramer* and *Ordinary People*—that, where a mother is absent or deficient, a reconstructed father can supply most of the absences and deficiencies—forms the principal idea of Leonard Nimoy's *Three Men and a Baby* (1987). The erstwhile committed bachelors of the title discover their nascent paternal aptitudes when a motherless baby appears in their midst. While they learn the nurturing arts of feeding their charge or cleaning up the nappy-soiling baby, the virtual absence of the baby's natural mother is rendered of little account.

The British film *The Good Father* (1986) once again offers for consideration a wife who seems to be the tougher partner in a failing marriage, dumping her child upon her husband and mocking the male who takes to wearing an apron and looking after the house. The unfairness of branding an errant wife an unfit mother is, however, brought out in the film's treatment of the intervention of legal justice in their private life—as, for example, when a judge entrusts their son to his father's care and decrees that the son is never to be domiciled with his mother. The husband himself distances himself from the judge's religious moralism (he is a high churchman with traditional views about female sexuality) by arranging to share custody with his estranged wife.

In the new world of treacherous womenfolk who are reluctant to fulfill the caring, nurturing roles apparently intended for them by Nature, male friendship gains greater attention in eighties movies. Bobby Roth's *Heartbreakers* (1984) centers on the friendship between the characters played by Peter Coyote and Nick Mancuso, celebrated usually with a game of racquetball followed by a snack together. Jill Forbes, in her review of the film, illuminates the problem of the male-friendship movie when she cites the reported remark by Jeff Kaltzenburg of Paramount on his introduction to the script: "But how do we know they're not homosexual?"[22] Forbes notes that writer-director Roth depicts these men an unerringly straight and that he claims that he has portrayed the new man, who is capable of "showing emotions" and "getting past his superficial macho."[23] What interests her much more, though, is the absence of a new woman to complement the heterosexual new man. Because of Roth's failure to conceptualize such a character as the new woman, she feels that these two men are gift-wrapped against reality instead of participating in it.[24]

Sexuality

The emphasis on monogamy implicit in such moralities as *Cujo* has already been mentioned in chapter 5, as, above, have the warnings about venereal disease and personal malaise in *The Last Married Couple in America*. More remarkable is the universality of the model of monogamy in Arthur Hiller's *Making Love* (1982), since the triangle here is made up of one woman and two men. Although the latter two, both married men, eventually choose each other, at least for a time, they do so not only against the possibilities of heterosexuality but against the apparent gay norm of one-night stands. When the rejected wife—a career woman from the opening of the movie—meets up at the end of the film with her former husband, she has not only remarried but has produced a child. He, meanwhile, is sharing his life with another man. He may have experimented with the gender of his partners, but that is as far as he seems capable of altering his views. He is as committed to monogamy, as distrustful of casual, recreational sex, at the end of the movie as he was at the beginning. The other two characters clearly think like him, in this at least. While the film may appear to be about alternative sexualities, it seems to reinforce the heterosexual norm, whatever the sexual orientation of its characters.

By the late seventies, the backlash against pornography is indicated by such movies as Paul Schrader's *Hardcore* (U.K. title: *The Hardcore Life* [1978]). Although Schrader has claimed evenhandedness in his portrayal of the Grand Rapids, Michigan, hero played by George C. Scott and of the porn industry's denizens, it is difficult to draw the same conclusion from the film's evidence. The emphasis on family and community on one side and rootlessness and anomie on the other is not easy to see in terms of balance. The treatment of the familial is hardly ironic, for example, in that the daughter's entire reason for defecting from the straight life to participate in porn is offered at the film's climax: her father failed to show her the love that he clearly felt. Thus, the lure of pornography, when it is not simply that of financial gain, is to be understood purely in terms of defiance of, or escape from, a world that could, in other circumstances, be all that is needed by such characters as the daughter. Since the charms of the family and small-town community are rendered evident, the absence of any understanding, or of explanation for the allure, of pornography surely does direct the spectator to empathize with the hero and thus with his values. His failure as a father is made good by his active-hero penetration of the underworld of pornographic exploitation; the family standard is restored by restoration of the protective father.

The Canadian *Not a Love Story,* made by Bonnie Sherr Klein in 1981, presents itself as an investigation of pornographic photographs, films, videos, and live acts in New York City. The phenomenon of pornography is discussed largely with opponents (such as Kate Millett and Robin Morgan). The stripper Linda Lee Tracey indicates to the director her growing disquiet about what she has done in posing for commercial photographs, and in so doing seems to become allied with the film's antipornographic objectives. While the enormous power of pornography is suggested in its economic importance (it is stated that, for example, there are four times the number of pornography outlets as there are McDonald's in the

United States), implicit condemnation replaces any will to investigate porn in terms of the appetites it creates or sustains.

This kind of judgmental approach to the investigative documentary on pornography is discoverable again in Paula de Koenigsberg and Lucy Winer's *Rate It X* (1985). The strategy this time involves interviews with men who voice their attitudes to male and female roles and to the representation of women in media images, interspliced with examples of exploitation movies, cartoons, advertisements.

It is condemnatory attitudes which prevail when there is any direct address of the issue of pornography in apparently nonpornographic fiction or documentary films. The function of Linda Lee Tracey in *Not a Love Story* seems to be to provide a figure from within the porn industry who will confess, open her eyes to her exploitation, and rebel against it. Georgina Spelvin, the star of the earlier *Devil in Miss Jones,* parodies this recantation of her previous sex-liberationist line in Gerard Damiano's *Midnight Blue* (1980) in a way which raises questions about the relationship of porn performer to crusading filmmaker in the Klein movie.

The hostility to pornography on the grounds of its commercial exploitation of sex and of its degradation of the performers within it finds an echo in those films which deplore prostitution, male or female. Paul Schrader again, in *American Gigolo* (1980), indicates by means of his mise-en-scène that Julian's (Richard Gere) ambience is the inferno, that his very success in exploitation of his sexuality produces self-loathing and sets him up for punishment. Colin Higgins's *The Best Little Whorehouse in Texas* (1982), despite its forthright title, manages to avoid direct consideration of its attitudes to prostitution through its bypassing of questions of the prostitutes' self-image, for example. Instead, it concentrates on the safer fare of the romance between the madame, Miss Mona (Dolly Parton), and the sheriff (Burt Reynolds). At the end of the film, the closing of the Chicken Ranch—because, it would seem, of hostile public opinion championed by opportunist politicians—has little resonance, in that Miss Mona sets off with her future husband to a more conventional existence.

Against the prevailing orthodoxies and pieties of those movies dealing with the sex industry in its various manifestations, Lizzie Borden's *Working Girls* (1986) proves surprisingly different. For one thing, it shows the "working girls" as intelligent and articulate, providing each other with a measure of emotional support, and demonstrates that their sexual exploitation by male clients is negligible in comparison with the economic exploitation practiced on

them by their (female) employer. The work that they do is compared
favorably with some of the other, low-paid, jobs which they might
be doing. The very willingness of the film to raise questions about
its subject, and to refrain from drawing the expected conclusions
about the girls' "work" is a sign of its difference from the others
mentioned above. Lizzie Borden asks in relation to it, "How do you
present a feminist statement about a situation that exists which is
itself a contradiction? It's like looking down both ends of a telescope."[25] At least Borden recognizes that a telescope has two ends.

Another, much earlier, film opens up questions about sexuality
and, in this case, the function of pornography as providing an
expression of what is directly inexpressible about a person's sexuality: Larry Cohen's *The Private Files of J. Edgar Hoover* (1977).
In it, Hoover is depicted as circulating pornographic materials
among Washington society. While he maintains a front of respectability, he refuses to recognize his abuses of power, and fails to
confront his own sexuality.

A more jaundiced look at "new man" pieties is also to be found,
though not often, in eighties films. One of the many paradoxes
focused on in *Sammy and Rosie Get Laid* (1987) is that Sammy
professes sexual freedom and is too "new" to be seen to want to
deny it to Rosie, yet he mourns the loss of intimacy and commitment in his primary relationship, with her. The West German film
Men (1985) dissects the relationship of men to each other in revolution around the same, female, object. It dissects the husband's
double standard in denying that his infidelities are as blameworthy
as his wife's. So short is the hero finally of being a reconstructed
"new man" that he feels murderous jealousy of, and competes with,
his wife's lover. Doris Dörrie's German film dares to suggest what
only a few entertainments of the eighties will admit, that beneath a
surface of greater sensitivity or openness lurk the same old attitudes to women as possessions. Where this is so, male friendship
constantly threatens the male friends, in that their masculinity
needs confirmation by women, and without them constantly threatens to turn into homoeroticism.

Thus, the violence shown to women, old and teenaged, as well as
to a homosexual male, in Penelope Spheeris's *The Boys Next Door*
(1984) is explicable in terms of the anxiety conjured up in, for
example, Bo's (Charlie Sheen) affection for Roy (Maxwell
Caulfield). ("I don't want to sound like a fag or nothing, but you're
my best friend.") Bo eventually shoots Roy dead, but only after Roy
has shot the woman with whom Bo has made love. An example of
the bolstering of the male ego through his Casanova-like attitude to

the women he encounters is offered by Blake Edwards's *Skin Deep* (1988), where there is no alienation of their uncritical affection for him in the women who have been rejected by the hero.

Further evidence of the absence of any real change in men's need to overpower and possess women is offered by the inability of the male intellectuals of *The Decline of the American Empire* to consider relations between the sexes in terms other than those of power. While the women of the film declare war on the male ego by their casual approach to sexual liaisons and their scorn for male weakness, the men's quest is to subjugate and control women through sexual relations. This continuing need for power as proof of their masculinity is rendered more overt in Adrian Lyne's playing out of a recognizably sadomasochistic relationship in *9½ Weeks* (1985), while the psychiatrist hero of Nicolas Roeg's *Bad Timing* (1980) carries his urge to control the heroine to the extent of physical assault and almost necrophiliac rape of his victim. As the Billie Holiday song lyrics sung in the film underline, this seemingly bizarre and distressing tale is "just the same old story."

A similar old story of lust and of (otherwise) an emotional vacuum, filled by acquisitiveness, is told in Lawrence Kasdan's *Body Heat* (1981). The film, being self-consciously in a *film noir* tradition, has the avidly desirous hero (William Hurt) only apparently fulfilled by his object of desire (Kathleen Turner). She has used his desire to set him up as her husband's murderer so that she can enjoy a pampered life-style without the inconvenience of either husband or jealous, possessive lover.

In Mike Leigh's *High Hopes* (1988), the one element that seems to cut across class (and even taste) divides is sexual desire. The relentlessly vulgar Burkes try to simulate passion for each other through half-playing out fantasy scenarios, though the lust which the husband feels for his "bit on the side" registers as more sincere. Meanwhile, the nouveaux-riches Boothe-Braines play erotic games with each other, using the language and behavior of babyhood. The only couple treated with less comic spleen, the contented socialists Cyril and Shirley Bender, spark off affectionate desire in each other, but in their case attention is focused on Shirley's wish to have a baby (while Cyril argues that the world is an unfit place for children). *Cocktail* (1988) is one of very few eighties movies to suggest that sexual "scoring" can be uncomplicated fun. Many eighties movies center on the appeal of sexual pleasure but regularly move beyond that basic position to consider the "results," social and psychological (though very seldom medical), of the satisfaction of sexual appetite.

Edward Zwick's *"About Last Night . . ."* (1986), for example, explores the situations set up already in the basis for the film, David Mamet's play *Sexual Perversity in Chicago.* Danny (Rob Lowe) and Debbie (Demi Moore) attempt to transform a casual sexual relationship into something more permanent. They encounter hostility from friends and former lovers but, more significantly, seem unable to articulate to each other their feelings and especially their causes for depression. Dialogue, which is worldly-wise with a wearily ironic edge, becomes a focus of interest in itself, being a mask for the more difficult conversations which the characters do not allow themselves to have.

A more unusual examination of sexual appetites and of their intersection with the wish for more permanent, and more exclusive, relationships is provided in Spike Lee's *She's Gotta Have It* (1986)—more unusual in that the pivot of the examination is female. Nola Darling (Tracy Camila Johns) candidly declares her enjoyment of sex. She has three men in her life and, not quite part of her sexual life though hovering on the edges of it, one woman. The men represent various aspects of masculinity within heterosexual relationships. One is "sensitive" and poetic (although this does not prevent his finally raping and attempting to humiliate and tame her). Another is self-absorbed and narcissistic. The third, played by Lee himself, is a mythomaniac who appeals to her by reason of his childlike qualities. Throughout the film, there are disjunctures between what people say they want and what it is intimated to the audience that they do want, and a playful consideration of a psychoanalytic explanation for Nola's tastes and behavior through on-screen discussions with her doctor and her father. The heroine has internalized disapproving judgments of her easy attitude to sex (this becomes evident in her nightmare of intruding females who set fire to her), but the film withholds any easy explanation or even unequivocal closure.

In this aspect at least, the refusal of easy judgment, the Spike Lee movie recalls the Australian movie *The Clinic* (1982). Directed by David Stevens, this chronicles the quotidian events within a medical unit dealing with sexually transmitted diseases and teaches, by means of an initially disapproving medical student, the folly of imagining that sexual expression can be controlled by censorious authority.

"About Last Night . . ." suggests the lethal nature of partners' inability to express caring attitudes to each other and, despite the tentatively promised happy ending, offers no solutions to the sapping of the will to care through hardheaded sexual casualness. *The*

Clinic, on the other hand, seems to explore the relevance of caring—from a different, professional (medical) quarter. It seems to agree that sexual pleasure probably excludes tender devotion but replaces what is missing in casual relationships with genuine concern from "caring professionals." Those movies which do center on the importance for lovers of mutual respect and sensitivity to each other seem to signal the unlikelihood of it in contemporary society by creating an element of fantasy to underline its near unattainability. Thus, Dustin Hoffman in *Tootsie* (1982) has to learn not just to cross-dress but to behave in a way that could be taken by his colleagues to be womanly before he gains access to women's need for understanding. More bizarrely, Carl Reiner's *All of Me* (1984) has the spirit of Lily Tomlin sharing a body with Steve Martin as the means to their education in complementarity. By its deconstruction of both femininity and, particularly, masculinity, the film allows its characters to transcend the apparent, but unreal, opposition of their genders. The element of the fantastic in this solution suggests a measure of pessimism about society's current thinking.

Finally, a consideration of sexuality as mediated through eighties movies would be incomplete without mention of new technology's relation to it. Two films of 1989—Steven Soderbergh's *sex, lies and videotape* and Atom Egoyan's *Speaking Parts* (from Canada)—pay particular attention to the role that technology plays in contemporary sex lives. Neither film seems certain of how to evaluate the mediation of sexuality by electronic processes. In the Soderbergh movie, there is a reversion to the notion that, since video (as was once believed of the film camera) is an impersonal mechanism, it has peculiar access to "truth." At the same time, it is to be distrusted because it threatens not merely to break into private lives but to participate in them at the level of sexuality. A similar point seems to be made by *Speaking Parts.* All human activity is at some level dependent on gadgetry. Sex is taken as a prime illustration, in terms especially of the telephone answering machine and the video camera. The central theses of both films regarding technology's intrusion into sexuality can work only if there is a degree of credibility to the notion that sex is "natural" and that therefore the emphasis given to machines in sex lives should be seen as intrusion and interference. The belief may be unpersuasive, but the films testify to its popularity within the societies in which the films were made.

8

Homosexuality

The Categorization of Homosexuality

Michel Foucault considers that the eighteenth and nineteenth centuries were the scene of a discursive explosion. Heterosexual monogamy occupied little attention, the legitimized couple being treated as a norm against which the sexuality of children, the mad, and the criminal was scrutinized.[1] One of the achievements of this period was the separation of certain aspects of sexuality from the norm (or the "natural") into the domain of the "unnatural." Thus, "there appeared on the one hand infractions against the legislation (or morality) pertaining to marriage and the family, and on the other, offences against the regularity of a natural function."[2] Foucault claims that homosexuality became a form of sexuality when emphasis shifted from the homosexual act to the notion of the homosexual person, "from the practice of sodomy" to "a kind of interior androgyny, a hermaphroditism of the soul," since, in this way, while the sodomite had been a "temporary aberration," the homosexual "was now a species."[3] Thus, for Foucault, the homosexual as category was born in 1870 with Westphal's article on "contrary sexual sensations."[4]

The creation of the homosexual marks a crucial moment in the history of social relations. Jeffrey Weeks, for instance, notes the tendency from the nineteenth century onward to regard sexuality as the very "truth" of our being, that by which we are defined socially and morally.[5] He also draws attention to the conception of sex as a unified domain, a thing in itself.[6] (He himself stands out against these cultural habits, arguing that sex is relational, shaped in social interaction and only comprehensible in a historical context in terms of those cultural meanings assigned to it.)[7]

The principal stimuli to investigations of sexuality in the nineteenth and twentieth centuries came from the practices of medicine and law. From the middle of the nineteenth century, nonprocreative sex was categorized by the medical profession under the heading of "perversions and deviations." Out of this larger category came the particular subcategory of homosexuality.[8] The medicalizing of homosexuality as an abnormal condition has a number of effects upon so-categorized homosexuals' perception of themselves. "If the law and its associated penalties made homosexuals into outsiders, and religion gave them a high sense of guilt, medicine and science gave them a deep sense of inferiority and inadequacy."[9] It also permits a liberal "treatment" of homosexuality as a problem requiring therapy rather than a moral evil requiring punishment. The medicalization of homosexuality as a condition further means the surrender of validation of homosexuality and homosexuals to medical practitioners. Then, too, as Greenwood and Young put it, "because medicalisation reduces social evils to personal failings, it produces a theory which cannot solve individual problems—rather, it obfuscates and bedevils them. . . . The practical solution . . . to the problems of efficacy, cost and size is a quasi-medical one—ghettoisation."[10]

The explanation of homosexuality through medical discourse has the effect not only of creating the homosexual in the first place but also of objectifying the person thus categorized.[11] This objectification diminishes, making the object of scrutiny less than normal through the attribution of sickness, inadequacy, misfortune.[12]

Against the medical explanations of homosexuality's causation in such features as chromosomal deficiency or psychological immaturity might be considered Freud's account of the development of sexuality from an infantile stage of bisexuality or, perhaps more accurately, polymorphous perversity. Heterosexuality is achieved by means of such societally produced, familial phenomena as the Oedipus and castration complexes. By this explanation, heterosexuality may be understood as the result of the repression of homosexuality. Interestingly, Freud himself seems to have felt some reluctance to take on the implications of his own account. Largely, the potential of Freudian psychoanalysis in relation to discourses of sexuality has been underexploited. This may be testimony to the investment society has made in the more conventional medical model of homosexuality.

Labeling, another term for categorization, whether by doctors, jurists, sexologists, or other forms of "expert," may be viewed today with justifiable suspicion, particularly by those groups which have experienced automatic objectification and diminution through the process of labeling. Edwin M. Schur puts the problem well: "Deviance issues are inherently political. They revolve around some people's assessments of other people's behaviour. And power is a crucial factor in determining which and whose assessments gain an ascendancy."[13] Schur notes that in a 1963 experimental study, when standard psychological tests were given to homosexuals drawn from the public at large, psychologists deprived of information about their sexuality found no greater indications of psychopathology in their results than in nonhomosexual control subjects.[14] This experiment suggests alternatives to the dominant habits of viewing homosexuality as sickness or of attributing, say, neurosis in homosexual subjects to the "condition" rather than to the stress of living in a heterosexist society. As Barry D. Adam writes, "The terms *Negro* and *homosexual* . . . [often accompany] 'scientific' and reductionist endeavours of nonmembers."[15] Mordechai Rotenberg, in his study *Damnation and Deviance*,[16] goes so far as to see a large part of the explanation for labeling into good and bad, successful and failed as being within the Calvinist scenario of division into eternal salvation and damnation.

Given that the wider purpose of the labeling of deviance may be to keep the bulk of society under control and out of the danger of deviant behavior of a more serious, political kind,[17] its common occurrence is easily appreciated. The dangers that groups and persons so labeled as deviant undergo by assenting to the practice and internalizing the categorization's meanings must also be apparent, though.

Weeks identifies Foucault's major contribution to the struggle for sexual liberation as his demonstration that such struggle requires "intervention at the level of definition of appropriate sexual behaviour."[18] Accordingly, Richard Dyer identifies the gay movement's key significance as being that "for the first time in living memory, gay people *themselves* determined that they would decide the definition."[19] The control of definition as an important element within understanding of one's own sexuality is, interestingly, suggested by Kinsey's researches, in that he discovered that roughly 25 percent of American males and 15 percent of American females had had at least one homosexual experience to orgasm, and yet only about 2 percent of females and 3 percent of males considered themselves homosexual (in the sense of exclusively so). Conversely, Blumstein and Schwartz found that nearly all of the sample of people who were self-defined as homosexual had enjoyed heterosexual relations at some time in their lives.[20]

Self-definition is not such an easy matter as these last examples might be taken to indicate. Stereotypes of homosexual behaviour cannot simply be dismissed, since homosexual people may well behave in accordance with them, thus seeming to confirm their truth.[21] If homosexuals cannot dismiss stereotypes, energy must still be devoted to developing alternatives and challenging the societally imposed definitions of homosexual behaviour and character.[22]

The quotidian understanding of male homosexuality is in terms of inadequacy, the failure to be masculine. Since masculinity is conventionally understood in terms of domination, this has peculiar consequences for the "untheorized" conception of homosexuality. Emmanuel Reynaud would claim a distinction between social attitudes to the active and passive versions of male homosexuality, and argues that active homosexuality has enjoyed legitimacy while its passive counterpart has been despised. "Whereas man can consider homosexuality in its 'active' form as a means of asserting his power, in its 'passive' form it is, on the contrary, a symbol of humiliation. . . . Man's fear of homosexuality is the expression of his fear of sexuality and his wish to dominate through sex."[23] This gives added credibility to Caroline Sheldon's belief that a gay man's crime is betrayal of the myth of the "real man," since the gay man is socially defined as female in consequence of the myth that gay men are passive.[24]

Homophobia, as a result of the mythology of homosexuality as nonmasculine, is easily explicable as a manifestation of masculinity's need to deny those qualities deemed feminine. We would do well to recall, "As long as a sense of masculinity is built upon the systematic denial of 'feminine' qualities, men are left in a continuous and endless struggle with themselves, in constant anxiety and fear of the revelations of their natures. They think they can control these fears within themselves, but they do so by projecting them . . . on to women, homosexuals, Jews, and blacks."[25] It could be added here that women who identify with masculine values and take as vital to themselves the benefits of, for instance, familialism will project psychologically with remarkable resemblance to men's cultural habits.

Gay Rights

The title of this section ought to clarify that a brief summary of only recent changes in thinking about homosexuality is being offered. Homosexual practices appear to be a part of sexual conduct from the beginning of recorded history, in that penalties for such practices are prescribed or even "enacted" in, for example, Old Testament story. Michel Foucault's work on sexuality would warn us against taking homosexuality, or for that matter sexuality in its diverse expressions, as a thing-in-itself. If we are impressed by Foucault's thinking, our endeavor must rather be to consider thinking about homosexuality, its various discourses.

Medical "experts" and sexologists last century and early in the twentieth had not merely labeled certain sexual practices as homosexual but also created the person, the figure of the homosexual. This century, thinking about persons categorized as homosexual has largely been in terms of their deviancy from an assumed sexual norm. This deviancy could on occasions be extended to embrace deviancy in terms of nationalist stereotypes. Thus, for example, in the United States in the fifties, McCarthyite thinking on homosexuality linked it with communism and stigmatized it as un-American. Even during the decade of far-reaching legal change in Britain—the sixties—the decriminalization of sexual acts between consenting male adults was not in recognition of "equality" or "rights" but in line with the Wolfenden strategy of attempting a clear legal distinction between public and private domains of conduct. (Penalties for importuning in public places were tightened up, for example, "public" being defined as relating to any situation where a third party was likely to be present.) The 1967 Sexual Offences Act was therefore capable of being supported by those who believed that homosexuals (so-called) were so deviant as to be sick and pathetic.[26]

The springboard for a different conception of homosexuality in terms, for instance, of gay life-styles was the rioting in Greenwich Village in June 1969 against the police raid of a gay disco, the Stonewall. The street riots culminated in a march up Fifth Avenue, this march being widely taken as a demonstration of gay pride. The "Stonewall riot" is usually accorded the status of a symbolic opening to a new appreciation of gay community and fellowship, as well as to gay rights movements both within and without the United States.

The thinking behind gay rights, which involved a radically new, positive evaluation of gayness, had tangible results in the seventies. Thus, for example, the American Psychiatric Association in 1973 removed homosexuality from its categories of mental disorders, and candidates who openly declared their homosexual preferences were elected to political office.[27] The success of gay-liberationist activism in raising public awareness was evidenced in the seventies also, paradoxically, by the public moves against it. In Britain, such moves could be identified in Mary Whitehouse's campaigns, particularly in her prosecution of Gay News, although, in common with several other crusaders taken to be antigay, she herself would deny this as a primary stimulus to action. In the United States, public opposition to gay rights was organized through such figures as Anita Bryant, whose virulently antigay stance is evident in her published work (to be dealt with more fully below). California voters in 1978 defeated the Briggs Initiative, designed to ban homosexual teachers and homosexual advocacy in public schools. Still, a measure of the backlash against gay rights was offered the following year in the leniently punished assassinations of the openly gay member of the board of supervisors of San Francisco, Harvey Milk, and of the mayor of San Francisco by an antigay former policeman and San Francisco supervisor, Dan White.

Jeffrey Weeks recognizes the immense achievement of the gay liberation movement in breaking down taboos about sex and in radical questioning of not only sexual behavior but of rigid gender divisions. Yet he also recognizes the problems within the kind of sexual liberalism that largely underlies such sexual reform movements. Gay culture, so-called, is celebrated by Dennis Altman as "an affirmation of sexual play and experimentation that goes far beyond the repressive norms most people in this society, including many homosexuals, have internalized."[28] The danger that Altman detects is the tendency within American New Right thinking to link gay liberation with abortion, ERA, pornography, all as examples of elements threatening the social fabric. Weeks, however, detects dangers internal to liberationist thinking itself, at least in its most common, liberal, form. He is particularly aware of the implicit belief in the fixed characteristics of men and women (whereby homosexuality remains a deviation), and of the consequent belief in reason, good sense, and proper education as the roads to reform, and he is dismayed by the absence of any historical sense of the changing nature of homosexual oppression.[29]

Whatever the intellectual problems in assent to the notion of the gay man or woman, and to the trappings of belief in "gay culture" or "a gay sensibility," certain aspects of alleged gay culture are easily identifiable in the sixties and seventies, above all. Thus, Richard Dyer identifies disco as the most widespread form of leisure activity for gays, both in terms of the dance activity as a means of expression and also in terms of venue, providing a space for social and sexual contact.[30] A potential problem, though, may be indicated in Altman's statement that "almost every discussion of the disco phenomenon, which swept most of the Western world in the late seventies, stresses its connection with gays. . . . thus reinforcing the idea of a self-evident gay culture and minority."[31] (So, for example, discos in movies centering even on ostensibly heterosexual characters have been read in terms of their fundamentally gay roots—a reading which is given added force by such movies as *Looking for Mr. Goodbar,* with its climactic murder by a closeted gay character picked up by the heroine at a disco.)

A more difficult discussion involves "camp" as an expression of a claimed gay sensibility. Susan Sontag concedes that, if there be any such thing as a natural mode of sensibility, then camp is not that mode, since its very essence is the love of the unnatural, at least as that is identified with artifice and exaggeration.[32] (It could be pointed out that there is a hiatus in her logic here, in that a love of the unnatural could theoretically be "natural" to those whose sexuality is deemed by wider society to be against nature.) The writer both distances herself from and shores up the belief that camp has much to do with a gay sensibility: "While it's not true that Camp taste *is* homosexual taste, there is no doubt a peculiar affinity and overlap. . . . Jews and homosexuals are the outstanding creative minorities in contemporary urban culture. . . . The two pioneering forces of modern sensibility are Jewish moral seriousness and homosexual aestheticism and irony."[33] (It is tempting to ask why, in that case, given her account of these phenomena and their sources, it should not be the other way around, too. Why not Jewish aestheticism and homosexual moral seriousness?) She believes that camp's function is as a solvent of morality, that it is encapsulated in the metaphor of life as theater,[34] with homosexuals pinning their integration into society upon the promotion of the aesthetic sense.[35] Richard Dyer discerns value in camp, in terms of its sensitivity to gender roles and its "refusal to take the trappings of femininity too seriously."[36]

Andrew Britton is markedly less impressed with the value of camp. He sees confirmation in it of an implied norm, rather than a radical critique of that norm. "Being essentially a mere play within given conventional signs, camp replaces the signs of 'masculinity' with a parody of the signs of 'femininity' and reinforces existing social definitions of both categories. The standard of 'the male' remains the fixed point in relation to which male gays and women emerge as 'that which is not male.' "[37] Britton recognizes within camp one way in which gay men have recuperated their oppression and advocates that it be criticized as such.[38]

Within the eighties, the disproportionate suffering of the gay community in relation to AIDS and the comparative neglect of the problem by government agencies in the United States have combined to give a new sense of purpose to gay organizations. The Gay Men's Health Crisis, aware of its political clout and willing to use it to raise funds, is the most obvious organized response to the inaction of government and of the medical world in the face of AIDS. According to Richard Liebmann-Smith, nearly all major American cities now have gay volunteer organizations which help people with AIDS in financial and legal terms or in terms of psychological support. A principal concern of these groups has been the setting up of gay hotlines and of public seminars to provide information about AIDS and about services relating to the illess.[39]

Just as it was possible, after the depredations on gay rights perpetrated by Anita Bryant, to argue optimistically in 1978 that she had stimulated a revival of gay liberation energy,[40] so communal resilience in the face of AIDS as well as of Britain's Clause 28 has been taken, perhaps in some desperation, to be the silver lining in the dense, dark clouds of the eighties.[41]

Liberal Attitudes to Homosexuality

One of the most succinct guides to liberal thinking in relation to homosexuality is provided by relevant British legislation in the sixties. The Wolfenden Committee made no attempt to challenge the moral indignation summoned up by homosexuality when it recommended the decriminalization of homosexual acts between consenting male adults (defined as of at least twenty-one years of age) in private. Rather, significant divisions were suggested between public and private acts, with public exhibition of homosexuality remaining legally punishable while private behavior became a matter of choice—just as a separation was held feasible between homosexual acts involving two adults and those between an adult (legally punishable) and a minor.[42]

To make a sexual act free from legal penalty does not necessarily involve its freedom from moral censure, or from the judgment that it is the act of "inadequates." The sixties legislation, noticeably, did not permit homosexual relations even in private to male adults in the merchant navy or the armed forces.

Right-Wing Attitudes to Homosexuality

Rightist thinking on homosexuality shares with liberal thought the notion that public display of it is abhorrent. So, those who conceive of homosexuality after the manner of Anita Bryant are particularly vociferous about questions of employment and housing in relation to homosexuals.[43] Male homosexuality is taken by the Right to represent a weakening of the proper virility of "White culture."[44] Hostility to homosexuality, conceived simplistically as effeminacy, is capable of rationalization as objection to the subversion of that which is accorded respect by virtue of its sober masculinity. "The effeminate/exhibitionist style of *some* gay men that has come to be their *collective* image represents the desertion of the repressed, serious and under-emotional style that has been 'masculine.' Instead gays offer a style that is playful, pleasure-seeking, indeed gay, a style that is symbolically a rejection of the work ethic."[45]

The Right's loathing of homosexuality is rationalized, as are so many of its loathings—of feminism or abortion rights, for example—by appeal to biblical teaching. Usefully in this regard, Andrea Dworkin claims that the clothing of homophobia in religiosity is unpersuasive. "There is nothing in the Old Testament to justify the vilification of homosexuals or homosexuality that began with Paul and still manifests virulently in the fundamentalist Right. . . . It takes the magical claim that the New Testament is 'concealed' in the Old to sustain the illusion of divine sanction for this special hatred of homosexuality. It is more than concealed; it is not there."[46]

When divine authority is difficult to adduce, then substitutes for it are found by the Right in Nature and in common sense. The argument that homosexuality is against nature, on the grounds that sex is designed by nature to have direct relevance to reproduction, founders on the point that all nonreproductive sex must be similarly perverted, that, in short, much heterosexual conjugation must by this logic be unnatural. Appeals to common sense have been characterized by Stuart Hall as the new symbolic version of the ancient principle of "divide and rule," whereby agents of control form a coalition with moderates through the use of a minority/majority paradigm (majority conduct and thinking being equated with the commonsensical).[47]

Another method used by the Right to discredit homosexuality is guilt by (claimed) association. Dennis Altman notices how opponents of feminism, which has been blamed for all the contemporary social evils summed up in the term "collapse of the traditional family," are almost invariably homophobic too.[48] He cites Kenneth Sherrill's claim that "homophobia accompanies opposition to a whole set of generally liberal issues, such as abortion, marijuana, open housing and decreased military spending," the rationalization being that these issues share the common dimension of "belonging to the new morality."[49]

Right-wing thinking in relation to homosexuality is usefully exemplified not only by Mary Whitehouse in her 1977 prosecution of *Gay News* but in the sycophantic account of her thinking and conduct in this relation by Michael Tracey and David Morrison.[50] Whitehouse sees herself as unjustly tarred with "the antihomosexual brush" through an organized campaign against her, that she is a victim of an alleged "homosexual/intellectual/humanist lobby,"[51] thus demonstrating the ease with which the victimizer can claim victimization when the victim attempts self-defense. Tracey and Morrison claim on her behalf, "What she was trying to do . . . lay not in punishing Lemon [Denis Lemon, editor of *Gay News*], nor in a sense in even bringing back to life the blasphemy laws. Both those were necessary means towards a much more profound end, which was re-establishing the role of God within social life."[52] It seems extraordinary that these authors believe that the reactivation of blasphemy laws might not be essential to the grand design claimed by them on her behalf. It also seems remarkable that it should be *Gay News* that was singled out for attack in the name of God's reestablishment in British social life.

The occasion of the prosecution was *Gay News*'s publication in 1976 of Professor James Kirkup's poem, "The Love That Dares to Speak Its Name," with its portrayal of carnal love between a Roman centurion and the crucified Christ. Tracey and Morrison, in this regard, mention—presumably in Whitehouse's justification—that there were adverse comments in that very periodical's correspondence columns about the poem. (It must be assumed that it would come as news to these writers that some of the oppressed in any society internalize the grounds for their oppression.)

The hollowness of Whitehouse's claim that she was not demonstrating homophobia in her legal defense of divinity against the incursions of homosexual carnality is pointed up by her statement in *Whatever Happened to Sex?:* "The natural repugnance which most people feel when homosexuality and lesbianism is mentioned . . ."[53] How does she know what most people feel? And why is repugnance "natural"? Once again, when divine authority is not invoked, Nature is dragged in to provide an alibi for prejudice. She claims to be sufficiently Christian to deplore the harshness of attitude attendant on such prejudice, but quickly she adds, "to go to the other extreme and elevate people suffering from such abnormalities into a norm for society not only threatens society but is dangerous to the individuals themselves, since it excludes them from consideration of treatment."[54] Whitehouse's concern with harshness of attitude is, thus, based on a conception of a heterosexual norm which is threatened by sick sociopaths. As the authors helpfully point out, she doubts neither the Bible's condemnation of homosexual practices nor the treatability of the pathological state of homosexuality.[55] The point of her campaign—which is claimed by herself and her hagiographers as not antihomosexual—is, apparently, to sublimate and control what the authors call "the darker instinct of man's nature"[56]—a phrase which, curiously, suggests that homosexuality may (in that it is instinctive, albeit darkly instinctive) be deemed natural.

The reason for the zealousness of such women as Anita Bryant (who launched a more forthright crusade in the name of God against gay rights during the same decade in the state of Florida) and Whitehouse in antigay and allegedly profamily causes may be taken by their supporters as obedience to the word of God, although the word of God is not only more difficult to interpret but less intensely selective than they take it to be. Less enthusiastic thinkers seek the reasons elsewhere.

It is obviously possible to argue that right-wing women's loathing of extrafamilial sex, a loathing that helps to explain their equally passionate antifeminism, is based on a belief that only within the family can they survive, and that only within the family is sex free of the concomitant danger that it is conceived to have beyond marital relationships. Sex manifestly may involve lethal danger beyond the family. On empirical evidence, however, it may involve danger within the family. It is hard to believe that married women share the law's hitherto obtaining difficulty in conceiving of the feasibility of violent rape within marriage. Moreover, statistics about sexual abuse appear to suggest that sexuality within the family may be a much less safe phenomenon than rightist women would appear to imply.

Andrea Dworkin explains the intense profamilialism of such campaigners as Anita Bryant in psychological terms, as involving displacement of their justifiable rage against those males who dominate them from within the family. "Having good reason to hate, but not the courage to rebel, women require symbols of danger that justify their fear."[57] By this argument, gay men were scapegoated by Anita Bryant in order to restrain her from reacting to pressures from within her family in a more direct fashion. (Bryant's subsequent history suggests that there may be more within Dworkin's suggestion than skeptics may at first credit.)

Whatever the wellsprings of her motivation, Bryant takes pains to present herself as a simple woman inspired (by God no less) to take on citified, sophisticated, "organized" gay militants. Her rhetoric here owes less perhaps to American movies about Joan of Arc or Bernadette than to the traditions of Frank Capra and, later, of those Doris Day vehicles where a cheerful, healthy, unintellectual housewife takes on the unscrupulous might of the railroad company or some other organization of the sort. "The footsoldiers were housewives and mothers . . . in opposition to a well-organized, highly financed, and politically militant group of homosexual activists," she writes,[58] as if she and the New Christian Right were innocent of organization, financing, and political militancy. Her aim, it is to be remembered, was to organize opposition to a proposed ordinance which she thought "if passed, would give special privileges to homosexuals in areas of housing, public accommodation, and employment."[59] This aim involved, she claims, "nothing political or militant."[60] She certainly sounds political and militant in her press release: "Behind the high-sounding appeal against discrimination in jobs and housing they are really asking to be blessed in their abnormal life-style by the office of the president of the United States."[61]

Her allegedly nonpolitical reasoning is that the issue which she has taken on cannot be deemed one of civil rights, since those who have "chosen to rebel against all responsible living" do not have civil rights. "It is simply not true that all human beings have the same rights," she avers.[62] (The truth of this observation may, incidentally, have been the point of the proposed ordinance.) But this is entirely proper, it seems. "Some human beings throw away their rights by throwing away their responsibilities when we no longer dare to say no and prove we mean it by enforcing it."[63] Righteous anger often interferes with Bryant's command of English, but the underlying meaning is clear enough. She groups homosexuals with adulterers, thieves, and rebellious children in order to ridicule the notion that they should have rights. Should there be, say, "extortioner rights" for thieves?[64] Since homespun naïveté is her forte, it may be missing the point here to accuse her argument of lack of sophistication. Nevertheless, it could be pointed out that adulterers may well have rights, but not qua adulterers. Rather, such rights accrue to them inasmuch as they live within a legalized family arrangement. (Presumably, the concept of adultery demands that one at least of the adulterers be married.) Her argument that "homosexuals" as persons be wholly identified with their sexuality or, even more crudely, with their sex acts is classic within Right conceptions of homosexuality, but it is no less gross for being classic.

In another classic Christian Right statement, she echoes the Mary Whitehouse line that true caring involves the demand that the sociopathic homosexual (there can be no other) seek treatment and cure. "It is tragic if the cultural surroundings provide more easily for homosexuality than for recovery of normal patterns. . . . It is far better to help an individual recover from his dejection—whatever has led him into such a debased way of life—restore his confidence, and help him return [sic] to full heterosexuality. A society that condones homosexual behaior is a society that is uncaring."[65] By this logic, Nazi Germany could well have refuted any insinuation that it was uncaring.

The work that Bryant put in against the Dade County ordinance turns out, though, to have been undertaken not just in the name of normality, not just for the sake of the family (which thinkers of her sort would equate with normality), but to protect children: "I felt I had to take a stand against this ordinance because of the effect it would have on my children, and on all the children of Dade County."[66] Why children? Because of her fears, dignified by her with the description "valid," of "widespread militant homosexuals' efforts to influence children to their abnormal way of life".[67] (Indeed, out of the Dade County strife came Save Our Children, Inc., and Protect America's Children, which moved on to further successes in Oregon, Minnesota, and Kansas.[68] At this stage, it must have been painful for Bryant to realize that the gingham, country-fresh image she had tried to give to her campaign had surely to give way to the actuality of a well-organized, highly financed, and poltically militant organization.)

Sometimes, Bryant's concern for children is in terms of fear of their being "exposed" to it. The metaphor is one of disease and contamination, a metaphor that may be highly signficant in New Christian Right thinking about AIDS. Her fuller explanation of her concern is more extraordinary, in that she shifts from Capra discourse to a set of images that belong surely in vampire movies. "The recruitment of our children is absolutely necessary for the survival and growth of homosexuality—for since homosexuals cannot reproduce, they *must* recruit, *must* freshen their ranks. And who qualifies as a likely recruit: a 35-year-old father or mother of two . . . or a teenage boy or girl who is surging with sexual awareness?"[69]

Such a statement deserves sustained analysis, in that it reveals so much about rightist conceptions of the dread figure of the homosexual. It contains a number of factual, not to mention logical, errors. Homosexuals can reproduce, for example, at least in the sense that men and women with strong homosexual tendencies can and do. The subtext of this statement seems to be that homosexuals would either produce ready-made homosexual children or, less improbably, that once these children were in their clutches, they would be forced into a life of unspeakable sexual exploitation by homosexual parents. (This is no more—and no less—credible than that heterosexual parents would recruit their children into their sexual service. Is Bryant more concerned about sexual abuse of minors, as is known to occur in many of her model families, or about exclusively homosexual abuse of minors?) It is also untrue that the recruitment of "our" children is necessary, absolutely or otherwise, for the survival, let alone growth, of homosexuality. The majority of homosexuals appear to have been born into ostensibly heterosexual families and to have found themselves increasingly identifying in homosexual terms. Even if homosexuality should be a disease, as Bryant believes, the source of the disease would seem to be from within the family, not in a sinister recruiting agent (recruiting to "freshen their ranks") from outside.

Bryant's unsuspected talent as pornographer is intriguingly suggested in her last thought and in her expression of it (the sibilance, assonance, and alliteration are highly reminiscent of pornographic writing style). Bryant may be an authority on whether teenagers do or do not surge with sexual awareness, but her rhetorical question about homosexual choice of teenagers or thirty-five-year-old parents would appear to say much more about herself than about the homosexuals on whose behalf she presumes to speak. Some homosexuals may be attracted to teenagers, others to thirty-five-year olds. The reduction of sexual attraction to questions of surging sexual awareness also says much about the impoverishment of that thinking which views sexuality in terms of exclusivity and of age (not to mention surge).

More significantly, she has created, in this quotation from her book, a monster, a creature of insatiable, morbid appetites, which needs young (virgin?) flesh in order to survive and propagate. No acknowledgment is made to either Bram Stoker or Bela Lugosi; without these gentlemen, it would be difficult for her allusiveness to work such a powerful spell on her readers, all the same.

God's Word is brought into the struggle by Bryant—as it so often is, at least as it is revealed to such authorities, by the Right. In her

letter to the Dade County Board of Commissioners, she refers it to
Leviticus 20:13, Jude 7, and, in the New Testament, to Corinthians
6, verses 9 and 10.[70] Her difficulty in claiming authority from the
Scriptures is shown by a perusal of Corinthians 6:9, where the only
remotely relevant condemnatory reference is to the effeminate.
Although Right thinking may equate homosexuality with
effeminacy, it is a difficult correlation to maintain. Homosexuals
may be effeminate, as may heterosexuals. Then, again, they may not
be.

Her conviction that God is on her side is demonstrated by her
interpretation of her near-involvement in a three-car collision as a
sign of His protection of her. (It could, of course, be interpreted in
quite contrary fashion as a warning of what could happen to her if
she persisted in her campaign. One is reminded here of the idiotic
conversation about divine providence in *The Big Bus* [James
Frawley, 1976] between a sweet old lady and the priest who has lost
his faith. Rejecting her conclusion that God has providently sat her
next to a man of the cloth on the bus journey, the priest rejoins, "If
your God is so powerful, why didn't He give you the window
seat?")

Her confidence about the workings of God extends to His creation of human sexuality. Because sexual identities have been ordained as "innate" to males and females, homosexuality must be a
twisting of divine order.[71]

Given the imperturbability of her confidence in herself and God's
plans for her, it is hardly surprising that in some quarters Anita
Bryant was laughed at, when, that is, she was not hated. Like Mary
Whitehouse in Britain, though, she sees herself as being victimized
by those whom she wanted to behave as helpless, "dejected" victims, and victimized by a conspiracy. Thus, she claims that there
was a "show-biz conspiracy" to laugh at her.[72] (A conspiracy to
laugh seems a particularly interesting conception.) She also detects
sinister sympathies between leaders of the ERA and NOW (National Organization for Women) and "militant homosexuals."[73]
Moreover, her director of press relations characterized San Francisco in a phrase worthy of Bryant at her most righteously angry, as
"a cesspool of sexual perversion gone rampant."[74] (There can be
few things more terrifying than a rampant cesspool.)

Finally, in just the same way as Mary Whitehouse's biographers
noted with apparent surprise that some *Gay News* readers expressed misgivings about the prosecuted poem of issue 96, Bryant
notes with obvious approval that some members of ("genuine")

minorities shared her antigay views. She writes that certain blacks, Hispanics, and others of many nationalities and religious backgrounds protested against homosexuals waving the flag of human rights. Moreover, these people sensibly called homosexuality by what she terms as its right name: "a perverted, unnatural, and ungodly lifestyle."[75] This exemplifies that divide-and-rule tactic whereby the insecurities of certain minorities are played on by those in authority so that they will align themselves with "legitimate" minorities, as determined by that authority. The tactic is particularly effective in separating recent immigrant groups from others, so that one (now more established) ethnic minority may permit or even participate in attacks upon another, more recently arrived. (A fine illustration of the point is made by the hostility between neighborhood blacks and the financially successful Korean family in their midst in Spike Lee's *Do the Right Thing* [1989].)

The point of spending time on the profoundly ignorant writings of Anita Bryant is to gain access to the sort of prejudices which are catered to and promulgated by the Right in both the United States and Great Britain. Bryant's success in Dade County is testimony to the political appeal of a package of unexamined beliefs within the arena of civil rights struggle. Among such beliefs, prominently, may be numbered these: that heterosexuality is innate, while homosexuality is an acquired perversion; that heterosexuality is both natural and divinely ordained, while homosexuality is unnatural and against God's order; that sexuality is divided into mutually exclusive heterosexuality and homosexuality (so that homosexuals cannot reproduce); that homosexuality is an illness and requires treatment; that homosexuality is contagious, particularly in the presence of children; that homosexuals have voracious sexual appetites, particularly for adolescents; that militant homosexuality deserves punishment, and that society is endangered if it does not react punitively; that, if left unchecked, militant homosexuals will conspire with other unnatural beings (feminists, notably) to subvert the approved way of life.

Since the United States and Britain in the eighties are placed under the paramount influence of right-wing thought, at a time when the mysteries of AIDS create a tempting vacuum in the understanding of sexuality itself, it is unusually important to grasp the prejudices and credos of the Right in relation to sexuality in general, homosexuality in particular.

Manifestations of Homosexuality in the Eighties

Section 28 of the British Local Government Act of 1988 states that a local authority "shall not . . . intentionally promote homosexuality or publish material with the intention of promoting homosexuality."[76] It is possible to interpret this as the kind of outcome Anita Bryant and Mary Whitehouse dreamed about in the latter seventies. On the other hand, what is indicated by the clause may be less clearly antigay legislation than a new manifestation of the old liberal thinking whereby private homosexual relations were nobody's business other than that of the (two) consenting adults, while public "display" of gayness was to be avoided. Interestingly, the British Social Attitudes Survey for 1987 shows a greater reluctance than in 1983 to see homosexuals banned from, say, the teaching profession, at the same time as it chronicles more widespread disapproval (74 percent in 1987; 62 percent in 1983) of a "homosexual relationship."[77] Jeffrey Weeks concludes that it is not homosexuality which troubles the British public so much as a kind of equalization of homosexuality with heterosexuality. If this is so, he goes on to state, then Clause 28 is remarkably in step with public opinion, since it did not try to criminalize homosexuality but rather attacked what it called the promotion of a "pretended family relationship."[78]

Even a cursory examination of Anita Bryant's writing about homosexuality reveals the prevalence of the disease metaphors in her conception of it. In this, she is part of a long, stubborn tradition. In the midnineteenth century, for example, Ambroise Tardieu thought of homosexuals as being exposed for what they were by their diseased and exhausted bodies, victims of their sexual excess, which led to disfigurement or death.[79] In the twentieth century, Bryant's thinking about the sapping of American society's strength through the unchecked power of the diseased homosexual is prefigured by Himmler, on the threat posed to Nazi Germany by the disease of homosexuality: "He regarded it as an infectious disease that could at any moment spread throughout Germany. Homosexuality, if unchecked, would mean the end of the Germanic race."[80] "We are faced with an aggressive social epidemic in this country."[81] The country this time is the United States, the source Anita Bryant.

A major achievement of the eighties was the releasing of a persistent and powerful metaphor—homosexuality as contagion—from its metaphorical trappings, thanks to the advent of and to a particular understanding of AIDS. Edward Albert notes that while homosexuals have "always been perceived as morally contagious, the medical metaphor has been reified in the media such that gays especially are now seen as concretely contagious as well."[82] Richard Goldstein sees the emergence of this new sort of conception in the eighties in terms of the New Right's moral agenda. "In their reign of terror, I sense a return to the premodern idea that illness is not 'an expression of the inner self' but a punishment and a sign."[83]

9

Movies and Homosexuality

Dominant Representations of Gay Men

In his useful summary of his impressions of dominant representations of gay men, Stuart Marshall finds that these are almost entirely abusive and insulting. Yet, he notes, there is a lack of theoretical work upon such mainstream, visual representations as well as upon ideology and culture, other than unfocused debates about "stereotyping" and "gay sensibility."[1] (Exceptions to this general rule of untheorized, vague discussion are given by Marshall[2] as *Gays and Film*[3] and *The Celluloid Closet*.)[4]

While women, according to Marshall, are abused in dominant media by a surfeit of representations, from control over which they are excluded, gay men are starved of representation in these media. When gay men are represented, it is normally within avant-garde "minority-audience" films or in the "unrecognized" though clearly popular domain of pornography. (This might well have the effect of not only further marginalizing them but also more closely associating them with criminality.) Their representation in dominant media is usually within dramatic fiction, in secondary roles, with their principal signification being degeneracy, and threat to the stability of family and thus of society. Degeneracy and threat are embodied by such versions of the gay male as the child molester, the pathetic queen, or the effete spy. The problems which such gay characters betoken within the narrative are resolved normally with their deaths.[5]

Unlike the bulk of work on dominant visual representation, which largely critiques it in terms of the inadequate notion of the stereotype or investigates it in terms of "gay archaeology," *Gays and Film* and *The Celluloid Closet* attempt to read "against the grain." Thus, they attempt to recover from classic Hollywood the homosexual characters, themes, and meanings which cannot be voiced or addressed by dominant film criticism and theory.[6]

Marshall argues that the visual domain is of exceptional importance to gay politics, claiming, for example, that the gay pride march is "its own political effect." Insistence on visibility represents a refusal of the confinement, demanded by the law, to a private domain.[7]

Dominant television representations, as discussed by Simon Watney, seem clearly similar to the dominant visual representations discussed in general by Stuart Marshall. Watney notes that while it is estimated that at least 10 percent of the British population is gay, representations of gay persons take up 1.85 percent of television actuality broadcasting time and 0.93 percent of radio actuality time.[8] Generally, gays on British television are represented as subjects of scandal, humor, or humanist pathos.[9]

Certain soap operas seem to attempt a critique of the exclusion of gay men from the social consensus. Channel 4's *Brookside* is one example, BBC1's *EastEnders* another, but there is always noticeable tentativeness about such endeavors. The principal gay character in *EastEnders,* played by Michael Cashman, managed to be a reasonable spokesperson for gay dignity and was yet treated by others in Albert Square with either ill-veiled hostility or the humanist pathos that Watney detects in many "well-meaning" series. (This could be taken as a matter of "realism" in relation to the diegetic world of this soap opera or in the interests of keeping up good audience ratings. Both possibilities suggest that the makers of *EastEnders* believe that homophobia is endemic in the majority of the British public.) Most notably, gay characters seem to have been written out of the scripts of both British soap operas.

The vagueness of soaps' good intentions and the apparent nervousness of the makers about their public's tolerance are again suggested by *Dynasty*'s treatment of Steven, on the other side of the Atlantic. Armistead Maupin clearly believes that at least the makers of soaps view them as a barometer of public intolerance: "Hollywood . . . had a period when AIDS caused them to back away like crazy from gay subject matter. That's when Steven Carrington turned straight on *Dynasty*. Now he's going gay again, so I guess the worst is over."[10]

Robin Wood claims that there was a brief moment in the latter seventies when a number of movies concerned themselves with the theoretical program implied by gay liberation.[11] However, this tendency was soon halted by movies that involved reactionary, and thoroughly traditional, versions of gayness, wherein it was equated with degeneracy and criminality. Wood points to *New York after Midnight,* in which a woman entering a gay disco may expect the men to stop dancing and try to rape her, and to *Windows,* in which a principal female character seems to believe that if a man is paid to rape the object of her erotic interest, she will turn to lesbianism. In particular, Wood cites *American Gigolo,* in which the hero tries to forget his presumably inglorious past, when he used to "trick with fags," and in which the villain is black and homosexual.[12]

Wood also identifies *Can't Stop the Music* as marking a return, at the start of the eighties, to the "clandestine."[13] The gay subtext, which largely dares not speak its name, is especially interesting when it is taken as one particularly obvious example of the constant "threat," in dominant cinema, that the gay undercurrent may break through into overt expression. When Steve Neale claims of mainstream cinema that "male homosexuality is constantly present as an undercurrent,"[14] he is not talking about identifiably gay characters or situations but about the operations of the gaze. Largely, the gaze in dominant cinema has been of particular interest to feminists in their analysis of women as objects of it. Yet male characters and the male stars personifying them must be gazed upon too by cinema spectators, even if within the diegesis they are active bearers of the gaze. The principal distinction between looking at women and men, according to Neale, is the refusal in the latter case to acknowledge eroticism. Eroticism involved with the look at men must always be oblique, or such looking (which is likely according to the usual accounts of cinematic looking to be "masculinized" even if the spectator is female) must be given an alibi (such as admiration of strength in a single-combat sequence, for example). "Were this not the case," Neale observes, "mainstream cinema would have openly to come to terms with the male homosexuality it so assiduously seeks either to denigrate or deny."[15]

Mainstream cinema has indeed assiduously sought to denigrate its own subterranean homosexuality (and presumably its legions of homosexual employees have sought to deny theirs) by shouting loudest against the figure of the homosexual. In the sixties, despite the decade's popular association with sexual liberation, the revision of the Production Code in 1960 simply permitted formerly banned words such as "faggot" and "dyke" to be uttered on soundtracks, and gay characters continued to be viewed as alien.[16] If Paul Schrader bears a share of the blame that Wood heaps upon *American Gigolo,* he may be implicated again when Vito Russo picks out *Hardcore* for a scene in which George C Scott, upon beating up a gay man, is told by the police lieutenant that he will not be arrested for this because "they don't care about some faggot hustler."[17]

Russo claims in 1987, "In popular films, anti-gay prejudice may be more prevalent now than at any other time in our history. Never have Hollywood screenwriters felt so secure in their belief that it is acceptable to insult homosexuals, and nowhere has fear and hatred of gay people been more evident than in commercial, mainstream motion pictures, which reflect[18] and encourage the prejudices of their intended audience."[19] He notes, for example, the insistence on degeneracy and criminality as represented by gay characters in *The Name of the Rose* and *Blue Velvet,* and the particularly odious use of antigay dialogue and humor by black characters and actors in *Hollywood Shuffle* and *Beverly Hills Cop.*[20] Perhaps—at least to a more casual observer than Russo—the homophobia revealed by mainstream movies' humor seems no more virulent in the eighties than it was previously. What may render the continuing diet of such material disturbing and depressing is that it should be continued unquestioningly into a decade where societal homophobia has been given a measure of "validity" by right-wing, allegedly Christian interpretations of the meaning of AIDS and in an industry which has greater reason than many to know that meaning, as well as alternatives to it.

At one particular point in the early 'eighties there seemed to be some attempt to consider gayness in the context of popular entertainment. In 1982, *Tootsie* and *Victor/Victoria* raised questions about homosexuality, antigay and misogynistic prejudice, the nature of femininity, masculinity, and androgyny. A number of less prestigious entertainments around this time—such as *Making Love, Partners,* and *Personal Best*—also seemed to revolve around matters of gayness. Even if these, and *Victor/Victoria,* were unpopular enough with the public to be commercially unsuccessful, their appearance deserves consideration.

Robin Wood pays particular attention to the setting for *Victor/Victoria,* a sort of never-never land represented by Paris in the thirties[21]—the kind of setting which makes the male homosexuality shown in the very first shot less immediate. He recognizes that the movie undermines its audience's entrenched attitudes through sympathy and laughter. The dialogue also criticizes homophobia—as, for example, when Julie Andrews says that the only people who consider homosexuality sinful are "respectable clergymen and terrified heterosexuals."[22] Yet, largely, *Victor/Victoria* panders to one tenacious myth, that homosexuals and heterosexuals are quite distinct species. There are indeed such moments as those where the heroine indicates the likelihood that the James Garner character must have had doubts about his sexuality,[23] or where Garner, instead of fighting, ends up as a buddy of the laborers of whom he had disapproved.[24] Yet these instances make little impression in a film which insists on the complete separateness and mutual exclusivity of heterosexual and homosexual, and which ends by making the heterosexual couple serious, the homosexual couple comic.[25]

In *Making Love*, Wood notes that homosexual lovemaking is presented as matter-of-factly as heterosexual, and says of the film: "its very existence as a popular entertainment, its very format of compressed soap opera, its public display for general audiences, all suggest the growing acceptance of gayness, its potential respectability."[26] He also points out that the screenwriter, Barry Sandler, felt able to "come out" during the film's making.[27] Yet, once again, the movie seems to confirm the separateness of two sexualities. Although the Michael Ontkean character appears at the beginning to be happily married, he finds in the course of the movie that he is "really" gay. The homosexual male played by Harry Hamlin is permitted to defend promiscuity, but ultimately the only life-styles granted visibility are those of heterosexual monogamy or its imitation, of the homosexual variety. Normality is restored, according to Wood, by the elimination of ideological threat and the teaming up of both the woman and her former husband with father figures.[28]

What even the more liberal, better-intentioned films about gayness thus seem to suggest is that gay characters, even gay couples, may survive and find a place in the world, provided that it is the proper place under patriarchy. The subversive potential of possible bisexuality is closed down in both *Victor/Victoria* and *Making Love*, much energy being expended on the establishment of two exclusive possibilities. "By merely reproducing the notion that everyone is, in some inexplicable way, either exclusively one thing or the other,"[29] such films reinforce and perpetuate that notion, so fundamental to the working of patriarchy.

The overall impression of eighties movies in relation to homosexuality is not as entirely negative as Vito Russo affirms. If the gay movies' cutting edge is considerably blunted by their liberalism, by their pandering to dearly and long-held beliefs about sexuality, at least they are made within an ideological climate that is manifestly "difficult." There are other aspects of eighties movies to consider also.

One of these is the apparent creation of a female gaze, largely through the adaptation of male objectification from gay-male homoerotic contexts. Suzanne Moore notes the camera's lingering over Richard Gere's body in *American Gigolo* and talks of the "ritual of getting dressed, the pampering and preening of the male body" so that this becomes a mechanism by means of which "movies from *Mean Streets* to *Saturday Night Fever* could effectively relocate the cinematic gaze within the strict confines of narrative structure. Standing in front of the mirror, masculinity could legitimately be displayed."[30] "Legitimately" as a term masks the need for further work, all the same, both on the implications of women looking at men (the lack of which work Moore recognizes) and of the devices by which men-as-spectacle may be rendered for a female gaze without the "problem" of identifiably summoning up the erotic male gaze. Whereas Steve Neale argues that the anxiety created by such male spectacle may be dispelled through sadism or punishment in mainstream cinema, Moore points out that we increasingly see male bodies coded as erotic spectacle without an attendant narrative violence.[31]

Another element of "progressive" potential, if only potential, in certain movies of the 'eighties, and arguably in movies generally, is the exposure of the acting involved in "passing for straight." Jack Babuscio takes passing as the successful imitation of heterosexuals and therefore an acting success.[32] (Here, it may be that the writer underestimates the element of acting, albeit acting to a less spectacular degree, necessary for heterosexuals to succeed in the field of passing, not so much as heterosexual but as masculine or feminine in the terms which society has adopted as appropriate.)

If, moreover, such eighties movies as *Victor/Victoria* and *Making Love* disappoint by raising possibilities of bisexuality which are finally jettisoned for the firmer establishment of the necessary separateness of homosexual and heterosexual, feminine and masculine, they do at least raise these possibilities. While Suzanne Moore seems justified in recognizing an increasing tendency erotically to objectify the male figure within entertainment, even without "compensatory" or obfuscating narrative punishment, one critic at least claims that there has long been the possibility within cinema of heroizing the man with feminine characteristics, primarily within the sphere of comedy. Andrew Britton observes how comedy may criticize and transform traditional gender roles "and the extent to which characteristics assigned by these roles to women can be presented as being desirable and attractive in a man."[33] He then goes so far as to claim that Cary Grant, principally in his comedies of the late thirties, embodied something akin to a positive image of bisexuality: "In what other male star, classical or modern, is the realisation of a man's 'femininity' endorsed so specifically and explicitly?"[34]

Gay "Documentaries"

It is in the "minority-audience" films and videos made (usually by politicized gay filmmakers) with an evident intention to confront heterosexist assumptions about homosexual men and women that consideration of not only gay life-styles but of heterosexual behavior may be undertaken from a challenging new perspective.

Several of these films' titles indicate their oppositional stance by their appropriation of sensationalist tabloid descriptions of the gays who are centered on in the films—boldly announcing their subject matter but also disarming prejudice and subverting homophobic discourse by foregrounding it in the alien context provided by a homosexual ambience. Such titles would surely include Rosa von Praunheim's *Army of Lovers, or Revolt of the Perverts* (1979), the (Australian) "One in Seven" Collective's *Witches Faggots Dykes and Poofters* (1980), and the Lesbian and Gay Youth Video Project's *Framed Youth—Revenge of the Teenage Perverts* (1983).

The apparent aim of many of these works is to consider the conceptions of gays which fuel homophobia and which help heterosexuality to sustain itself in its position of brutal domination. Thus, *Framed Youth* produces a collage of views of heterosexuality in Britain but from the perspective of gay and lesbian youth. Among other techniques used to explore the straight world of Britain is that of interviewing "average" British citizens. These interviews indicate homophobia and its almost inevitable companion, profound ignorance. Consistent with the belief that the personal is political, there is emphasis in the video upon the makers' revelation of experiences of love, violence, and strained relations with parents.

The Alternative Miss World (1980) is, as its title promises, a parody from a different perspective of the heterosexual ritual known as the Miss World beauty contest. The gender ambivalence of the master of ceremony's (Andrew Logan) costuming, so that he appears half-male, half-female, is an indication of the essential means by which the ritual is critiqued, through sexual-identity confusions that undermine the basis for such a celebration of masculine desire.

Melanie Chait's *Veronica 4 Rose* (1982), televised on Britain's Channel 4, centers on young women's discussion of their attempts at "coming out" as lesbians. Unusually, the "realism" or "truth" of these filmed discussions is problematized through inclusion of scenes in which, in a screening room, the same women watch and debate these filmed sequences. As Mandy Merck puts it, what is chiefly placed in focus here is the point that sexuality is a struggle of competing representations, which then somehow become "identities."[35]

Many of the eighties gay-made films are, though, attempts to recapture or to create gay history. The West German *Army of Lovers,* for example, attempts to outline the increase in gay militancy from the fifties to the seventies, with the Stonewall riot being treated as a watershed in the evolution of gay consciousness. Attention is directed to not only such enemies of gay liberation as Anita Bryant but to strife within the broad movement, exposing the difficulties created for it by right-wing, materialistic bourgeois, and closeted gays. The 1984 documentary *Before Stonewall* is, as its title might suggest, an attempt (by Greta Schiller and Robert Rosenberg) to compile a visual and aural record of gay experience from the early years of the present century up to Stonewall. What is foregrounded in the attempt is the difficulty of reclaiming visual material from people who were strongly encouraged to remain invisible. Also, icons of straightness (Dwight Eisenhower, Ronald Reagan) are here looked at differently; in the new context, they seem as alien as they would wish the participants in the documentary to seem. Robert Epstein's *The Times of Harvey Milk* (1984) centers on the optimism that Milk's election on to their board of supervisors inspired in gay citizens of San Francisco and the anger that the lenient punishment of his "voluntary manslaughter" by Dan White occasioned among the same people. *Witches Faggots Dykes and Poofters* deals with the persecution of gays in Australia during the seventies, including police brutality and imprisonment without charge, and savage medical treatment—lobotomy.

While most of the above works could be termed "documentaries," even if that term is vastly more problematic than its casual use might suggest, Isaac Julien's *Looking for Langston* (1989) could not be, in that users of the term "documentary" normally have a notion, however nebulous, of documentary style in mind. This would not apply here. While Julien's film is another attempt to recapture a suppressed piece of history—all the more hidden since the subject is black as well as gay—the film is more poetic than documentary style customarily permits. Langston Hughes, the principal poet of the Harlem Renaissance of the twenties, is explored, particularly in terms of his highly private life. As Kobena Mercer indicates, "coming out" was not a feasible solution for him, in that homosexuality was regarded then as a "sin against the race."[36] Isaac Julien's film, with its amalgam of poetry and music and its stylized monochrome shooting, has to move beyond those other films which reconstruct gay history by uncovering the, as it were, double invisibility of a gay black artist.

Lesbianism

The representation of lesbianism in mainstream entertainment cinema is a very different matter from its treatment in, say, *Veronica 4 Rose* or in Lizzie Borden's *Working Girls* (1986), where the heroine's relationship with her black lover, Diane, is treated as matter-of-factly as her working life in a brothel.

Largely, lesbian relationships are seen through the eyes of the "normal" and measured against the standard of "normality," as that is identified apparently with heterosexual monogamy. So, John Sayles's *Lianna* (1982) frames its narrative of lesbian love with a "normal" woman as sympathetic onlooker, so that, presumably, the threatened strangeness of the narrative is disguised or reduced. Robert Towne's *Personal Best* (1982) pits a tender lesbian involvement between women athletes against individualistic competitiveness, to suggest that personal success is jeopardized by emotional commitment, that the achievement of one's "personal best" is compromised by same-sex entanglement. The movie does not warn against entanglement as such, since the female athletes move on to more conventional, patriarchal relations with men without suffering impairment of their athletic success. Perhaps its unconscious subtext is that heterosexual relations are less damaging because they are inevitably shallower, thus less demanding.

Dominant movies' difficulty with deciding about the viability of lesbian relations is again suggested by the sudden closing down of visual representation of lesbian lovemaking in Randal Kleiser's *Summer Lovers* (1982). Also, because the film is set in the time of summer vacation within a Greek landscape that suggests the temporariness of its delights, it may be spared confrontation with its implications, just as Robin Wood argues, by another route, of *Victor/Victoria*. In both cases, the romances are placed within a kind of never-never land, even if the time setting is precise and the locations are discoverable in an atlas of Europe.

A similar question could well be raised about Donna Deitch's *Desert Hearts* (1985). For all its refusal of conventional heterosexist moralism, its insistence that lesbian romantic entanglements are little different in nature from the heterosexual variety (one woman has come to the end of her marriage, another has been sexually pressured by her male boss), the drama is played out during the heroine's temporary stay in Reno, Nevada. Steve Jenkins usefully points out that the setting is a sort of limbo, the Nevada desert being at one point described as "God's backyard," and that the sense of limbo "is heightened, paradoxically, by the film's historical setting."[37]

An indication of the difficulties faced by even would-be "progressives" in uncoupling their conceptions of lesbianism from those imposed by the homophobic culture in which lesbians are forced to operate is offered from within the narrative of *Sammy and Rosie Get Laid* (1987), perhaps as some illumination of the problems of portraying gay relationships within mainstream narrative cinema. Sammy theoretically wants his wife to enjoy a sexual freedom equivalent to that which he accords himself but is clearly rendered insecure by his knowledge of her physical attraction to another man. The lesbian couple welcomed into Sammy and Rosie's home mirror their benefactors in the dilemmas that they face and, like them, succumb to the insecurities that freedom within a more vicious, individualistic wider society must engender, in that one betrays the other. The Kureishi film seems to be suggesting that oases of freedom and sanity cannot for long exist within a society that violently opposes both notions, that there must be a tainting of idealism through that necessary contact. Hence, perhaps, the reason why happy gay relations seem to be permitted, in movie terms, in magic isolation from the homophobic world, and why there is always a suggestion of their being unsustainable beyond that world, or indefinitely within that world.

Fiction "from Inside"

The title of this section is not meant to imply any special knowledge of or undue interest in the personal sexual histories of the directors, actors, writers, and so forth, involved in making the following films. The reference is more to the ideological placement of the spectator's identification in the experience of these films. Against the habit of dominant Hollywood cinema, in particular, these films construct a world in which heterosexism is seen as an outside force impinging to a more or less serious degree upon the lives of the principal characters and where, through the psychological processes of identification, spectator sympathies are aligned with gay characters, this alignment allowing the force of the "normal" world to be rendered strange and able to be felt as such.

Possibly the film apparently least concerned with the pressures exerted by "normal," heterosexual social standards is Frank Ripploh's West German *Taxi zum Klo* (1981). In this movie, the director, together with his former lover, Bernd Broaderup, attempts to create an ostensibly autobiographical account of his leaving the teaching profession in order to take up filmmaking full-time.

Through that filmmaking, he unapologetically celebrates his gay life-style, warts and all, exposing his "driven" promiscuity, his public-lavatory and public-park encounters, his occasional flippancy in the face of serious political causes when he feels too horny to show his customary dedication. In these respects, the film has a much less earnest surface than, for example, Ron Peck and Paul Hallam's *Nighthawks* (1978). This British film also features the central character's life of one-night stands, and its narrative pivots on the problem created for him by his pupils' discovery of his homosexuality. Yet, the laid-back atmosphere of Ripploh's movie masks the force of dominant attitudes to his life which, indeed, help to explain his choices and living style. As the film indicates, Ripploh was in one sense induced to leave teaching, since disciplinary action was taken against him. His awareness of and albeit sardonic responses to antigay propaganda in the society in which he finds himself are clearly indicated in the film. He may be amused rather than angry when a neo-Nazi on television calls for the revival of work camps for homosexuals, but the inclusion of the clip indicates that the film's largely heterosexual-free concentration on sexual pleasure has still to be placed within a social and political ambience of incomprehension or outright hostility.

Again, while the action of Derek Jarman's *Caravaggio* (1986) largely unfolds in contexts which show themselves to be relatively indifferent to bourgeois morality, this morality is still represented as important within the wider art world through the figure of Baglione. The latter spouts well-nigh modern-day right-wing moralisms and innuendoes against Caravaggio, hiding his jealousy of Caravaggio's skill beneath a veil of scandalized outrage. James Ivory's *Maurice* (1987) is true to its source, Forster, and its period in communicating the unspeakability of "unnatural vice" and the blight which their sexuality produced upon homosexuals at a time when any sexual activity or importuning was liable to criminal prosecution. Yet, it does not seem a period piece, even if it looks like one, in the latter half of the eighties. Rather, it foregrounds the pseudoscience of the early sexologists and the horrors of a return to pre-Wolfenden thinking in a period in Britain when, for example, a return to Victorian values would surely mean at its most literal an unlearning of even the liberal interpretation of homosexuality.

Paul Bogart's *Torch Song Trilogy* (1988) also feels curiously like a period piece, although the period is much more recent than *Maurice*'s. A film of today dedicated to the chronicling of the tribulations of gay—and, in this case, transvestite—experience in the United States which does not mention AIDS must inevitably seem to be about a bygone age. Since the period of the movie is the seventies, it is true to that decade in not centering on mortal illness, although as Mark Finch points out, intimations of mortality are easily discoverable within the mise-en-scène.[38] The film, after all, opens with the camera panning over a cemetery in Brooklyn, and the climactic "torch-song" scene is played out at the cemetery where the hero's mother (Anne Bancroft) attempts to deny her son (Harvey Fierstein) the dignity of mourning his dead lover. Drag becomes, in this context, a mark of defiance although, like camp in Andrew Britton's analysis of it, a defiance that gives power to patriarchy by reinforcing its oppositions, albeit in parody form.

Possibly the least apologetic and most "inside" of the eighties movies about gay experience is Stephen Frears's *My Beautiful Laundrette* (1985). It is noticeable, for example, that the film reverses a long-lived feature of such liberal-humanist movies as *Victor/Victoria*, whereby the heterosexual romance is accorded the respect that a homosexual relationship is not. The latter may be treated with twinkling-eyed indulgence, but its inequality of status is clearly signaled by its treatment as somehow amusing in itself. In the Frears film, however playful the physical relationship between Omar (Gordon Warnecke) and Johnny (Daniel Day Lewis) might be, especially in the final water-throwing sequence, it is felt as "real," while the September romance between Nasser and his white woman friend is made to look slightly absurd. The achievement of this reversal may seem at first glance to be by the substitution of ageism for sexism, since the homosexual lovers are young and conventionally attractive, while the heterosexual lovers are signaled as definitely middle-aged. The sequence in which the launderette is ceremonially opened depends on more than that, though. While the male/female couple waltz in the presence of the waiting crowd, showcasing their romance (daring only in its cross-color aspect), the male lovers, out of sight in the back of the launderette, are resting after their less ritualized mating. Their being hidden and their need to cover up their bodies and to deflect Nasser from what their half-nakedness means show that homosexuality is not an open experience of the sort that the Nasser-Rachel coupling might be. Yet, their momentary embarrassment is only that—momentary— and social embarrassment rather than guilt. This is the sort of embarrassment that an unmarried couple might indicate if disturbed by father in a British family comedy of the fifties.

The Thatcherite values which the Asian family has embraced and which permeate white/black relationships in the film's present (despite National Front tensions at school in the film's past) act as a solvent of racial positioning and clearly confuse the lines of sexual acceptability to the point where economics would appear to govern the rightness or otherwise of sexualities. Nobody in the film's world other than the parental generation of the Asian family appears to be "hung up" on questions of sexual morality, perhaps because the conventional domination/submission pattern that governs masculine/feminine relations is discernible here in the scenes, whether erotic or otherwise, between the young men. The launderette is by being "beautiful" (and its misspelling in the title emphasizes its specialness, the way that it fits particular personalities) a peculiar form of the never-never land which has been detected as providing a setting for "impossible" relations in other gay films. Yet it also functions as a very ordinary laundry, with its attendant problems of work rota and economic viability. The film, while sharing some of the wishfulness and otherworldliness of, say, *Desert Hearts,* is also surprisingly hardheaded and thoroughly localized in time and space. (It leads, incidentally, so clearly to the picture of greater fragmentation and confusion in *Sammy and Rosie Get Laid,* possibly through the important contributions of Hanif Kureishi to each film, that the hostile critical treatment of the later film seems perverse.)

Equally precise in its sense of time and place is Ron Peck's short, *What Can I Do with a Male Nude?* (1985). This is not just for the obvious reason that the invisible narrator complains of the pressures he has been put under for his obsessional desire to view and photograph frontally nude male models, particularly from the police and also from feminism, during a decade when the power of British Customs and Excise over what may or may not be imported, read, viewed, displayed, has been allowed to grow apace. An underlying point (though neither AIDS nor homosexuality is explicitly mentioned) is that visual pleasure has been made unusually important by the ban on "unsafe sex" that the AIDS crisis has demanded, so that extra moral and legal pressures placed on the consumer of images of maleness have become especially intolerable.

These films all share an oppositional ideological position. In them, the "normal" is largely gay. The heterosexual norm is either experienced as insensitively hostile (spectator positioning would then mean that an awareness of threat from that quarter is inspired or increased in the spectator) or, somewhat more radically, as "other." This positioning deserves to be clearly differentiated from that created by those films which are "sympathetic" to gayness. *Dog Day Afternoon* (1975), for example, proves unusually bold for a mainstream movie in having its identification point revealed—too late in the narrative for an audience to withhold its sympathy?—to be gay and in having that identification point played by a major star, Al Pacino. Yet, as Robin Wood points out, from the time that the Pacino character is known to be gay he is conceived as neurotic, worthy of sympathy but not of full empathy.[39] Also, gay militants are portrayed in a way that would gain approval from Anita Bryant. Thus, while the comfortable assumptions that an audience brings to a film centering on gay characters are dented, they are not for long damaged.

A somewhat audacious mainstream movie such as this offering from Sidney Lumet raises questions about the possibility or otherwise of dominant movies' doing other than reproducing the prevailing understanding of homosexual and heterosexual if identification is not from the beginning and throughout the movie drastically altered, after the manner of *My Beautiful Laundrette,* which makes no apology for and refuses to "explain" its young heroes' gayness.

Homosexuality as Second-Best or Pathetic

The question of identification, and also of the understanding of homosexuality, is raised with special relevance in Hector Babenco's *Kiss of the Spider Woman* (1985). A number of spectator positions are made possible. This is not only because the movie centers on Luis Molina (William Hurt), a highly "feminine," unintellectual, apolitical homosexual, and his cellmate, a "real man," Valentin Arregui (Raul Julia), a heterosexual who succumbs at length to Molina's blandishments, with the bigger star playing the lower-status character. More importantly, Molina takes delight in recounting the plot of a Nazi propaganda film in a way which concentrates on glamor and physical allure and shows no awareness of the mechanisms by which the Third Reich is made appealing and the French Resistance repellent.

Within the Babenco film, the Nazi film as recounted by Molina is shown, as a film-within-the-film, complete with luscious, stylized images of an improbably glamorous heroine (Sonia Braga) and of the handsome Werner (Herson Capri), the Nazi head of counterintelligence and creature of her (therefore Molina's) dreams. Since mainstream film normally works by processes of identification, and since the Nazi propaganda film clearly uses the methods of dominant cinema to elicit sympathy for its crude messages, that film must be "made" for somebody within the Babenco film if it is to be seen to work. Since *Spider Woman*'s audience is confused about the way that the fictitious Nazi film works, it experiences a measure of confusion about the loyalties that are presumably being set up in the movie proper. Is the audience positioned in such a way that it is largely distanced from the over-the-top theatrical, "camp" Molina or is it taken in to his world via his film's imagery (and thus placed in an empathetic relation with Arregui's final seduction by Molina)? That these are problems recognized within the film itself is remarked by Kim Newman, who points out that Molina expressly identifies with the star, the Sonia Braga character, in the Nazi film, thus leaving open the possibilities of Arregui's identification with one or other of the more active male principals.[40] The choice of identification point certainly seems clear to Molina. "Tell the truth, who do you identify with the most, the clubfoot patriot or the handsome Werner?"

These questions may be academic, though, in relation to a more important one—whether Arregui's "real man" status is compromised or not by his falling for the obviously "feminized" Molina. Here may be an example of that phenomenon noted by Emmanuel Reynaud[41] whereby the "passive" partner in a homosexual relationship is deemed truly homosexual, and despised for his attributed effeminacy, while the "active" partner is credited with manliness—which, in turn, means that he cannot be homosexual. The distinction made throughout the bulk of the movie between the men in terms of masculinity and "activity" is not necessarily, by any means, compromised by the lovemaking between the men. This is, after all, prison and, without female company, even "real men" are traditionally thought to seek the closest thing to it. Whatever sympathies are created for and around Molina are further complicated by the fact that he is manipulable by higher authority even through his "private" sexuality, so that he takes on an Eve-like quality of treacherousness at his most loving.

The understanding of a homosexual relationship through standard heterosexual means, whereby one is dominant, freer, more "masculine" by virtue of that fact, the other submissive, tied, more "feminine," crops up again in Stephen Frears's *Prick Up Your Ears* (1987), where the tensions between Joe Orton and Kenneth Halliwell are predicated on their marriage "roles" and particularly on Halliwell's nagging-wife insecurity. This may be because the voice setting out the route into the Orton-Halliwell relationship is that of Vanessa Redgrave's Peggy Ramsay, Orton's literary agent, who in actuality described Halliwell as Orton's first wife. (The popular—

and, through his biographer, popularized—understanding of Orton as the playboy genius dragged down by his drab shrew of a wife is not unchallengeable. As interesting as the "facts" of the matter might be, it may be more useful to consider what function the traditional version of Orton-Halliwell may serve. One obvious example is precisely that an unconventional relationship can be placed in a comfortable heterosexual niche, making moral judgment far easier for conventional observers.)

The traditional thinking, which would explain homosexual couples in terms of masculine and feminine and therefore in reassuring notions of "natural" complementarity even in relations that have "gone wrong," reappears in Philip Saville's *The Fruit Machine* (1988). Here, the runaway boys are "camp" Eddie (Emile Charles), with his love of opera and old films, and "butch" Michael (Tony Forsyth), a hustler. Moreover, Eddie finally dies, as his way out of the "trap" in which even he himself recognizes that he is.

Certain late-seventies movies that attempted consideration of homosexuality flatter dominant understanding of it. Thus, in Paul Aaron's *A Different Story* (1978), homosexuality seems to be a stage in a transition toward a more mature version of sexuality, namely heterosexuality. If that transition represents progress, so too, presumably, does the hero's increase in "masculinity," whereby he leaves off being a version of a housewife to take up a job. The French film of the same year, Philippe Vallois's *We Were One Man,* centers on a strange friendship between a wounded German soldier and his French benefactor. The friendship is strange not only because the time is 1943 and the friends (who eventually become lovers) are on opposite sides in a world war, but because the Frenchman is an escaped lunatic. This somewhat narrows the sexual-political significance of the affair. As is common in otherwise conventionally conceived films about homosexual relationships, one of the lovers is killed by the end of the narrative.

Condescension to gay characters continues in the eighties. In Alan Johnson's *To Be or Not to Be* (1983), one of the characters threatened with extinction in a Nazi concentration camp is treated as deserving of sympathy precisely because, as ultraeffeminate, he is capable of being conceived and protected in "little-helpless-woman" terms. The dancer who turns out to be gay in *A Chorus Line* (1985), while not refused dignity, is still rendered in "sympathetic" terms of guilt, anxiety, and, basically, helplessness. In view of his failure in "masculinity," it comes as no surprise that he is the dancer who sustains serious physical injury when he attempts the athletic kind of dancing required of him for the Broadway show.

Homosexuality as Comic

Comedy can, as Andrew Britton points out, unseat certainties about gender's relation to sexual differentiation in conduct, appearance, and sexual choice. On the other hand, it just as easily may not. There are many film comedies involving homosexuals that keep gayness where it has nearly always been, firmly in the closet or, if ever allowed out, at the mercy of crude oversimplifications by a heterosexist, homophobic society.

Edouard Molinaro's *La cage aux folles* (1978) surely owes a considerable part of its box-office popularity to its confirmation of (for a heterosexist society) the comforting notion that homosexuals are really women trapped in men's bodies. Vito Russo points out that its success in the United States may be explained as "a testament to the durability of the old-fashioned expansive femininity used to type male homosexuality."[42] This wretched entertainment spawned two sequels, *La cage aux folles II* (Edouard Molinaro, 1980) and *III* (Georges Lautner, 1985), the latter of which had the subtitle *"Elles" se marient*. The reduction of the Michel Serrault and Ugo Tognazzi characters to versions of "she" is already accomplished in the 1978 film. The public declaration of it in the subtitle is both witless and oddly (since it was hardly a secret before) depressing.

The reduction of homosexual men to screamingly camp caricatures, as a method for making otherwise not too hostile treatment of gay characters acceptable to a public of precarious sympathies, is discoverable in *To Be or Not to Be,* in *Victor/Victoria,* and in Peter Medak's *Zorro, the Gay Blade* (1981). The suggestion in most of these films seems to be that persecution of such frail, less-than-feminine creatures would be inapposite, and that they are so unthreatening as to deserve some guarded indulgence from a wary audience. Uncle Monty in Bruce Robinson's *Withnail and I* (1987) is not frail or particularly effeminate when he plays that other ever-popular stereotype, the predatory gay male. Nevertheless, he is fat, middle-aged and obviously no match physically for the young man whose virtue he threatens physically. The anxiety that the actively gay male seems regularly to conjure up, particularly in men who could not easily be overpowered, is activated by Uncle Monty but also "contained" safely within the young men's physical capabilities and also the predominantly nostalgic attitude here presented to the period of the sixties—a time when sexual energies might have been released as seldom before, but a time which was, significantly in this film, coming to an end.

Homosexuality as Sinister

The reduction of what is recognizably feminine as a component within homosexual relations to effeminate, making it ridiculous or pitiable, obviates the threat—an ever-present threat for heterosexuals, if Freud's explanation of sexuality's development is to be credited—of recognition or of points of contact between homosexual and heterosexual experience. A different tactic may be used for dealing with masculinity within homosexuality, in which it is made strange by extending it and distorting it into violence, murderousness, sadism.

In Sidney Lumet's *Deathtrap* (1982), for instance, the male lovers do not feel simply desire for each other but a sexual possessiveness and jealousy which results in murder. Martin Donovan's *Apartment Zero* (1988) has former hired killer Jack Carney (Hart Bochner) desired by Adrian LeDuc (Colin Firth). After Jack has killed a man that he has picked up in order to obtain his passport, after the pair have cooperated in disposing of the corpse of a woman who could identify Jack, Jack is shot dead in a struggle between the lovers. The film ends with the survivor, Adrian, corrupted. At least that seems to be what is suggested by his choice of leather clothing and his conversion of the art cinema into a porno palace.

Not all films which show a sinister side of homosexuality need be read straightforwardly as homophobic, however. Just as some movies attempt to deny the interconnectedness of homosexual and heterosexual within societal experience by a playing up of homosexual evil, there are other movies which permit their audiences to see the workings of homophobia as a motive force in the formation of a damaging conception of homosexuality.

Thus, the violence of *The Boys Next Door* (1984) is readable in terms of the boys' refusal to acknowledge their erotic attraction and their violent denial of it. They pick up an openly gay man and allow themselves to be invited back to his apartment, where one of them fights with and kills him. The origin of the violence which they unleash on the girl who has to endure a terrifying ride on the bonnet of the car seems to be the hurling of the insult "Queer!" The violence in these young men, which seems at one level to be arbitrary, is deemed to be only if we do not follow up the clues.

The hero Jesse (Mark Patton) of *A Nightmare on Elm Street, Part 2: Freddy's Revenge* appears peculiarly susceptible to dreams in which he finds himself in masochistic situations. At one point, he dreams that he is in a gay S/M bar, in which he allows himself to be picked up by his coach. He is led back to school by the coach, who is promptly murdered by Freddy in Jesse's sight. Moreover, when Jesse wants to confide he turns not to his girlfriend but to a fellow pupil who has been bullying him heretofore. It seems entirely appropriate that such a teenager should eventually have his body possessed by Freddy and that Freddy should commit violence when the teenager's consciousness is off guard (as when he drops off to sleep).

Possibly the most interesting of the violent-homosexual movies of the eighties is William Friedkin's *Cruising* (1980). In it, an apparently heterosexual patrolman Steve Burns (Al Pacino) goes underground into an S/M homosexual milieu in the hope of tracking down a serial killer of gay men. The film was the object of demonstrations by gay activists during its making and then during its exhibition in New York City. Yet it seems to be far from the straightforwardly homophobic work that it may superficially be taken to be. A film about homophobia need not on that account be itself homophobic.

Robin Wood's analysis of the movie is typically evenhanded and cogent. He is particularly impressed with the way that Burns seems to take pleasure in the gay disco, with his almost undeniable attraction to the young gay man who becomes the last murder victim, and with his diminishing interest in his girlfriend Nancy (Karen Allen). He also notes that the New York cops use their power to have, for example, a transvestite perform fellatio upon them and that the S/M fans dress as New York cops for one event. This would suggest that the choice of dress is not simply perverted fancy, but that the gay men draw on a knowledge of the closeness of police sexuality to their own when they choose to impersonate them. The final killing is of the gay man whom Burns befriended. As the murder could not have been committed by the serial killer now apprehended, there must be more than one killer operating by the end of the movie. That this killer is Burns is never stated, and it would be impossible on the film's evidence to establish that as an unassailable reading. Nevertheless, the possibility is most certainly not ruled out, and the possibility is also foreshadowed in, for example, the way that sequences involving Burns's being drawn into the S/M world are intercut with the violence unleashed against one of the murder victims.[43]

Dennis Altman's view of the work is indicated by the opening of his sentence: "Just as the gay world plays out the general sexual fears and fantasies about sadomasochism (which William Friedkin probably sensed when he decided to film *Cruising* and unfortunately for him could never properly articulate) . . ."[44] What inhibits Friedkin's articulation may well be that a mainstream movie is tackling one of the great secrets of patriarchy, that it projects on to gays and women that which may not be admissible in men. Wood concedes that there are no positive images of gay culture in this movie, but he also notes that there are no positive alternatives of any kind to the corrupt, disintegrating society featured here.[45] His findings could be corroborated by an appeal to authorial considerations. In Friedkin's 1973 *The Exorcist,* the uncontaminated priest at the climax of the film takes evil into himself in order to destroy it by his self-immolation. In the later film, Burns less altruistically may take evil into himself.

There is one interesting area in the film which Wood takes as virtually unreadable—when Burns during his shaving at his girlfriend's apartment nicks his throat and she, not he, dons the SS uniform that Steve has brought back. Wood wonders how she could have contracted the "disease" from him.[46] By rational logic, she could not, but by the kind of post-AIDS thinking that flourishes with right-wing encouragement, the scene makes a different kind of sense today, if read metaphorically. If Burns had contracted the HIV virus from his contact with the gay subculture, Nancy could easily contract it through sexual contact with him. His nicking of his throat underlines this point, in that the flow of his blood would endanger her and would also symbolize the opening of his body to infection. That the film could not be read in exactly this way in 1980 is obvious. The reading is offered not to suggest that Friedkin has the gift of prophecy or that the film magically prefigures dominant thinking about AIDS. Rather, the attempt is to show how beliefs about the contagiousness of homosexuality and the transmission of the contagion to even the most "innocent" and uncontaminated of parties, beliefs which were only latent in the years before AIDS, surface with full force in the years following the "discovery" of the HIV virus.

10

AIDS

Some Data about the Illness

As early as 1979, doctors in New York and California (principally Los Angeles and San Francisco) who had already begun to notice long-term enlarged lymph nodes in several of their gay patients had to deal with gay men suffering from Kaposi's sarcoma and pneumocystis carinii pneumonia. The virulency of KS and PCP was particularly noticeable in men who were young and had been in full vigor before their illnesses. (KS when encountered elsewhere was seldom fatal, but the group of New York men suffering from it were dying within eight to twenty-four months of the diagnosis.)[1] The underlying cause of both illnesses was taken to be a breakdown in the immune systems of the sufferers. Such immune deficiency had already been encountered by medicine in the cases of organ-transplant patients whose immune systems had been deliberately interfered with by drugs (in order to prevent organ rejection) and of cancer patients who had undergone chemotherapy.[2]

The *New York Times* of 3 July 1981 "broke the story" under the headline "Rare Cancer Seen in 41 Homosexuals." The introduction of the public to the story by the news media was thus in terms of the connection of KS (for a time known as "gay cancer") with homosexuality,[3] and a strong connection was suggested between the illnesses and sexually transmitted disease.[4] One of the key terms in the early days of medical and media inquiry into the complex of KS and PCP was GRID (gay-related immunodeficiency), as well as AID (acquired immune deficiency).[5] In the first quarter of 1982, the labeling of patients suffering from a complex of symptoms relating to depressed immune systems was in terms of "GRID," despite the fact that intravenous drug users, hemophiliacs, and Haitian immigrants into the United States were now numbered among such patients.[6]

The appearance of the mysterious illness in the late seventies is recognized by Sander L. Gilman to have provided a clearly desired link between two hitherto unrelated social concerns of the time: an upswing in sexually transmitted diseases after a sustained period of decline and growing public awareness of the gay liberation movements, especially in large population centers, from the time of the Stonewall riot.[7] Gilman finds evidence of the desire to form some kind of similar link in the short-lived attempt in the seventies to use genital herpes as a way of providing a morally repulsive disease for a disapproved life-style.[8] GRID provided the link far more dramatically than herpes could. Despite the variety of immune-suppressed patients, the complex was associated from its earliest publicity with homosexuality and was often referred to by the media as "the gay plague."[9]

The connection stressed by the media helps to explain, though not to excuse, the reticence of public leaders on the subject of the "plague," even when over a thousand cases were reported in the United States and Europe within a period of eighteen months. "Almost without exception public leaders evaded the epidemic, avoiding even the usual expressions of compassion and concern. It was as if the sexual orientation of the victims made any involvement risky, and the politicians directed their courage and energies elsewhere."[10] Kevin M. Cahill, M.D., convicts the organized medical community of a parallel evasiveness for as long as the complex seemed to be associated exclusively or paramountly with homosexuality.[11] The inaction of the American government and medical community, but above all the forging of an adamantine link between a particular sexuality and vulnerability to the illness, may help to explain why it is reported in 1990 that the rate of HIV infection among homosexual and bisexual men is falling while cases of heterosexual infection, though much fewer in number, are on the increase.[12]

The acronym AIDS (acquired immune deficiency syndrome) was officially adopted by the Centers for Disease Control in 1982.[13]

Commentators on AIDS generally offer statistics to suggest lines of inquiry, or of medical or political intervention. The statistics published include the following:

June 1981: 26 cases of KS were reported in the Centers for Disease Control's *Morbidity and Mortality Weekly Report*; 5 cases of PCP (caused by protozoan parasites) were reported.[14]

5 October 1982: 634 Americans had AIDS, with 260 dead.[15]

"End of 1982": The Centers for Disease Control reported the documented AIDS cases in the United States as nearly 900.[16]

July 1984: The total number of United States cases reported to the CDC was "in excess of 5,200," of whom approximately 45 percent had died.[17]

"Late winter 1984": The number of AIDS cases identified in the United States had reached about 3,600, and the number of dead was known to be over 1,300.[18]

April 1985: According to the CDC, there were about 10,000 cases in the United States alone.[19]

"Mid-1985":" There were just over 11,000 cases in the world, 9,000 of these being in the United States.[20]

2 October 1985: 12,000 Americans were dead or dying of AIDS, with hundreds of thousands "infected."[21]

"Beginning of 1986": The world total of AIDS cases had doubled to over 22,000, with 2,500 new cases per month being diagnosed. New York City was reckoned to be the "AIDS capital of the world," with between 400,000 and 500,000 "infected with the virus," according to Dr. Charles Rabkin, 40,000 of the 75,000 infected American women being in New York.[22]

"Early 1986": The CDC reported more than 19,000 cases nation-wide, and more than 10,000 deaths from the illness since it was "identified in 1981."[23]

April 1986: More than 19,000 cases were reported to the CDC, with more than 10,000 cases dead. (These statistics, which seem to repeat the information provided immediately above, are followed by a prediction: "Experts expect that a total of 14,000 to 15,000 new cases of AIDS will be diagnosed in 1986 and that at least 7,000 AIDS patients will die.")[24]

Between 1981 and end 1985: The United States went from one case to more than 15,000.[25]

Between December 1983 and the beginning of 1986: The United Kingdom went from 58 cases to almost 300.[26]

In November 1987, a collective work by ACT-UP (the AIDS Coalition to Unleash Power) was displayed in a window of the New

Museum of Contemporary Arts in New York. It was entitled, for reasons made obvious within the work itself, "Let the Record Show. . ." The text starts as follows:

> By Thanksgiving 1981, 244 known dead . . . AIDS . . . no word from the President.
> By Thanksgiving 1982, 1,123 known dead . . . AIDS . . . no word from the President.

It continues in this vein until the final entry, which records that, at Thanksgiving 1987, there were 25,644 known dead, upon which President Reagan said:

> "I have asked the Department of Health and Human Services to determine as soon as possible the extent to which the AIDS virus has penetrated our society."[27]

April 1990: The number infected through heterosexual intercourse nearly doubled in the year previous to this point, according to the Department of Health in Britain. Only 6 percent were reckoned to have been infected in this way, but the department warned, "within a few years' time, it is possible that over half the UK cases of AIDS could be in the heterosexual contact and injecting drug categories." Heterosexual-contact cases increased from 90 to 172 within the past year, and those among drug users sharing the same equipment from 48 to 99. In the same period, the increase among homosexual and bisexual men was from 1,769 to 2,530.[28]

A number of observations could be made about the battery of statistics offered above. There seem to be discrepancies in the 1984 statistics and again in those of 1985, while there seem to be major differences between ACT-UP's figures and the CDC's. Far more importantly, perhaps, new talk of a "virus" and "infection" come into being in the course of the reports of data, with that crucial development in "knowledge" of AIDS where, between 1983 and 1984, French and American researchers isolated and identified the human immunodeficiency virus (HIV) as the main causative agent of AIDS.[29] The tenacity with which the virus and the "full-blown" syndrome are held to be connected as cause and effect, respectively, helps to explain medical statisticians' fondness for prediction and is of vital significance for the formation of attitudes by doctors and PWAs (persons with AIDS) to the disease. The so-called AIDS test involves the search for HIV antibodies with the use of protein extracted from the inactivated virus. Donor blood has been screened in American blood banking by means of a similar process. The significance attributed to the HIV virus as *the* explanation for AIDS means that, in media parlance, little distinction is made between the virus and the syndrome. There is remarkably loose talk of "the AIDS virus," by means of which people who test positive are encouraged to believe that they are under a virtual death sentence.[30]

Another statistic of significant interest is that upon which the 1990 data may be seen to center: the distribution of "infection" and/ or AIDS suffering among the population. Writing of early 1986, for example, Edward Albert reports the following distribution:

Approximately 72%	Homosexual or bisexual men
Approximately 25%	IV drug abusers
5.5%	Haitian immigrants
1%	Hemophiliacs
6%	"Noncategorizable persons"

The fact that the figures add up to well over 100 percent is explained by the overlap in some categories. The residual group making up 6 percent are explained as including, for example, blood recipients and children of drug abusers.[31]

Because of the crucial significance accorded to the HIV virus and the investment of medical confidence in that significance, scientists have concentrated, since its isolation and labeling, on seeking ways to inhibit replication of the virus in order to prevent its spreading from one cell to another within the body.[32] Since AIDS is largely viewed as incurable (though possibly treatable), the emphasis is heavily upon education to stop its spread. That education is obviously also heavily dependent on what passes for knowledge and is crucially linked with the intimacy of the association claimed between HIV infection and the development of the believed-fatal syndrome.

There have been voices, both lay and "expert," raised against the viral-agent orthodoxy, all the same. Thus, Bob Cecchi, one of those interviewed in Lon G. Nungesser's book of interviews with "ordinary people" who suffer from and/or think about AIDS, says of the viral notion: "I think there's a virus that does the final job, that makes it irreversible. I think there is a condition where you're susceptible to the virus that is reversible. . . . My feeling still is HTLV-III or LAV is another opportunistic infection."[33] Casper G. Schmidt is more forthright in his rejection of the solution of the AIDS mystery by means of a virus. He reminds his readers that every single disease entity for which no adequate explanation can be found has been attributed at some time to viral origin. His alternative hypothesis posits a psychosocial origin for the AIDS epidemic, which lies on the cusp between immunology, pathology, and psychology. He considers that the groups identified as being at greatest risk may develop severe, mostly masked, reactive depression, of which immune deficiency is one facet.[34]

A continuing battle against HIV as the "cause" of AIDS has been waged by, among others, the molecular biologist Peter Duesberg. The argument of "anti-HIV" specialists is that their voices cannot be heard because of the vested interests in "the AIDS industry," particularly as that is identified with drug companies. Duesberg's counterhypothesis, which seeks an explanation in drug overuse (the drugs referred to being both "illegal" and "legal," particularly antibiotics) leading to "intoxication," is unimpressive to other experts in the field. Duncan Campbell states that Duesberg's criticisms of the orthodoxy, that the HIV virus is the causative agent, "have repeatedly and effectively been refuted," and is particularly appalled at the implications of his often-stated view that "AIDS is a behavioural disease," since this is not only offensive to persons with AIDS but also "flies in the face of the well-established patterns of transmission via blood and its products to transfusion recipients, haemophiliacs, and their partners."[35] The doubts which Duesberg raises about the explanatory value of HIV need to be considered, all the same, particularly in his interpretation of statistics and his undermining of HIV-based predictions, not least because these allow seropositive persons greater hope. (According to Duesberg, only 1.5 percent of HIV positive cases have developed AIDS.)[36]

In the years since Schmidt suggested a psychosocial origin for AIDS, there have been considerable advances in the understanding of AIDS, as well as considerable controversy stirred up by Peter Duesberg and his fellow thinkers. Schmidt's reasoning, nevertheless, shows, as one of its virtues, sensitivity to the combination of late seventies New Right militancy and the emergence of a baffling new ailment. His explanation is one of the few that attempts to consider why certain groups, of precarious social "fit" in the United States (homosexuals, drug abusers, immigrant Haitians), seem particularly to be targets of AIDS, always excepting the possibility that AIDS is another term for the wrath of God. (Nobody has yet explained why God is so wrathful with Haitians or, for that matter, so particularly well-disposed toward lesbians.)

In brief, Schmidt argues that AIDS is a typical example of epidemic hysteria and that the epidemic has at its core the group fantasy of scapegoating, by which the poison feelings of a whole group may be injected into certain scapegoat containers, the destruction of the containers relieving the group of its bad feelings and ensuring its purification of guilt and sin.[37] He identifies the proximal cause as the vast conservative swing in public opinion since 1977, culminating in the Reagan years.[38] He identifies a national sacrificial witch-hunt in which the hunters are the Moral Majority and other conservative groups, while the hunted are America's drug addicts and homosexuals. The hunted, like the hunters, act out roles, the acting out being beyond their awareness. The result is an epidemic of depression based mostly on shame, the reduction of cell-mediated immunity being a typical sign of severe depression.[39]

He recognizes that the greatest theoretical challenge to researchers of the phenomenon is that perfectly normal and seemingly healthy people are caught up in such epidemics. "The disconcerting possibility that this raises is that we are all susceptible."[40] The virus, he claims, is probably just another opportunistic infection. The unconscious social conflict which AIDS is called upon to resolve is twofold: (1) the bad feelings stirred up by, for example, unconscious homosexual fantasies in the general population are projected outward, onto scapegoats; (2) guilt over, for instance, sexual excesses both within the general population and within the scapegoated subcultures.[41] Interestingly, too, Schmidt cites the triad of promiscuity, poison blood, and poison sperm as being in vogue in the Middle Ages to explain the origins of leprosy.[42] Schmidt is struck by the coincidence of the time of the appearance of AIDS and the new public hostility to homosexuals expressed in such campaigns as Anita Bryant's crusade in Dade County: the "whole catalogue of threats delivered into the public arena (starting with Bryant's campaign materials which contained a paper entitled, 'Why Certain Sexual Deviations Are Punishable by Death') points to one end, which is 'Death to the Homosexuals.' And this was indeed the message they picked up."[43]

There are obvious problems with Schmidt's account. Even if we leave out of account the difficulties of explaining AIDS in hemophiliacs and recipients of blood transfusions, he has particular difficulty with explanations of child AIDS sufferers (usually taken to have had infection spread to them by their mothers). His argument is that these children suffer from severe anaclitic depression (through deprivation or neglect) and that the pathophysiological mechanism by which they become ill is identical with that by means of which adults fall prey to immune deficiency.[44] What, then, of babies born with the illness? Some of the answers are obvious, one being that testing of newborn babies' blood would be for the presence of HIV antibodies, which could prove irrelevant to whether or not they developed AIDS. Another one, not mentioned by Schmidt, might be that because the mother's immune system is "really" damaged because of group-fantasy scapegoating, the baby is born with "real" damage to its own immune system. Whatever the credibility or incredibility of the details of his thesis, however, the crucial contribution for which Schmidt deserves recognition is his awareness of the interdependence of somatic and psychic health and his attempt to illuminate the means by which those who are socially marginalized seem to be specifically picked out to suffer an epidemic of this gravity.

AIDS' Historical Setting

Schmidt's article itemizes a number of historical shifts which make the need for scapegoating the more acute. He considers, for example, that the buildup of nuclear weapons too destructive to be used in war places a curb on phallic assertiveness, which in turn creates a feeling of gender dysphoria, which is then projected onto the nation's homosexuals in fantasy. He identifies America's sense of "impotence" with the Carter years, Reagan's brief being to turn this around, which he did through such tactics as the invasion of Grenada.[45] Britain's Falklands War is interpreted by him as a dress rehearsal for this invasion. (Thatcher's war was referred to by Alexander Haig as "a turning point in a long and dangerous night of Western passivity.")[46]

He notices too, the huge changes in American family life, with women's demand for orgasmic satisfaction and the growth of recreational sex in the seventies producing a massive buildup of fear and guilt.[47] "The sexual revolution and the freeing up of heterosexual conduct was parallel to that in the homosexual community, but it was the latter that was chosen to represent those impulses we wished to disavow and punish."[48] The late-seventies clampdown, to fit the pattern for such clampdowns, demands a phase of internal sacrifice followed by a phase of external sacrifice (usually a war). Schmidt believes that the former phase began about 1975, intensified by 1977, and was made into a formal doctrine with the introduction of Reaganomics in 1981.[49] Homosexuals assented to the scapegoating ritual by playing masochists to the New Right's sadists and turned their aggression inward upon their bodies, Schmidt believes.[50]

Lloyd deMause argues that there is good evidence for America's need for punishment for sex in such campaigns as those, before AIDS "emerged," for the so-called chemical castration of rapists. AIDS was a much better catalyst for antisexuality, however, since the castration of rapists was "too limited in scope to make a really powerful group-fantasy."[51]

Thus, the New Right and uncritical devotees of its interpretations stood the obvious possible meaning for the emergence of AIDS on its head. Instead of consideration of its scapegoating as a likely explanation for the sufferings of the socially marginalized, the signification given to AIDS was that it symbolized "the perils of living outside the norm" and "the fruits of permissiveness."[52] AIDS has an explanatory and terroristic value to the Right well beyond the obvious sphere of sexual morality. "Denunciations of 'the gay plague' are part of a much larger complaint, common among antiliberals in the West and many exiles from the Russian bloc, about contemporary permissiveness of all kinds." Thus, the basis of such denunciations is not simply homophobia but "the utility of AIDS in pursuing one of the main activities of the so-called neo-conservatives, the Kulturkampf against all that is called, for short (and inaccurately) the 1960s. A whole politics of 'the will'—of intolerance, of paranoia, of fear of political weakness—has fastened on this disease."[53]

Although the interpretations of AIDS as the result of scapegoating rituals or as an irresistible metaphor for America's neoconservatives might seem to some readers too farfetched, Jeffrey Weeks considers the coincidence of AIDS' "discovery" and of the historical setting in relation to the need for proper treatment of the crisis helpfully when he writes: "The epidemic would have been a personal and social disaster whenever it had occurred. The fact that it manifested itself first of all in the community that was in the frontline of the moral backlash in the U.S.A., at a time when anti-gay rhetoric was being legitimized by a whole swathe of New Right propaganda, and during a period of serious cut-backs in welfare services and medical and social science research, meant that the health crisis also became a symbol of an era which preferred moral certainty and individual salvation to the rational addressing a painful human need."[54]

The officials of the Reagan administration in the first half of the eighties ignored the health crisis and the pleas of government scientists, while the press avoided discussion of AIDS until it reacted to fears about the safety of "the general population". In 1982, *Newsweek,* for example, covered the danger to a two-month-old hemophiliac under the heading "Homosexual Plague Strikes New Victim."[55] By the time of Reagan's reelection, he had not spoken publicly about the crisis.[56] It is estimated that 20,849 Americans had died of AIDS before he delivered his first speech on the epidemic.[57] Reagan's deafness to word about the epidemic seems both to have been for the specific reason that he did not want to be seen to help those who, in New Right thinking, had brought their illness upon themselves, but also on the general neoconservative lines, that people should look out for themselves if they were ill. His feeling seems to have been that federal health agencies should find ways to combat AIDS without further help—by, for example, diverting money from less urgent projects. In addition, if it is true that Reagan succeeded in making himself the benign center of America and placing malignancies outside its borders,[58] then there is a powerful psychological reason for his refusal to acknowledge the existence of AIDS within his borders—or else to regard those suffering from AIDS as, by that fact alone, beyond the pale.

While the energies of such citizens as Elizabeth Taylor went into raising private money through AIDS benefits, the Reagan administration did nothing.[59] Reagan's ideological arguments that "private initiative" was appropriate for scientific research and health care are dismissed by Douglas Crimp as attempts to excuse and perpetuate the state's irresponsibility.[60] New York City mayor Edward Koch did offer the official welcome, on the other hand, to the symposium gathered with his encouragement to seek a "solution to the most frightening epidemic we have faced in recent years."[61] Kevin M. Cahill, M.D., gives voice to the thought that the health of drug addicts and poor Haitian refugees was seen as insignificant by the health professions, and that only the realization that the disease could spread to the general population through blood transfusions awakened interest.[62]

Even this awakening seems to be resented by some, as an exaggeration of the importance of the epidemic and an unnecessary disturbance of public tranquillity. Gerald R. Connor appears to be criticized by Harry Schwartz for developing a strategy that emphasized the public aspect of the disease rather than that AIDS strikes mainly homosexuals.[63] "Aided by a small number of special interest groups, particularly homosexuals (who sought increased funding for research and for the support of its victims), and by some research scientists, for a few months the media made AIDS into a frightening specter haunting the American public," he writes.[64]

Meanwhile, on the other side of the Atlantic, AIDS received its first official report in 1983. The report, combined with news from the United States, is said to have started a wave of AIDS panic in "the always-hysterical British press."[65] While the health minister, Kenneth Clarke, called reaction among the British public to the crisis "almost medieval," the Conservative government did remarkably little until, as in America, there were fears that AIDS could pass into "the general population." Near the end of September 1985, Barney Hayhoe announced that £910,000 was to be provided for "sensible measures" against AIDS. Still, Professor Michael Adler of the Middlesex Hospital gave notice that much more money was required if counseling and testing on the scale that he had become used to was to continue. In December 1985, £7 million was promised, largely to help AIDS counselors and to finance a campaign of public education. The government's response, in the provision of finances, was likened to "ad hoc Scrooge-like unpocketing of small sums of money."[66]

Both governments' promotion of self-interest had a curious effect in relation to AIDS. Not only did the positive valuing of selfishness mean that those already on the fringes of society were starved of the resources that might have been put their way, but self-interest was given the added value of being simple medical prudence.[67] The relationship of "standing on one's feet" to individual success in business terms but also in terms of good health may help to explain why "better-educated, upscale professionals in their thirties" seemed in 1984 opposed to the notion of changing their "unsafe" sexual habits after the manner of homosexuals. "With a certainty that would make John Calvin proud, this group appeared to link their success to a sense of immunity to AIDS."[68] Since business success and individual self-sufficiency have clear connections in eighties thinking with virility, it is perhaps not so surprising that such porn stars as Bill Margold refuse, despite their occupation, to think about improving "safety": "My whole feeling about 'safe sex' and about disease in general is that if you are unhealthy, you deserve to be dead!"[69]

Given the importance accorded to business success and productivity in the eighties, it is perhaps not surprising either that some spokespersons on behalf of the funding of AIDS research have to resort to arguments about the loss of productivity consequent upon AIDS deaths. The dean of the School of Public Health at the University of Michigan, for example, is reported to have said: "We are losing a generation of well-trained and exceptionally talented men, and humanity cannot afford to lose even an iota of trained talent in these troubled times."[70] The CDC is said, also, to have calculated the loss in productivity through AIDS at over 4.8 billion dollars.[71]

The Conceptualization of AIDS

"AIDS does not exist apart from the practices that conceptualize it, represent it, and respond to it. We know AIDS only in and through these practices."[72] This statement by Douglas Crimp clarifies the reasons why the conceptualization of AIDS is of crucial moment for every doctor, every PWA, and indeed every person who attempts to offer an opinion on it. While Crimp never contests the reality of painful illness and death, he is surely right to insist on the startling truth that AIDS, far from being a medical "fact," is a construction, based on a series of inferences from observation of, notably, immunity collapse and the presence of HIV antibodies in certain bloodstreams.

Susan Sontag agrees. She calls AIDS "a clinical construction," taking its identity from "a long, and lengthening, roster of symptoms . . . which 'mean' that what the patient has is this illness."[73] In addition, she points out, "the very contention that AIDS is invariably fatal depends partly on what doctors decided to define as AIDS—and keep in reserve as distinct earlier stages of the disease."[74]

It is possible that this realization is literally a matter of life and death. One HIV-positive American asserts, for example, that the very politically active, angry PWAs in New York are still alive, while the people who have accepted the death sentence and who actually seem to him to want it because they feel that they deserve it are going under.[75] (This observation lends further possible credibility to Schmidt's belief, reported earlier, in AIDS as a psychosocial phenomenon.)

One consequence of surrendering the conceptualization of AIDS to medical expertise is to reactivate the processes by which the homosexual was invented in the first place by doctors and sexologists of the late-nineteenth century and early twentieth. As Michael Lynch puts it, "Gays are once again allowing the medical profession to define, restrict, pathologise us. What used to be a psychiatric pathology is now an infectious one."[76]

The immense practical value of turning away from passive dependence upon a government which seemed not to care about the epidemic and even from a medical profession whose views on AIDS were heavily influenced by their conceptualization of homosexual sufferers can be demonstrated by the creation of the Gay Men's Health Crisis to fill the vacuum of caring, counseling, and treating in the United States in the first part of the eighties. (This may help to explain the otherwise bizarre conceptualization of AIDS by one individual, who sees it as the way that gays have chosen to get their civil rights.)[77]

Because of the claimed near-obsession of investigators of the syndrome with the sexual practices and life-styles of its most evident American and European sufferers, the relevance of poverty and malnutrition, highlighted as a probable cause particularly of Third World AIDS, has been played down.[78] This may seem like a fatal isolationism in reviewing the illness within the ranks of North American and European medical experts and politicians. Given the Americano- and Eurocentric dimension of AIDS' conceptualization, it is hardly suprising that an explanation of the illness in terms of American bacteriological warfare upon them, a warfare that got out of hand and whose consequences returned upon the perpetrators, has found popularity in Zaire and other countries of Central Africa.[79]

The cruciality of AIDS' conception, demonstrated strikingly in neglect of AIDS during a period when the New Right deemed sufferers from it to deserve their "punishment," makes it the most political of illnesses.

The fear of AIDS can—and clearly has been—exploited in relation to notions of racial, as well as sexual, purity. The perceptible need is for a border, between the polluted (here diseased, contagious) and the pure (disease-free, taken in this case to be HIV negative). The profound psychological need for belief in this border means that sexuality can be rendered less diffuse and permeable, so that it is balkanized into two utterly distinct spheres, heterosexuality and homosexuality (with the bisexual man an imponderable entity, conceived in terms of sly treachery to heterosexuality). The border can usefully be aligned, however, with national boundaries. Thus, AIDS was, in the understanding of many countries, an invasion from outside, which encouraged calls for clampdowns on immigration, as well as for legally enforced "testing" of the aliens within the midst of the country. Aliens could be literally understood, or identified, as those elements which the prevailing ideology deemed to be "other."

Jean-Marie Le Pen called, in France, for mandatory nationwide testing and quarantining of those carrying the HIV virus,[80] even though the French in 1981 generally saw the invasion as due to

contacts with Americans,[81] rather than, for example, with the
North African and Arab immigrants who occupy so much of Le
Pen's thinking. The United States, in the meantime, projected its
fear and loathing on to a revivified notion of "the dark continent"
but most especially and specifically on to the Haitians. Haitians
were popularly associated, in any case, with voodoo and ritual
involving the use of animal and human blood.[82] "Authoritarian
political ideologies have a vested interest in promoting fear, a sense
of the imminence of takeover by aliens—and real diseases are
useful material."[83] Aliens may be Haitians if you are North American, or American if you are French, but the principle is simple. The
borders constructed within the body politic are less capable of
geographical, let alone moral, justification, but AIDS gives these
borders a new credibility, contrasting polluted city with pure small
town, polluted homosexual with pure heterosexual, polluted black
with pure white.

Evidence of the rigid border taken to delimit "safe," where
normal people are on one side and "polluted," deviant people on
the other, can be found in press attitudes to the reporting of the
disease, especially in its early days. The principal tactic was silence
on the subject until, that is, it was suddenly feared that it might
attack "the general population," at which point, especially in 1983,
the press became saturated in AIDS reports. In other words, reports about people dying of AIDS became important only when
people on the right side of the border seemed likely to be affected.
Harry Schwartz, who has figured before in this chapter as a useful
illustration of dominant thinking, actually explains the press's silence as being due to homosexuals' wise decision to keep their
pollution quiet, and then explains the sudden explosion of information in the press as being due to a conspiracy of homosexual
publicists who hid the information that AIDS was "largely a homosexual disease."[84]

Generally, the press saw AIDS as a way to reinforce the borderline which it had customarily drawn before the advent of the
illness. According to the *New Republic* in 1983, AIDS as a metaphor "has come to symbolize . . . the identity between contagion
and a kind of desire."[85] Edward Albert suggests that the media
"medicalized" deviance, by this means filling out its portrait of a
pariah subgroup and also distancing readers from the sufferings of
ill persons within this subgroup. He explains "medicalization" as
involving "a redefinition of the offending behaviour or condition
from one of 'crime' or 'sin' to one of 'illness.' "[86] Distancing of the
group most in need of help from those apparently unaffected by the

illness was achieved by the American press in the early days of reporting by, for example, portraying the group as bizarre, deviant in sexual habits, and interesting but isolated (thus not threatening),[87] and also by suggesting that the gay community was under siege, that its institutions were crumbling, that its life-style was altering perforce.[88] The glaringly obvious difference between those at risk and those protected by their normality and purity was emphasized visually by the concentration on AIDS sufferers as "gay" and/or wasted.[89]

Albert concludes, "By emphasizing the deviant lifestyles and highlighting the differences between 'at-risk' and 'not-at-risk' groups, AIDS sufferers were symbolically isolated from the rest of society. Such isolation served (and still serves) not only to protect the population at large from an unbounded fear of contagion but to reaffirm the already present ambiguity in attitudes toward the central characters in the AIDS epidemic, homosexual men."[90]

Homosexual men were defined in the eighties within a largely hostile, homophobic British popular press by their association with AIDS. "Via the relay of AIDS, the image of the gay man has been woven through with some of the most terrifying representations of degenerative disease. Death and homosexuality are now inseparably linked in public consciousness."[91]

The Symbolization of AIDS

Susan Sontag has proved to be particularly aware of the metaphorical language used to characterize illness. She understands the force of these metaphors (and of their associations) in relation to the understanding of illness and to the formation of attitudes to the illness as well as to those suffering from it. She notes the predominance of warfare analogies and military metaphors in connection with cancer and its treatment.[92] She also notes that illnesses may be used as metaphors for evil, the most popular illnesses for such use being syphilis, tuberculosis, and cancer.[93] The result of such metaphorical thinking in regard to illness is clear to her: "The move from the demonization of the illness to the attribution of fault to the patient is an inevitable one, no matter if patients are thought of as victims. Victims suggest innocence. And innocence, by the inexorable logic that governs all rational terms, suggests guilt."[94]

Sontag sees the principal metaphors arising from AIDS as those of invasion and, when transmission is discussed, pollution.[95] Invasion is easily capable of conception in the eighties in Reaganite terms of "star wars" and even of space invaders.[96] The medical belief in a latency period between HIV infection and the onset of "full-blown" AIDS lends itself to metaphorical notions of contamination and mutation.[97] Sander L. Gilman has discovered another metaphorical association with AIDS—depression. He notes that the traditional iconography of melancholy or depression is powerfully employed in illustrations of AIDS discussions or articles. He finds it, for example, in the popular scientific journal *Discover* (September 1986) in the illustration of a major update on AIDS. He believes that this depiction of the depression of the AIDS sufferer helps to characterize the hopeless male (obviously, in context, homosexual) as the victim and source of his own pollution. This in turn is an attempt to counter the fear that AIDS may become a danger to heterosexuals, since the writer is attempting to refute the notion that the disease is a danger to everyone. (The essay is subtitled "Still No Reason for Hysteria.")[98]

AIDS is popularly linked (because it is so linked by the media and by certain politicians) with deviancy, as if the disease were explained purely by reference to behavior deemed by some version of a moral majority as not fitting—the behavior of people on the wrong, alien, side of the borderline. The mystery and the fear of it are dispelled at the same time as the warning against seduction into the unnatural is reinforced, when a simple cause-effect relation is affirmed between "deviant" sexuality and AIDS. A striking example of the tendency may be found in the *New York Post* of 24 May 1983: "The poor homosexuals . . . have declared war upon nature, and now nature is exacting an awful retribution." This was written by Patrick J. Buchanan, who went on to become an assistant to President Reagan.[99] For the New Right in general, the essence of homosexuality was taken to be promiscuity. Disease was an inevitable consequence of promiscuity. Thus, the connection between homosexuality and AIDS is easily comprehensible. One explains the other. The matter is put succinctly by Viper, a porn actress: "They want to broadcast all the warnings they can about AIDS, because they really believe it's a faggot disease, and it's filthy and faggots are perverts."[100]

Even those who would dispute the link created between deviant sex and AIDS fall into the trap of using a discourse that exposes belief in a borderline, between "them" and "us." Note the use of (implied) third and first person in the following extract from Hancock and Carim: "We can allow ourselves no longer the stupid gratification of blaming one or another minority group within our community for the sudden appearance of the disease. We can, in short, pretend no longer that this is anyone else's problem but our own. This is uniquely *our* virus—a reflection of our own lifestyles and of the world that we have fashioned. We have unleashed it, given it its headstart, provided it with fertile soil to take root and spread amongst us."[101]

Deviance may, of course, be characterized in political as well as moral/sexual terms. (Le Pen is reported as having dismissed some of his political opponents by use of the term "sidatique"—SIDA being the French acronym for AIDS.)[102] However, what is striking about the metaphorical use of AIDS is that not only homosexuality but sexuality itself has been stigmatized as dangerous or, more accurately, as lethal. Hancock and Carim, again resorting to the first person plural, believe that AIDS whispers "to us" that "the days of wine and roses are over."[103] Susan Sontag thinks that sexual coupling has become "a chain, a chain of transmission, from the past."[104] Life itself, in the form of blood and sexual fluids, has become the bearer of contamination.[105]

It is a short step from seeing AIDS as an inevitable result of deviance to claiming that sufferers from AIDS have brought it upon themselves, and, by another short step, that AIDS is a just punishment for the sin of deviance. Long before AIDS, illnesses were interpreted as punishment, although generally medical practitioners have dissented from that notion.[106] Within this century, thanks to Reich on Freud, cancer has been interpreted as the punishment for repression,[107] making the cancer sufferer in that sense responsible for the disease. While it may be true that any significant disease whose causality is unclear and which is difficult to treat is given a moralistic meaning,[108] AIDS has been particularly irresistible to the moralizing tendency, since it is widely taken to be a sexually transmitted disease and since it is taken to fulfill the New Christian Right warnings of the late seventies.

One of the first to make the obvious link between the disease and God's just wrath against homosexuals was Jerry Falwell. In a news conference of July 1983, he called AIDS God's punishment upon homosexuals for breaking His laws and those of nature. He further accused the gay community of using its political influence to prevent officials from stopping the spread of the disease (by, for example, closing the bathhouses in New York and San Francisco). Falwell urged health authorities to outlaw homosexuals from donating their blood.[109]

Falwell's utterances are a clear sign of the "moral panic" created around AIDS. This form of panic may be defined as dealing with widespread fears and anxieties not by seeking the real causes of the problem but by displacing them on to "folk devils."[110]

An obvious problem for exponents of AIDS-as-divine-retribution is that nonmembers of the punished group also fall ill. Examples of such "undeserving" sufferers are children and hemophiliacs who are known not to be drug abusers or homosexuals. Hancock and Carim once again fall into a trap when they ask, reasonably, of children suffering from AIDS, "What have they done, these ill-starred infants, to deserve such a bleak future?"[111] Their question summons up the likelihood that there are others facing a bleak future who have done something by reason of which they deserve that future. Press stories about AIDS have concentrated heavily on the "undeserving" victim, attempting by that concentration to elicit sympathy for those caught up in the horror of AIDS through no fault of their own. (The implication is obvious.) When they deal with women, they tend to divide these, in traditional patriarchal fashion, into wives and mothers, on the one hand, and prostitutes, on the other, characterizing the latter as a danger to clients and clients' wives alike. Research would indicate that prostitutes are unlikely to be infected because they are less likely than the general population to permit sex without their partners' use of a condom.

Although "plague" references are absent from American press reports after December 1983,[112] as long as AIDS is interpreted moralistically, the links with classic plague thinking stand revealed. In ancient Greece, plagues were capable of interpretation as instruments of divine wrath. The readiness with which Falwell's analysis of the AIDS crisis was given credence raises questions about the distance between current New Christian Right thinking and the popular thinking about plague from which such ancient Athenians as Thucydides, historian of the plague at Athens, distances himself. Dennis Altman makes the point, fairly: "Both the ways in which the state, the media, the medical profession and the affected communities respond, and the irrational fears and prejudices aroused by the disease, bring into question how far we have progressed since the great plagues of pre-modernity."[113]

When AIDS is seen as a plague, it is not surprising if, in the absence of explanation for it other than God's righteous anger, it is dwelt on for its horror potential. The following account of a visit to "an AIDS ward" seems to suggest a scenario for a splatter movie, since its imagery goes somewhat beyond that of David Cronenberg's movies: "When they see fungus in a person's eye and see him or her bleeding from every place it is possible to bleed from; when they see and hear strong, healthy people in the prime of life vomiting blood, losing their hair and being transformed into wizened bags of skin and bone within a matter of months, then they will understand the extent to which human dignity is still at the mercy of minute specks of mindless matter."[114] The aim, as so often with the writing of Graham Hancock and Enver Carim, seems laudable enough, but the writing itself, as often too, betrays the passage's roots in Rightist and even fundamentalist thinking. (Why should scientists bother to explain that specks of matter—presumably in reference to the HIV virus—are "mindless"?)

They continue in what can be thought of as their Old Testament mode: "The sight of professional scientists, artists, businessmen, farmers, pastoralists [?] being reduced in such an ignominious way to listless cadavers slithering in a stench of incontinence is more than enough to bring home the indiscriminating nature of this disease. It respects no international borders, it is not confined to any particular race, and it doesn't give a damn about the person's social status or sex."[115] Surely there must be more helpful ways of making the fair point that the virus does not discriminate. (To suggest that it doesn't give a damn reinvests it with a personality, perversely.) Surely the reader does not require a Dante-esque vision of the Inferno to get the basic point.

When "objective observers" of the health crisis are so imbued with plague imagery and the fundamentalist outlook, what hope is there for a rational debate and a genuinely sympathetic approach to the catastrophe?

11

Movies and AIDS

"To speak of sexuality and the body, and not also to speak of AIDS, would be, well, obscene."[1] The aim of this chapter is to see whether movies, in clearly talking about sexuality and about the body, do also speak of AIDS, however circumlocutively.

Douglas Crimp declares that art has the power to save lives,[2] pointing to ACT-UP's "Let the Record Show . . ." (discussed in chapter 10) as an example of such art. Rather than the personal, elegiac expression which dominates the art world's response to AIDS, he calls for an art, and practices, that are critical, theoretical, and activist.[3]

An example of photography's response to AIDS can be found in the 1989 British *Bodies of Experience* exhibition at Camerawork. The exhibition gave six photographers the opportunity to record their impressions of the effect of HIV infection upon their lives. Thus, for example, John Cole offered photographic records of life at the London Lighthouse (a hospice for both inpatients and out-), suggesting the warmth and community the Lighthouse creates for patients and visitors. (Philip Core, reviewing the exhibition, felt, however, that there needed to be a more somber balance to these photographs, recording, say, the closing of AIDS wards at Saint Stephen's, or the overcrowding at Westminster Hospital.[4] This balance would indeed have fitted with the energy created by anger at American government attitudes to the AIDS crisis in ACT-UP artists, for example.)

AIDS has impinged on videomakers' consciousness and practice, to judge by E. Ann Kaplan's mention of several videos made about the disease (even if none of these appeared on MTV, as far as she is aware).[5] In October 1987, the American Film Institute Video Festival included "Only Human: Sex, Gender, and Other Misrepresentations," organized by Bill Horrigan and B. Ruby Rich; three programs in the series were devoted to videotapes on AIDS, with the objective of providing counterimages and counterrhetoric to challenge those purveyed by dominant media.[6] Stuart Marshall's videotape *Bright Eyes,* aiming to contest the homophobia underlying dominant media's representations of AIDS, was broadcast on Britain's Channel 4 in December 1984 in *The Eleventh Hour* series.[7]

In the theater, AIDS-oriented dramatic works include Jeff Hagedorn's *One,* Bob Chesley's *Night Sweat,* Larry Kramer's *The Normal Heart,* and William Hoffman's *As Is.*[8]

AIDS awareness impinged on eighties television. It became public knowledge that, for example, the stars of *Dallas* and *Dynasty* (on which Rock Hudson had appeared in a principal role not long before his death) had undergone blood tests for the presence of HIV, and that Barry Lowen, an executive of the company making *Dynasty,* had died of AIDS.[9] At the end of 1983, *St. Elsewhere* included a story about a young politician suffering from AIDS.[10] The dominant-media treatment of AIDS in terms of personal melancholia, on the part of the ill homosexual, and, perversely, in terms of family problem, is well illustrated by NBC's *An Early Frost.* In this television drama about a young Chicagoan afflicted with AIDS, his suffering is treated after the manner, as Simon Watney puts it, of such terminal-illness romance films as *Dark Victory* and *Love Story.*[11] On the other hand, his male lover is soon edited out of all consideration, to give place instead to the sick man's family, and particularly to the reconciliation of a father, complete with Reaganite macho values, and son. The son's return to Chicago is followed by the closing of family ranks.[12] The illness has been a problem for an otherwise "normal family" rather than for the PWA and his lover, apparently.

A treatment of AIDS thought by some commentators to be overtly homophobic was provided by PBS's *AIDS: A Public Inquiry.*[13] On the other hand, Peter Adair and Robert Epstein's *The A.I.D.S. Show,* broadcast in 1986, was a version of San Francisco's Theatre Rhinoceros's review;[14] still, it remained an example of the personal, elegiac art against which Douglas Crimp calls for artists to organize themselves.

While awareness of AIDS is manifested again and again in eighties popular culture, that awareness brings with it not simply fear of the illness but fear of the associations of "weakness" that the illness's popular inseparability from homosexuality (and the popular conceptions of that sexuality) carries along with it. This may explain Eddie Murphy's remarkably insensitive references, which he attempted to excuse on the grounds of humorous intentions, the suppurating sores on the face of *Dune*'s homosexual villain,[15] and certain (male) porn stars' daredevil attitude to the "virility test" of AIDS: "People are not interested in going to see X-rated films coated in rubber any more than they are interested in going to the Coliseum to see the Christians against the tabby-cats. . . . There have been studies on the X-rated industry which have basically concluded that the X-rated performer, *per se,* is psychologically programmed much the same to a bullfighter, a sky-diver or a race-car driver."[16]

Fatal Illness (and AIDS) in the Movies

The difficulty that dominant movies experience in facing up to AIDS as an issue relevant to their depiction of carnal desire is suggested by the jocularity of those moments where knowledge of the danger of AIDS is, however briefly, acknowledged. The remark to the Richard Dreyfuss character of *Stakeout* (1987) by his fellow cop, "I trust you practiced safe sex," is more a buddy-buddy mock-serious testimony to their machismo in discussing Dreyfuss's amorous success than a sign of genuine concern. Hollywood has trouble, in any case, in concentrating sympathetic attention on a "real man" suffering fatal illness. When a man of reasonable youthfulness and apparently full vigor is faced with the news of his being fatally ill, in Burt Reynolds's *The End* (1978), his collapse into hysterical tears once he is alone is treated as a matter for broad comedy. (Reynolds is one of the more interesting "macho" stars, in that he often punctures that image by having his real men turn into cry-babies or quivering wrecks when there is nobody around to see the transformation.)

Another example of evident consciousness of AIDS being masked by a comic approach and an evasive treatment of the subject is discoverable in George Miller's Australian movie *Les Patterson Saves the World* (1987). Here, Dr. Charles Herpes (Henri Szeps) has discovered an antidote to a disgusting skin ailment called by the acronym of HELP. Meanwhile, a certain Colonel Godowni is spreading the fatal illness by infecting toilet seats which are being exported to the United States. The cocktail of suppurating sores, fatality, contagiousness, and sexual double entendre makes the inspiration crystal clear. Even if the comedy turns therefore on misinformation, it is popularly credited misinformation (that, for example, AIDS is "merely" a sexually transmitted disease and that sexually transmitted diseases can, paradoxically, be caught from toilet seats). The comic distortion is likely in turn to strengthen the prevalent conceptions of AIDS in the film's audience.

Arthur J. Bressan, Jr.,'s *Buddies* (1985) and Bill Sherwood's

Parting Glances (1985) square up to the fact that they are dealing with both AIDS and gayness—which in itself may explain why these have enjoyed far narrower circulation than the macho-comedy oblique versions.

The central character of *Buddies,* David (David Schachter), becomes involved with AIDS issues when he moves from the theoretical—he is writing a book on the subject—to the practical, by becoming a "buddy." The PWA to whom he becomes buddy, Robert (Geoff Edholm), has not relinquished his long-term interest in gay politics or his "up-front" frankness about this political commitment and the carnality of his sexuality. "Coming out" becomes an issue for David. Encouraged by Robert, he takes this step. The interview in which he has to come out and which he knows will be published is undertaken because he is assured that it will be of benefit to people with AIDS. When Robert dies, David takes up a stance alone, bearing a placard, outside the White House. The movie is true to Robert's professed politics in that it was made with extreme rapidity in order to raise money for AIDS organizations. The address is not only "from inside" but to an audience that is assumed to be politically aware and able to share Robert's viewpoints on sexual pleasure, gayness, and its political dimensions.

Parting Glances is another "made-from-the-inside" movie which effectively refuses the dominant notion of homosexuality as problem by taking it as the norm, at least in so far as the characters and milieu of the film are gay and function as such without any appearance of problem. The film's commentary on and condemnation of those artists morbidly fascinated with fatal illness is the nearest it comes to taking a political line. Instead, it concentrates on the dilemma facing Michael (Richard Ganoung), who has to choose between a lover who is leaving the country for two years and a much more giving potential lover who is dying of AIDS. While *Parting Glances* offers as its identification points men who think unproblematically in terms of homosexuality, the barriers to identification are not so much in their particular sexuality as in the precision of their location within a particular urban class: "New York yuppies to a man, they are able to move from jogging to party to disco to Fire Island, swapping gay anecdotes with their respective employers along the way. Inevitably, those unacquainted with this life style may react less enthusiastically than those New Yorkers who experience the thrill of recognition."[17]

It seems inevitably to be the case in mainstream movies that AIDS is looked at "from the outside," since AIDS is assumed to be a gay disease. Whether that outside is from normal-family perspective or through heterosexual vision, it is, paradoxically, as if AIDS cannot be looked at for any length of time—or at all. The seventies take on some of the appearance of an alibi for this evasion. Although *Cocktail* (1988) does not expend energy on establishing its period as the seventies, its sexual attitudes are those of a less anxious period for New Yorkers. The screenplay by Heywood Gould is based on his own book, which relates to the writer's experiences in the previous decade. *Torch Song Trilogy* (1988) would have to foreground its time location in the seventies (as it does) for questions not to be raised about the absence of AIDS, even in terms of AIDS anxiety, from its narrative. As noted in chapter 9, *Trilogy* does, though, have an elegiac feel to it, focusing on death even more than its "act-two" narrative would demand.

A film such as Blake Edwards's *Skin Deep* (1988), which treats womanizing as unproblematic and even heroic, is also difficult to take, if not to make, however. Kim Newman's remarks on it show that awareness of AIDS, at least potentially as a heterosexual issue even when it is not allowed to surface as such, underlies reception of eighties entertainment movies: "Aside from one jokey and smug reference to AIDS, the film ignores modern sexual mores and assumes that Zach's [John Ritter] promiscuity is of vital interest only to himself and to Alex [Alyson Reed], his preordained soul mate. . . . Most of his cast-off women remain adoringly indulgent of him."[18]

Horror Films and Their Possible Connection with AIDS

A markedly new trend in seventies and especially eighties horror films is the emphasis on destruction of the human body; although violence, mutilation, and destruction have been visited on human bodies from the beginnings of the horror movie, the novelty resides in the source of the destruction—in that the source lies within the body itself. Nearly all of David Cronenberg's movies center on the notion that lurking within the body—usually a well-cared-for, comfortably off, middle-class person's body—is pestilence.

Although from the midseventies Cronenberg was making films about parasitic growths within the body whose eruption out of it caused lethal damage to its former host, probably the most famous such sequence is in the work of another director, Ridley Scott. In Scott's *Alien* (1979), a parasitic life force has managed to take up residence in the body of the John Hurt character. When he has "given birth" to it inside the spaceship—it tears its way out of his belly into the light of day—he loses his life. His body is of no further use to the creature, and may thus be discarded.

Incidentally, one of the contemporary nightmares that gives special potency to *Alien* is that a clear border is indicated in the early sequences, between the "safe" world of the space vessel and the dreaded world of alien life forces beyond, and yet the safety of this sacred limit (which the heroine, played by Sigourney Weaver, attempts to protect) is breached by the permitted reintroduction of the fatally contaminated Hurt character. One of the formerly "safe" human beings whose environment must be hermetically sealed for its survival is the source of the all but triumphant threat to that environment and thus to their lives. This can be read straightforwardly as playing on, for example, British fears about the breach of quarantine arrangements because of kindly impulses (concerned, in this context, with the protection of domestic pets from the relatively long-term isolation demanded by British quarantine regulations), and about the introduction of rabies to islands that appear to be free of a pest which has terrified the continent of Europe. It is almost impossible, though, not to see in the dread of a borderline's breach the concern shown in the late seventies in American New Right thinking to establish a demarcation line between familial and extrafamilial, between sexual normality and sexual perversion, wholesome and deviant practices. The overwhelmingly powerful augmentation of this concern with the "discovery" of AIDS makes it well-nigh impossible to undertake a retroactive reading of *Alien* without consideration of the maintenance of a border—the purpose of this border being to prevent the unconscious introduction of life-threatening parasitic organisms. (A more specific version of that reading would have John Hurt as the bisexual who brings back destruction to his formerly pure family.)

John Carpenter's *The Thing* (1982) goes beyond *Alien*, while it much reduces the narrative impetus of the Scott movie in order to intensify concentration on the process of body invasion and destruction by a life force which appears to have no other aim than survival. Carpenter encourages the interpretation of this particular body horror in terms of cancer, but since cancer is one of the forms through which AIDS kills by the closing down of the immune system, it would be nit-picking to deny that the film produces much of its audience's repelled fascination by playing on its repelled fascination with the suffering produced by AIDS, as that is relayed by sensationalist media.

In the same year, *The Beast Within*, mentioned by Philip Brophy among other, more famous examples of body-destruction horror films, details the agonizing transformation of a boy in his hospital bed until a creature erupts out of his body in full view of his mother, presumed "father," and a doctor.[19] Here, as Brophy seems to suggest by his summary, the monstrous birth (from a male body, as in *Alien*) happens in environments normally taken to be reassuring, that of the family and that of the hospital, with its "caring professionals." Here, this 1982 movie makes more explicit suggestions already detectable within Ridley Scott's space vessel. The space travelers of *Alien* behave as a family by, for example, eating together at the point of the alien's birth from Hurt's body and by having an all-controlling computer known as Mother. Then, too, the social rooms of the spacecraft are all gleaming, clean surfaces, suggesting, if not an advertising-world modern kitchen, a clinic or hospital.

Pete Boss believes that at the heart of much contemporary horror is the notion of physical helplessness, frequently at the hands, or implements, of a brightly lit and hygienic institution.[20] He believes that this is due to several interacting cultural conditions, such as contemporary horror films' obsession with the destruction of the human body, paranoid or conspiracist tendencies within social and political thinking, and the complex of negative images which informs popular attempts to address problems of death and dying, especially in relation to medical technology and institutional bureaucracy.[21]

Since Boss's article was published in 1986, it is surprising that these valid observations are not brought together under the explanatory umbrella of AIDS thinking. Paranoid, conspiracist thinking is clearly evident in the New Christian Right's hostility to gay rights activists (their success would be likely to destroy America, the Right suggests), and Anita Bryant freely talks about conspiracies against her. (There are counterparanoid beliefs, too, that AIDS is a CIA-inspired plot, gone somewhat wrong, against homosexuals or Africans.) The way that the "front-line" AIDS victims were identified with gay life-styles and sexuality in America reinvigorates the paranoia of the Right in dealing with people and claims categorized as rigidly "other." Death and dying are considered with a peculiarly negative cast of mind when deaths are taken to be the result of body destruction "from inside" (the body and the life-style of the body). So far, too, medical technology that has proved increasingly effective in the treatment of certain kinds of cancer has failed to do much more for AIDS than to identify those believed to be doomed to die because they are seropositive.

Boss rightly draws attention to the antinomy within, especially, Cronenberg's films: body health and body destruction. Body health is signaled by jogging, aerobics, and so on, while body destruction is aligned with cancer.[22] The particular notion of body health's alignment with the sort of self-help indicated by aerobics classes relates, with unusual intimacy, body horror to dominant thinking. Jogging and aerobics, like squash, volleyball, and tennis, could be thought to represent the emphasis of the Right, taken with particular seriousness by yuppies, on personal responsibility for individual health, and could also be thought to increase the always present tendency to blame ill health on the patient's wrong choices or attitudes.

That self-help exercise is not always contrasted with body destruction from within the body itself could be illustrated with reference to Michael Crichton's *Coma* (1977), though. Here, the victim has been practicing aerobics just before she is rendered brain-dead by deliberate malpractice within a hospital's operating theater. It may, paradoxically, be the health of her body which makes her an attractive victim, on the other hand. This provides a different irony from the more usual one, of the apparently healthy being unaware of their invasion by lethal organisms. The latter is directly applicable to the way that the media have handled the AIDS epidemic, as cutting down young gays apparently in the full vigor of life, and is a ubiquitous image in the notion of HIV-positive persons being "really" ill although the illness may not manifest itself for many years.

In body-destruction fantasies, as Boss points out, there is a reduction of the self to the body, "a closing-off or reduction of identity to its corporal horizons."[23] In this aspect, horror movies are following a trend in thought which is manifested with particular force by the New Right, in its apparent inability to separate persons from the physical (sexual) acts which they perform. (Bryant's fascination with the oral consumption of semen is particularly revealing here, as she justifies her campaign against human beings' rights by recourse to arguments concerning physical experience alone, as if that were a final court.) In turn, the New Right is merely emphasising a tendency that seems ubiquitous in nineteenth- and twentieth-century thought. The invention of the homosexual (person) out of homosexual acts is an excellent illustration of the tendency to reduce the self to the body. Even Foucault, in his dissection of the discourse by which sexuality is understood, appears to leave "the body" intact, as something irreducible to power, the body thus achieving a kind of reality which is denied other social phenomena.[24]

Boss takes particular interest, following Foucault, in the constitution of the body as not just a subject but an object, as a knowable quantity for physical and political regulation, and in the relation of that constitution to the methods of modern medicine.[25] He takes such movies as *Coma* and *Terminal Choice* (1984) as offering graphic fantasies of the body's subjection to an alien, totalitarian regime,[26] which produce their horror from the ease with which subjects are turned into objects, people into things.[27] Interestingly, he points out the audience's emotional implication with the victims of these changes, in that it is placed, for instance, under the descending scalpel in *Blind Date* (1984).

This consideration of spectator positioning in relation to the body-destruction fantasy helps to modify Boss's opinion that it is difficult to see, with Robin Wood, any political progressivity within such fantasies of physical degradation and vulnerability.[28] He believes that Wood, by focusing on the figure of the monster as "Other," leaves the discourse of corporeal destruction taken for granted as somehow determining the extent of the monster's "monstrousness."[29] Yet there is surely more to say about notions of "progressivity" within body-destruction fantasies than taking Wood to task on this point would allow. The aligning of the spectator with the victim, for one thing, however fleetingly this may be done (Freud's work on fantasy would suggest multiple identification and positioning as practically a sine qua non of fantasy, especially sadomasochistic fantasy), must damage the media attempts to render AIDS suffering as something that happens only to "them," never to "us." The way that undeserving and, by implication, deserving sufferers have been created to make good the potential gaps which the hemophiliac or "AIDS baby" might open up is further evidence of media (and, thus, politicians') determination that AIDS will be something that either happens only to "them" or else happens to "us" only because of "them."

The notion that AIDS is never more than a construction and that its construction may operate to the advantage of medical personnel (and drug companies) has been voiced openly by Casper G. Schmidt and Peter Duesberg, for example (see chapter 10). Therefore, making surgeons in horror movies into psychopaths or turning well-funded medical institutions into totalitarian regimes with new uses for human bodies is a means of unsettling the received wisdom, which, after all, is the wisdom of medical "superiors." There is a perceptible pessimism at the heart of much contemporary horror, suggesting our inability to be more than our bodies, which may encourage hopeless passivity, a tendency that could also be encouraged by loss of faith in institutions, as well as in persons, that had been taken to be all-knowing and ever-beneficent. Yet for those who are already in actuality expected to be bound in passivity and silence because they are not allowed to be more than their bodies and because medical expertise is allowed to remain unchallengeable, the revelation of other possibilities could be seen as highly progressive. As usual, the suggestion cannot be allowed to remain that "progressivity" is an unproblematic term. We have to ask, progressive for whom? in what ways? And even when we have answers to these questions, we must beware of the notion that a film is capable of a universal, and unified, reading. What may be clearly negative in one reading may be as clearly positive in another.

The progressivity or otherwise of horror in general, of body-destruction horror in particular, ought to remain an important debate among students of popular culture. However the political relevance of body-destruction fantasies is to be viewed, the repetition of themes of parasitic growths and alien invasions at a body-internal level within body-destruction horror movies is surely to be remarked.

Perhaps the least "disguised" of the horror movies in relation to AIDS is Chuck Russell's *The Blob* (1988). This is partly because, in this new version of the fifties tale of a growth that retains life by attaching itself to human beings, the Blob comes into being as the result of a germ-warfare experiment that goes wrong (a widespread belief in Central Africa and in gay circles in relation to AIDS). It is also significantly because a central figure in the tale is the fundamentalist Reverend Meeker (Del Close), who intends to use the Blob fragments he has collected to effect the "Rapture," or destruction of the sinful world.

Hancock and Carim tell their horrified reader that the HIV virus has now "broken out" of the immune system to find "a sanctuary" in the brain.[30] (The imagery of much AIDS writing owes a considerable debt to the horror genre, which, it must be remembered, was literary before it was cinematic.) Even without this intelligence, Frank Henenlotter's *Brain Damage* (1987) would be difficult to consider without reference to AIDS fear and to the relay of AIDS information. Brain damage is inflicted by a parasite called the "Aylmar" (affectionately dubbed Elmer), which lives by means of the consumption of brains. Elmer chooses to live with Brian (Rick Herbst), a resident in the same building as his original hosts, because the latter offer it only animal brains. Elmer injects an ecstatically hallucinogenic substance into Brian's brain, and in return, Elmer is taken into the city—to feed on human brains, unknown to Brian. The most notorious sequence from the movie is where the parasite, while Brian is kissing his girlfriend, darts out of his mouth and consumes her brains. (The scene gives new meaning to the make-out term of "sucking [someone's] brains out" and other variants!) At the end of the movie, although Brian chooses suicide, his brain refuses to die.

One of the most striking elements in *The Thing* is the absence of female characters. The Antarctic setting permits the absence to be naturalized, as it were, but the victimization of male bodies by something lurking in the bodies of other men suggests an analogy with the popular conception of AIDS transmission. The experiment within the diegesis to test for infected blood interestingly precedes the advent of such a test for donated blood supplies. While *Alien* has female crew members, and has one such female as the only human survivor, the "family" within the spaceship is distinctly asexual too, in both heterosexual and homosexual terms. Mother may be their computer, but the nearest person to a biological mother is the male crew member who unorthodoxly gives birth to the alien from within his body. (*Alien* itself gives birth, too, to James Cameron's *Aliens* [1986], wherein a mother-child relationship is strongly suggested among the human beings on the space vessel.)

The notion of monstrous birth is at the center of Cronenberg's *The Brood* (1979), where, for example, rage generates "the brood" on, and then from, the heroine's (Samantha Eggar) body. Early in the film, a male patient is made to expose the sores on his upper body. In view of the film's treatment of the genesis of cancerous tumors and of the explanation for her brood in the heroine's psyche, these sores are a manifestation of inner torment, which the doctor-hero (Oliver Reed) is attempting to cure.

Cronenberg's *The Fly* (1986) is most persuasively to be claimed as "an AIDS movie" when it centers on bodily declension (at least when considered from the human point of view) and the negotiation of disgust between the erstwhile lovers, Seth (Jeff Goldblum) and Veronica (Geena Davis). The rationalization for drastic bodily change is found here in a private experiment that goes wrong, in which a fly has become trapped in the machine Seth uses for his teleportation. Since his genes become intermingled with those of the fly, he becomes less recognizably human as his metamorphosis continues, regurgitating his food in order to digest it, losing human limbs in the process of the mutation, for example. The film largely concentrates claustrophobically on the process of change and the problems that it sets up for human emotions (desire, compassion) as well as the questions that it raises about the advisability of Veronica's termination of her pregnancy by Seth. All of these elements—physical declension, the stress on loved ones to keep on "recognizing" the loved one, the fear of transmission to another generation—are dreadfully familiar within the context of AIDS.

Cronenberg denies himself the title conferred on him, "King of Venereal Horror." Perhaps critics who accuse him of disgust at the human body project their own reactions on to him. He says of his concentration on the processes of human bodily change: "It's not disgust. It's fascination, but it's also a willingness to look at what is really there without flinching, and to say *this* is what we're made of, as strange and as disgusting as it might seem at times."[31]

What may be part of this fascination with the human body is the proximity created in, for example, *The Fly* between sexual pleasure and the danger (or promise?) of bodily change. Seth is inhibited in his experiments with teleportation until his physical relationship with Veronica liberates his energies and confidence. That this liberation results in hyperactive overconfidence may or may not color reception of the relation between physical experience and, in this context, the release of individualistic energy.

Whatever Cronenberg may be saying about the proximity of sexual experience and drastic alteration in human physicality, it is observable that eighties movies frequently draw a connection between sexuality and mortality. It is glaringly obvious, for instance, that the hero's girlfriend falls victim to the parasite Elmer in *Brain Damage* when she returns his kiss. Vampire movies have always pivoted on the inseparability of sexual desire and of mortal danger. The notion reappears in Tony Scott's *The Hunger* (1983), where the vampiric couple played by Catherine Deneuve and David Bowie go to a nightclub and pick up a pair of punks for what looks like a standard big-city one-night stand of sex. It is the hero's insistence on kissing the mysterious young woman whom he has just met in Kathryn Bigelow's *Near Dark* (1987) that explains his descent into vampirism.

Vampire movies also dramatize the need for blood and the "otherness" of vampire blood. The almost-vampire hero of *Near Dark,* in order to revive himself, has to drink blood from the wrists of his beloved. The notion of the particular danger for vampires' survival from polluted blood is treated for comedy in *Love at First Bite* (1979), set not coincidentally in a New York of, to the vampire, shockingly loose sexual morals. ("Okay, but it will have to be a quickie," says the heroine almost immediately after the Transylvanian hero [George Hamilton] has begun his old-fashioned seduction of her.) In *A Return to Salem's Lot,* the community has developed a distaste for human blood and has taken to drinking the blood of cows, on the grounds that cows do not take heroin or transmit AIDS.[32]

Even more conventional thrillers, such as Harold Becker's *Sea of Love* (1989), betray a new level of anxiety about the connection of one-night stands and death. The hero's fear of being shot dead by the heroine's newly discovered gun seems to represent more than the long-standing equation of the sex act with death, but rather, in AIDS thinking, an analogy with Russian roulette.[33]

A Major Movie Star and AIDS

Rock Hudson died on 2 October 1985. News of his death but, perhaps more dramatically, the publicizing in the summer of 1985 of his fight against AIDS, made the affliction markedly more "real" than the media had allowed it to become when it maintained a border between "natural victims" and others. Also, by exposing Hudson's (at the least) "compromised" sexuality, carefully manufactured as wholly straight by his publicists in the Code-bound (and McCarthy-threatened) fifties, his death forced a number of public attitudes to emerge. Either Hudson himself was a charlatan, a whited sepulcher who presumably deserved death for his deception as well as his deviance, or the studio peddled lies about the stars, or both. Alternatively, the public was afforded a rare potential opportunity to see the price paid by stars for their need to embody what official ideology demanded—in this case a certain version of cast-iron masculinity.

A still more interesting revelation could be discerned in the newly rewritten story of Rock Hudson—that masculinity or its lack is not something innate but something which is constructed. It is a construction, most probably, in all cases where masculinity is displayed, but in the case of a star known to be bisexual or homosexual, the process of construction becomes uniquely obvious. This is not because a man who is bisexual or homosexual cannot be, in terms of social definitions, "masculine" without tuition. Rather, it is because popular myths about homosexuality would demand that he be viewed in "nonmasculine" terms—so that a particularly cast-iron version of masculinity needs to be created by those with a strong economic interest in ensuring that their star is as widely acceptable as possible.

The account of Rock Hudson offered under the names of the star and Sara Davidson[34] reveals more than they may themselves be aware both about the manipulation of this star's image and about star images in general. The belief that stars are special beings, with such well-nigh meaningless attributes as "animal magnetism," is attested by fellow actor George Nader's opinion of Hudson. "Every major star has a tremendous motor inside that can generate animal magnetism. They rev that motor up and the emotion comes out through the eyes, through the senses—we don't know how—but it can reach off a screen and touch people sitting in a darkened theatre." This "magical" account of stardom, which may indeed well declare "we don't know how," is common in Hollywood's (and its publicity departments') accounts of itself. It obfuscates the star's constructedness, through publicity skills, lighting, choice of star vehicle, and so forth. Nader's account of Hudson's success as a star residing in "indefinable" inner qualities which the screen "lit up" is belied by talk in the book of the effect that the announcement from the Paris hospital of the star's having AIDS would have on his carefully preserved "image." It is said that he "planned, plotted and protected" his image as romantic hero for thirty-six years. Further, the constructedness of the star image is clearly indicated by the remark that "Rock was an actor and he played two roles— one in public and one at home. In public, he was guarded, but at home, he could be what he called 'a secret libertine.' "[35]

This last remark indicates that his sexuality was importantly concealed for the preservation of his image. Then again, there is the intimation that both Hudson and Nader knew that, to be stars, they had to present an image "without a chink, without a suggestion of softness." The rationalization for this self-presentation is that the public would find it impossible to believe in any love scenes that a star revealed to be homosexual would have with an actress. What is less obviously indicated, too, is that masculinity admits of no softness, and that masculinity and homosexuality are intrinsically opposed. How this masculinity, "without a chink, without a suggestion of softness," was created is revealed as partly due to the talents of the studio photographers who supplied material to fan magazines. Hudson was normally photographed with his shirt off, as "the beefcake king," stripped to the waist but also undertaking some activity—such as watering his garden, washing his car, or painting the house. A typical caption is offered as, "Looking at him from any angle, the conclusion is: "What a man!" Being such a man, he inspired one paramount thought in his female fans, apparently: "So you'd like to be Mrs. Hudson?"[36]

Incidentally, the embodiment of machismo that was created by the fan magazines may not have found its way directly into his fifties movies. Although his virtues of quiet dependability and assurance are observable in some of his Douglas Sirk roles, especially in *Written on the Wind* (1956), he is cast as less stable and more "sensitive" and "intuitively" understanding of women, a man with whom a woman would be "safe," in, for example Sirk's *All That Heaven Allows* (1955) and *The Tarnished Angels* (1957).

It is clear from the book alone that the creation of Hudson's heterosexual image was expected to dovetail with the social expectations of manliness popular in fifties America. It is indicated, for example, that men had short hair, held their cigarettes between thumb and first finger, and that the military look, post-Korea, was in. So were homophobia and homophobic jokes. Another dearly held popular belief in the fifties was that one was either "normal" or "queer," with bisexuality being a cop-out. The consensus was that a bisexual had simply not emerged from the closet.[37]

At this very time, the Kinsey report told the public something quite different, namely that "males do not represent two discrete populations, heterosexual and homosexual." Most men fall between the extremes of exclusive homosexuality and exclusive heterosexuality. "For the first time, homosexuality was validated by a respected scientist, an impartial observer."[38] However, such conclusions from the Kinsey report seem to have made no dent on public homophobia.

Some of that public homophobia appears, not surprisingly, to have been internalized by Hudson. We are told that he was attracted to women but preferred men. He preferred men who were "tall, well built and manly." Moreover, a man who "liked women" was rendered by reason of that propensity more masculine in Hudson's eyes.[39]

It may be surprising, in view of Hudson's awareness of his image and ability to analyze it even as he found himself complicit in some of the thinking which produced it, to find that the biography he and Sara Davidson produced believes, as all showbiz biographies seem to believe, that it can achieve truth. "It's time to tell my story," Hudson says. "It's time to set things straight." Davidson appears to credit this. Although she declares that she has "put together" the narrative "from many views," her aim is no less than "to find out: what was the truth?"[40]

She takes the central question in Hudson's career as whether his marriage to Phyllis Gates was "real" or not—an odd identification of centrality. In making this choice, she must be aware of being doomed to disappointment in her quest. She notes, in this regard, that because one principal is dead and the other unsure what happened, the question is "still unresolved." Gates's opinion—"I don't believe it was genuine. . . . I used to say he did better acting at home than at the studio"—seems clear enough, on the other hand. The notion that underlies Gates's remarks, that there are acted and entirely unacted, "genuine" emotions, may seem naive in any context but especially in that of Hollywood. Yet it is a notion that also evidently underlies the biography itself. Davidson goes on to offer her conclusion, that he did genuinely love Phyllis, that he did not marry her "with cold calculation," and that, as a romantic with romantic ideas about marriage and family, he had intended the marriage to last.[41] What this fanciful reconstruction has to do with the kind of "truth" that she is seeking is difficult to determine.

Davidson is, on the evidence of her writing alone, "positioned." Like Anita Bryant, though for quite different reasons, she presents herself from the position of ordinary common sense and of "normality." "What was I getting into?" she asks the reader as she recounts what she explicitly characterizes as the bizarre life-style of Hudson's household when she first interviewed him. In describing her encounter with Marc Christian, whom she describes as "bisexual," she finds his evasiveness sinister, because "people don't usually forget the way they met their lovers."[42] The imposition of her "healthy, normal" standards upon an interviewee who has to produce answers that he knows will be public property must limit the practicability of her ambitions to truth telling.

If the writer is, as all writers must be, socially, sexually, and politically positioned, so must be those who speak with her. Her blithe unawareness of the role played by her own history is almost replicated in her attitude to her interviewees. She does, admittedly, indicate some awareness that stories change as the tellers' motivation may itself change. Davidson is given good advice. Nader tells her, for example: "There are many Rock Hudsons. He projects what will appeal to the person he's with." A friend offers a caveat that seems essential for all writers of oral histories: "You never know who's telling you what for what reason." Yet, implicit in her approach to this biography is an expectation that she can arrive at "the truth." This would be a fond hope in any context but unusually foolish in the context of acting and image making and image preserving. As Marc Christian is reported as saying, "Rock always had to live his life in secrets. . . . He kept things from everyone."[43] Presumably, he would keep things from his biographer in particular, given her attitudes, since these seem to mirror attitudes popular in his fans.

It would be less surprising if Phyllis Gates, rather than Sara

Davidson, found the question of the "reality" of Hudson's marriage with her to be "central." She takes it upon herself to write a book about the event, with Bob Thomas.[44] Once again, it is her presentation of herself that may be more interesting than the "real story" purported to be told. Gates portrays herself as a simple, sweet ingenue dazzled by Hudson's charm and puzzled by his friends and by his evasions. Thus, her first date felt "like high-school" ("He was the best dancer I had ever known."). Yet, she records an evening with Hudson, "handsome blond" Craig Hill, and his agent, Henry Willson, in quite other tones. "The three maintained a giddy conversation of total trivia, laughing merrily at their lame *bons mots*."[45] The picture given here is of the disapproving heterosexual dejected by the "giddiness," "triviality," and "lame wit" of three men enjoying what is evidently coded to represent a gay evening out together.

While her judgments seem in this case designed to flatter homophobic prejudice, Gates evidences awareness of some problem in her account of herself, even at the time of the marriage as well as at the present day. A disappointed heterosexual woman who has not remarried seems called on to furnish an explanation, if her readers are the sort that the book seems to be written for. "Over the years there have been other men in my life. I almost married one of them. But I could never bring myself to fall in love again." She also troubles to explain—and to render beyond suspicion—her close friendship with another unmarried woman. "I tossed the bridal bouquet to Pat, of course, since she was the only unmarried woman there. I knew that she was wishing her own wedding would come soon." She also feels impelled to explain her lack of children since, even by her own admission, Hudson did fulfill his conjugal duties. She claims that "naturally" she wanted a family, but that "at thirty, Rock and I were still fairly young."[46]

It should be stressed at this point that the present writer has no knowledge of Phyllis Gates, her sexuality or her personality, and attention should be directed to the definite possibility that what is written in her name may not be her unghosted words. There is no suggestion that she is not presenting her thoughts on marriage, childlessness, and absence of remarriage candidly. What is being pointed out is that there is an urge evident in the book to placate the censoriousness and inquisitiveness of the kind of public who could be expected to side with her in her suffering in the presence of giddy, trivial young men.

Gates's account of homosexuality, and of what she takes to be its essential component, effeminacy, says much about the prejudices which she embodies, or which she assures her readership that she embodies. Hudson's agent, while not effeminate, was "not exactly what you would consider manly," because he loved gossip and could be "bitchy" about people that he avowedly did not like. She finds the relationship between Hudson and his mother embarrassingly cloying. When Hudson was in a dour mood, she says, "he seemed almost overcome with self-loathing." She also attributes jealousy to him (of James Dean) and reports that he cried over Dean's death, "blaming himself" for his jealousy. She reports his misogyny—in particular his revulsion from female genitalia and in his slapping her.[47]

Yet after she has completed a picture of a man suffering from all the "typical" vices of the male homosexual, she reports her amazement about the *Confidential* magazine threat to publish a story about a homosexual gang bang in which he was allegedly involved. She refuses at this late point in their relationship to believe that he could be homosexual because, amazingly, "He had always been the manliest of men." She had fewer doubts about Henry Willson. When Henry calls her a bitch, she reports that she could not resist the retort, "Well, Henry, it takes one to know one."[48] For her, homosexuality is a matter of nonmanliness, while heterosexuality, the only possible converse, is a matter of manliness.

While she claims difficulty in recognizing Hudson's homosexuality, the book offers a heterosexual's account of the genesis of that homosexuality. Thus, she takes it upon herself to report the absence of Hudson's father and the overprotectiveness of his mother, the influence of the less-than-manly Henry Willson ("Rock was his consenting Galatea"). His sexual intercourse with her is described in terms of effort—"He did manage some lovemaking." She notes that he indulged in no physical activity other than gardening.[49]

The "official" record on Rock Hudson (from Ronald Reagan) presents a somewhat different picture of him. "Nancy and I are saddened. Rock Hudson will be remembered for his humanity, his sympathetic spirit and his well-deserved reputation for kindness. May God rest his soul."[50]

Because Hudson was a star who was inevitably, given the economic pressures attendant on Hollywood success in the fifties, created for homophobes and who, tragically, goes on being interpreted "from the outside," in the light of heterosexual conceptions of homosexuality, of masculinity and femininity, and of AIDS as a gay disease, his physical sufferings were much increased by a sense of shame. "He felt he'd committed a crime against his public. That was his main concern—that the public would find out. He said one night, 'I hope I die of a heart attack before they find out I have AIDS. If only that would happen . . .' "[51] The tabloid press in Britain, as he might have expected, obliged by denouncing the star's "dishonesty" and his "betrayal" of his fans' fantasies, and by imputing a sense of his own responsibility for his illness.[52]

If AIDS gained "reality" through his death—"the world is tuned in to AIDS because of you"[53]—it was a peculiar kind of reality which he brought to it. He was conceived as a particular kind of male star and forced to remain within that conception of maleness even after his death, where his meaning remains filtered through, and manipulated by, heterosexist assumptions about his entire life and illness. Even without these considerable factors, there is another problem. Randy Shilts accepts that Hudson's death is a watershed for American attitudes to AIDS. However, "by the time America paid attention to the disease, it was too late to do anything about it."[54]

12
Some Key Films

What appear to be key films, in relation to the peculiar moods of the eighties in the United States and Britain, may be thought to appear that way because of individual predilections and observations. In other words, what seems a key film to one person may seem anything but to another. It would be fair to suspect that significance is in the eye of the beholder.

All the same, it is worth remarking that four out of the seven films touched on in this chapter were released in the last year of the eighties. Three of these were prestigious films or else highly popular at the box office. The other one of these, *Society,* could be thought to be headed for that peculiar form of future existence—the cult movie. Cults are difficult to predict with any certainty, however. The principal reason why it has joined the other three 1989 films is that it seems to qualify as the down-market, popularized version, in many respects, of the distinctly up-market, self-consciously "arty" *The Cook, The Thief, His Wife and Her Lover.*

It may seem like overcompensation for the concentration on the end of the eighties that one so-called key film actually precedes the eighties. *Shivers* has been chosen because today it apparently predicts, or rather foreshadows, the kind of plague and sex = death thinking that underlies popular reaction, with press encouragement, to fear of AIDS.

The other two movies—*Fatal Attraction* and *Planes, Trains and Automobiles*—belong to the latter half of the eighties. While there is no direct allusion to AIDS—paradoxically, there seems to be clearer reference to it in *Shivers* at a time when such reference is "impossible"—in *Fatal Attraction,* the movie is saturated in sexual and familial ideology which is by no means limited to the eighties but which is a key part of the undercurrents which flow beneath the worst excesses of AIDS rhetoric. The John Hughes comedy clearly comments on the familial in distinction to all that "territory" out there over which planes, trains, and automobiles drag the hapless husband-hero, introducing him to experiences which he largely loathes and which were undreamed of by him before the comedic nightmare begins. This is one of the few ostensibly light-entertainment movies that directly confronts what middle-class familialism excludes, and takes on these attitudes during a decade that has given political currency to "family" while it silences all that is excluded by that term (at least as it is used by politicians).

While another commentator might make quite other selections in the name of "key films," these very different kinds of films chosen here convey a surprisingly full set of images of the eighties. The movies may look relatively expensive *(Born on the Fourth of July)* or relatively cheap *(Shivers);* may wear their serious intentions on their sleeves *(Born; The Cook, The Thief, His Wife and Her Lover)* or discourage audiences from taking them seriously *(Planes)*; may seem like a war movie *(Born)* or a thriller *(Fatal Attraction)* or an extended pilot for a sitcom *(Parenthood)*; but there are definite resemblances among them which cross genres, as well as the divide between art movie and schlock horror.

Born on the Fourth of July (Oliver Stone, 1989)

Adapted from his own published account, the movie is uncontroversially a version of the experience of the paraplegic Vietnam veteran Ron Kovic. It starts with his early experiences in Massapequa, New York, concentrating on his tenth birthday on 4 July 1956, where he watches a patriotic parade involving disabled veterans (among others). Later, he is with his family as they listen to JFK's inaugural address on radio. His school life—embracing such incidents as his losing a public wrestling bout, the visit of a recruiter for Vietnam, his "gate-crashing" of the senior prom to enjoy one dance with his childhood sweetheart, Donna—is recorded. So is his experience in Vietnam, particularly his shocked witnessing of the "mistake" of a massacred Vietnamese family and his own mistake in shooting dead a combatant from his own side. After his spinal cord is severed by a sniper's bullet, his failure to reintegrate into his family and nation, once he has emerged from the hellish experience of a filthy, uncaring veterans' hospital, is dramatized. So is his period in Mexico, where he drinks and, as best he can, whores along with his disabled erstwhile buddies. The film centers on his self-reaffirmation through his antiwar politics. He fights back when he is ejected from the Republican Convention at Miami in 1972 and becomes a media celebrity through his appearance on television.

The film's climax appears to be Kovic's address to the 1976 Democratic Convention as an honored guest.

Ostensibly, then, the film's subject is Kovic and, because Kovic
became an anti-Vietnam celebrity who cast into doubt the values
taught him by his lower-middle-class family, his school, the Catholic
church to which his mother was so devoted, and gung-ho movies of
the fifties, the film seems of necessity to be anti-Vietnam, casting
into question these same values. Not surprisingly, the film's fiercest
critics seem politically motivated (not least of these hostile critics
being the Reagan administration). Because the film is taken to be a
bio-pic, which happens to support Kovic's line on himself and on
the war which nearly destroyed him, it is attacked for its "falsity" or
"bias." Reagan's spokespersons take Kovic and thus the film to task
for several alleged inaccuracies in its portrayal of real people or real
incidents. One of the most mean-spirited reviews comes from
Pauline Kael, who regularly reacts venomously to movies which
question establishment thinking from what she detects to be a left-
wing (and therefore, to her, inevitably exaggerated) position. Kael's
line is one where she seems to imagine that a free market in
ideology operated for Kovic in the fifties. Surely he could have read
Mad magazine if he wanted a counterblast against the chauvinistic
pieties which, after all, his own brother did not swallow whole.
Even the less obviously conservative attacks on the film attempt to
take the line that everybody already knows that Vietnam was "a
bad war." Everybody clearly did not know it, at least at the time,
surely. Why else would the United States have been so bitterly
polarized by the war?

Further thinking is called for regarding the relevance of attacks
on Stone's film from the point of view of historical inaccuracies. A
critic as knowledgeable about Vietnam as John Pilger attacks this
and other American movies on Vietnam for failing to set the record
straight about the exploitative nature of American involvement and
for deliberately obfuscating the far greater significance that this war
had for the Vietnamese, of the South as well as of the North. Yet he
may be missing the point. Vietnam for American consciousness has
become a matter of media representation. Belief about Vietnam,
the way the story is now told and believed to have happened, may
be crucial. Part of that belief is that America "made mistakes." The
character of Rambo was created as a way of shoring up confidence
in the wake of even that much-modified belief. It is probable that
young Americans in the late eighties gain their information about
the war from comic books and from the Stone movies as well as

from those where Sylvester Stallone redresses the unacceptable balance of history. In that sense, we clearly do *not* all know that Vietnam was a bad war. It may even be that some of the more uninformed film fans believe that the war was not lost by the United States (and South Vietnam).

Interestingly, Stone chose to make this film not in 1978, when he bought the rights to Kovic's book,[1] because that was a period of "national malaise." Although the upbeat ending of the film centers on Kovic's personal triumph at the 1976 Democratic Convention, and although that convention nominated Carter, Stone seems to realize that the United States did not see Carter's presidency in the triumphant light that the movie might otherwise imply. Moreover, the making of both *Platoon* and the present film in the later eighties may be significant. (It was possible to make a movie as disturbing as *The Deer Hunter* in the midseventies, after all.) Stone's account of Kovic's experiences and Kovic's politics is offered in the wake of the Rambo movies and at a time when British television viewers were being urged, through the screening of *Tumbledown,* to question the glory and glamour of the Falklands War as the Thatcher government portrayed it—at least in as far as its cruelly damaged (again, real-life) hero's being hidden away as the unacceptable face of war is concerned. *Born,* because it is markedly less about the Vietnam War than about public attitudes to it, public beliefs about it, also takes on the authority of church and family in a period when allegedly Christian, and therefore allegedly familial, values have made a political comeback.

It is a film which in some ways epitomizes present-day Hollywood movies but which, in others, represents an attack on Hollywood ideology. John Wayne movies, according to *Born,* helped to put Kovic into the war. Yet the questioning of militaristic, macho values is not restricted to criticism of fifties films. It is surely not possible for the fans of Tom Cruise, who plays Kovic in the movie, to dissociate him entirely from the Cruise who played the hero of *Top Gun,* the highest-grossing movie of 1986. The latter movie celebrated personal heroism, male glamour, machismo, following a tradition that emanates from long before the John Wayne movies and that finds expression already in the eighties with *An Officer and a Gentleman.*

The mistake of seeing *Born* as just another Vietnam movie may be signaled by the fact that only seventeen minutes of this lengthy work is devoted to the Vietnam conflict (shot, disconcertingly and antirealistically, as if the camera were mounted on a typewriter carriage). A crucial thematic in the film is winning/losing. This binary opposition is not merely to be understood in its obvious sense but in another—of the winner/the loser. Because a young school student loses a wrestling match, this does not in every society indicate that he is "a loser." In this film, it does, though. Kovic weeps when he cannot quite find the strength to hold out against his opponent. Significantly, his shame is shared by his family and girlfriend. The wrestling scene is an unusually economical indicator of why Kovic goes to war, and why his self-assessment undergoes such radical revision as a result of his being persistently treated as a war hero on his return. The notion of losing and winning is easily comprehensible. The conversion of losing and winning into the identities of the loser and the winner is a different matter. (The same person can be a winner if he plays the part of brave veteran, a loser when he "gives in" to self-pity.)

In an obvious sense, the United States lost the Vietnam War. The dread of being "a loser" permeates seventies society in a way which helps to explain the national experience of the late seventies and thus of the Carter years. The dread is not met head-on in the Reagan years but is bypassed. America is allowed to "start feeling good about herself." The invention of Rambo—and Reagan's publicly voiced approval of the movie hero and of his tactics underscores this—was almost a cultural necessity in the eighties. As J. Hoberman observes: "While Stallone's perfect Nautilus-built pecs assuaged America's mutilated masculinity, Kovic's book, Stone's movie, and Cruise's gritty performance are all intimately concerned with the wasting of the body."[2]

This quotation provides a further clue to the "real" subject of the movie, a subject which it shares with several of the other movies discussed in this chapter—corporeality. Rambo's body must, importantly, be "perfect" and impregnable for the myth of his invincibility to restore American confidence. Kovic's body is not. He could not quite find the reserves to win the school wrestling match. When his spine is shot at, he loses the ability to walk, to be mobile without his wheelchair. He loses the power "to be a man," in that he cannot make love, at least in conventional ways. Most significantly, he loses his youth and beauty. The body degenerates and decays before the spectator's eyes.

"Who's gonna love me?" he yells at his father. The question goes well beyond the hero's plight. It draws attention to the interdependence of desire and physical functioning. It also draws attention to the peculiarly intimate, desiring relationship between cinema spectator and charismatic star. Tom Cruise's good looks and sculpted physique help to explain his appeal in such other eighties movies as

Risky Business and *Top Gun*. The question that the film dares to
pose is, Who's gonna love Tom Cruise when he loses his looks? He
starts by looking fresh-faced, clean-shaven, crew-cut. After his war
experience, he becomes scruffy, his hair becomes lank (and, worse,
he shows signs of balding). This is achieved by his donning of a wig,
but it proved so effective that Universal felt real anxiety that their
star looked so unappealing. The withholding of sympathy, and
certainly admiration, from a star who refuses to look like one
during most of the movie is an evident risk. That Cruise does not
sacrifice sympathy may indicate something about knowledge of the
star—that under the makeup and the balding wig he remains whole
and handsome—as well as his acting talents. Nevertheless, the fear
that his physical declension unleashed in the studio illustrates the
bond between approved physical appearance and humane sentiments. In this aspect of its operations, the film approaches *The
Fly*'s territory. Who's gonna love a man who does not look like one,
who may, therefore, not be one? The emphasis on the body and its
(non-) functioning after the usual fashions touches a sensitive
nerve. Is human understanding limited by physical recognizability,
in terms of what is culturally believed to be "natural" human
physicality? If it is, how much more limited can that understanding
be in a society which is encouraged to admire winning or to feel that
physical impairment is, at some level, attributable to the weakness
of the person physically impaired?

The emphasis on the collapse of the body helps to explain the
power of that central portion of the movie devoted to Kovic's
experience of the veterans' hospital, a portion which even the film's
detractors felt impelled to express some admiration for. The hospital is filthy. The floor is urine-soaked, rats scuttle about beneath the
patients' beds, the unattended sick can lie upside down, strapped
into their beds, staring at their own vomit until help belatedly
arrives. The body at the mercy of the uncaring in an environment
which seems paradoxically to encourage only the fittest to survive
has seldom been better illustrated outside horror or pornography.
While broken bodies suffer, junkies shoot up in the hospital closets.

Many have noticed that the black nurses and orderlies are
"disaffected." They care nothing for the war, for one thing. They
show little regard for the lives in their care, for another. Yet, the
critics of the film fail to tie in their disaffection with their social
status. Like the new Kovic, as he will reluctantly discover, his
attendants are seen as "losers" and learn to behave as such. The
sacrifice of blacks in the Vietnam War could be seen as dispropor-
tionately high. At one level, this makes the orderlies' contempt for

the war wounded less "acceptable." At another, it reveals a basis for their contempt for the war, its being also a contempt for the war's official ideology. Treated as society's refuse, the nurses and orderlies create an environment where they can act out that societal destiny. Kovic's physical unattractiveness and the Mexican-brothel sequences especially supply a counterpart to the hospital staff's creation of hell around them. In an obvious sense, the hell that is created is created *for* them by a governmental attitude that warfare is about heroes, whole heroes, who are admirable as long as they persist in looking like Tom Cruise and as long as they take their place in patriotic parades or make patriotic speeches in their hometowns. Kovic's difficulty in recognizing the human beings beneath the attitudes and appearances of the nurses and orderlies will be mirrored in the film by his family's inability to see him beneath the paraplegic he appears entirely to be.

The film may be read, with its emphasis on beauty and innocence before Vietnam and its contrast with ugliness and knowledge after it, in terms of the myth of Eden. Hoberman says of Massapequa in 1956, as filmed here, "It's the last American paradise."[3] The quality of a dream is repeatedly discernible in the 1956 sequences (and this becomes a romantic dream in the senior-prom sequence, where Kovic runs through the rain to his sweetheart to the music of "Moon River"). The sun is refracted in the trees, spring buds fill the air. The cinematographer, Robert Richardson, substantiates the reading of 1956 Massapequa as a dream of family, community, nation: "A heightened reflection of reality was sought after. We chose a dream-like interpretation of *Life* magazine photography. Atmosphere prevailed. We used an abundance of smoke, rain and pollen in the air. Shadows were reduced and the colors of a fairytale came to life. There was a golden ambience which symbolised the era and its innocence. . . . The lensing was wide and low to capture the sense of community from a child's perspective."[4] The dream is Kovic's. His dreaming serves to remove Massapequa from its geographical setting. Thus, it is beside the point to complain that the small town looks Midwestern rather than Eastern. (It also looks remarkably like the California town of Elia Kazan's *East of Eden* [1954].) His small-town dream is a dream of America.

If pre-Vietnam Massapequa is Eden, the Fall is the experience of Vietnam and also of immediately post-Vietnam suffering in the veterans' hospital and then back in Massapequa. Tom Berenger plays the charismatic recruiter who visits Kovic's high school, Berenger's being a face made familiar in similar contexts by *Platoon.*

The nightmare begins in Vietnam, with the fatal "mistakes" and the unheroic quality of the fighting, as well as Kovic's wounding. It continues with the rats-in-the-bedpans hospital, the return to a sexually repressive and chauvinistic family home, and the self-expulsion from the former Eden to the brothels of Mexico. The religious significance of the Eden myth, with knowledge and the Fall coinciding, is altered in Stone's film nonetheless. Knowledge comes slowly, after the Fall, after the expulsion, and the knowledge is liberating. The exclusion which is in one sense a fact is no longer internalized as such. It is as if the stress in the Adam/Eve story were placed not on the Fall from divine grace and the loss of the Garden but on defiance of God and an awareness that the Garden was only a wishful dream.

The Cook, the Thief, His Wife and Her Lover
(Peter Greenaway, 1989)

The title of Greenaway's film makes it evident that its characters are to be seen as embodiments, types that would be familiar within Jacobean melodrama, and not as psychologically rounded, idiosyncratic personalities.

The Cook (Richard Bohringer) has been taken, by Greenaway no less, to represent the filmmaker: "The Cook is me."⁵ He can be understood as a voyeur, a man who takes pleasure in watching the highly physical love affair developing between the Wife and her Lover. Perhaps more crucially, he can be seen as the artist of the kitchen, willing to swallow humiliation so that he can practice his culinary arts. The insults that he accepts from the Thief are of no account when these are compared with his need to express himself in his cuisine. Although this facet has not been picked up by critics or enunciated as such by Greenaway in his many comments on the film, it is not stretching credibility to see a commentary in this on the Thatcher government's encouragement of sponsorship as a means, other than state subsidy, for the financing of high art.

The Thief (Michael Gambon) is a free-market gangster who never stops talking for long. His incessant monologue of sexual and corporeal insults to his wife, and of contempt for his fellow-dining henchmen, is reminiscent of some of John Osborne's more tiresome heroes' soliloquies. His surname, Spica, has credibly been explained by Greenaway as a pun on "speaker." Although his violence—to a woman when he sticks a fork in her cheek, to a young boy when he tortures him in his quest for information about his

Wife's whereabouts—is presented as repulsive, it is the extreme irritation that is set up in the audience as he pollutes every dish with his wearisome monologue, as he indulges his lavatorial humor or demonstrates his crude power over the chef or his wife, his henchmen or unknown diners, that loses all sympathy for the character. (Violence in gangster characters can be notoriously appealing in films.) "There is a new philistinism in England, a new, vulgar attitude toward culture, toward any currency other than cash," Greenaway claims.[6] The Thief is self-evidently the most philistine and vulgar in his attitude to the Cook's arts, even as he admires them and attempts to make culinary awareness his own talent. What he controls, he controls less through his bouts of violence than by the sustained power of the purse. He "owns" his wife, the Cook's skills, his gang, even the diners through his part-ownership of the restaurant. (In a rare moment of self-assertion, the Cook insists on buying his own meat and fish when the Thief attempts to induce him to buy vanloads of it from him directly.) Some of the power of the narrative resides in its demonstration of limits to his ownership. Perhaps, though, the triumph of love and of culture are desperate moments of optimism, much as the final dispatch of the Thief seems to Greenaway to be (as if so much evil could be dispelled so quickly and easily).

Both *Born* and *The Cook* could be thought "phallically fixated" in the short shrift they give to their female characters. Ron Kovic's Donna disappears from the screen and from our, as well as his, thoughts after her part in a brutally suppressed student demonstration. While the Wife (Helen Mirren) of Greenaway's film is still on screen at the climax of the film and it is she who kills the Thief, Georgina is largely a victim empowered by physical love. At times, she is reduced to being a naked Eve, expelled naked from her version of Eden with her Adam in a van seething with decaying, worm-infested carcasses of meat. Her Lover (Alan Howard), while also victimized (he dies after an assault on him, by having pages of one of his beloved books stuffed down his throat), is provided with the burden of representing High Culture. He is seen as the antitype to the Thief. For one thing, he is silent for a remarkable length of the film's running time, even though within earshot of the ever-garrulous Albert Spica. He appreciates the food, consuming it at the same time as reading and apparently blocking out Spica's monotonous tirades of abuse. His nakedness in the van of rotting meat is more ambiguous than the Wife's, more self-assertive at the same time as it offers him up as an unarmed victim, the Leavisite man of culture rendered almost powerless in a world run by philistines.

More interesting than the representations of qualities and cultural characteristics through the types of the title may be the semiotic potential of the various parts of the restaurant building. What remains in the mind after the characters' speeches and motivations have become blurred are the tracking shots by which the camera enters and leaves each part of the restaurant area. These are, from left to right, the car-park area outside the restaurant proper, the kitchens, the dining room. Somewhere else in the building, behind the dining room and close to the kitchens, is the lavatory area. Somewhere quite else is the children's ward (where the tortured boy soprano of the kitchen scenes ends up) and the bookstore (to which Adam and Eve make their escape and where the Lover is killed). Each area has its own color coding and its own range of associations, in both temporal and painterly terms.

The car-park area has been aptly termed "post-industrial apocalyptic" by Adam Mars-Jones.[7] This is the area of scavenging wild dogs, refuse, and not even the pretence of lawfulness, where a man who has offended Albert Spica has dog turds forced into his mouth and is urinated on by him. It is part of the restaurant and yet not "recognized" by it, its squalor being explicable only in terms of the detritus from the restaurant, some of that detritus human in form.

The kitchen has a medieval air about it, a spacious cooking area which the camera prowls like a visitor anxious to sniff the beguiling smells from the saucepots and boiling pans. (Sean French, alternatively, sees the kitchen as essentially eighteenth-century.)[8]

The dining area of the restaurant is the most opulent of all. The diners wear Jean-Paul Gaultier creations. Above the diners is a massive reproduction of Franz Hals's 1616 painting "Banquet of Officers of the St. George Civic Guard Company," which seems to comment on the debased twentieth-century version, the Thief's nightly companions, within a room designed in nineteenth-century style. Greenaway sees the restaurant as a form of cathedral, where the table is an altar and there is a chancel, nave, and choir.[9]

By contrast with all of these, the most late-twentieth-century architecture is reserved for the lavatories, which are high-tech in design.

The whole ensemble as metaphor for Thatcher's Britain is difficult to resist: the vulgar opulence of the dining area and the lavatories, with their diners whose passport to this consumer paradise is simply money, the kitchen area with its servants (and artist) in their "proper place," the wasteland of the car-park, dependent on the restaurant and yet scarcely acknowledged by it.

The color coding of the areas is highly schematized. Thus, the car-park is shot in a cold blue light, the kitchen is colored green, the restaurant plush red, and the high-tech lavatories are pinkish-white. While the children's ward is colored yellow (explained as the color of an egg yolk by Greenaway),[10] the bookstore is brown, with gold to conjure up associations of gold leaf, the lettering on old book spines. That the architectural entities marked off by different design and color are ultimately meant to have explicatory power is indicated by, for example, the fact that Helen Mirren's clothes change hue as she leaves the restaurant for the lavatory.

It would be difficult not to see the film as "painterly" even without knowledge of Greenaway's commitment to the Great (and particularly Dutch) Masters. He himself points the way to a reading of the film not simply as an aesthetic experience but in terms of thematics. "Dutch painting revels in food as the epitome of satiated bourgeois aspiration."[11]

The film's alleged inspiration in Jacobean melodrama, its similarities to John Ford's 'Tis Pity She's a Whore, is explained by Greenaway not simply as evidence of the temporal coincidence of Jacobean melodrama with the golden age of Dutch painting but, once again, as evidence of his interest in corporeality.[12]

His vision has been seen as "cold" in all his film work, even in this film wherein passion both carnal and vengeful is explored. Certainly he eschews the traditional "grammar" of dominant cinema, in that he refuses point-of-view shots (at least as these are identifiable with human characters' points of view) as well as reaction shots. The camera provides little clue as to the identity of the perceiver. The perceiver would share a discarnated God's point of view if, perhaps, that point of view were not fixed largely at gut level in this most consumption-oriented of all his films. Greenaway would defend his decision not to allow his films to make emotional connections with their audiences by citing painting as an art form where intense psychological identification on the part of the viewer is not required.

Interestingly, a film about appetite and philistinism allied with conspicuous consumption is designed to be digested (or refused) by cerebration, even if its effects are unusually, for an art movie, shocking and, often, appealing to the senses. "The film's basic metaphor is the alimentary canal. . . . [The film] is about greed, power, sex and violence in our modern consumerist society; it's about how everything passes from the mouth to the anus."[13] He reveals a world in which everything can be consumed, including, finally, the Lover, or, initially, excrement, in which consumers will tolerate a barrage of verbal and even physical abuse in order to be allowed to consume.

Although all of Stone's 1989 film could be seen to turn on the mythology of Eden, a significant part of Greenaway's film pivots on it as well. The God who turns Adam and Eve, appropriately naked and ashamed, out of Eden is the free-market Thief. Their rescue is through the good offices of the Cook, who allows them to use the Thief's van of rotting meat for their getaway. (Inevitably, their hitherto corporeal beauty becomes potentially corruptible into rot and decay by the juxtaposition of their bodies with worm-eaten, stinking carcasses.) As with Stone's post-Edenic hero, they rebel sufficiently to establish their own version of the Garden in the book depository. Georgina rebels against and destroys her former God in the final act of the film's narrative.

Again, as the flight from Eden reminds us, the real subject of this work, as arguably of Stone's, is corporeality, the emphasis on flesh as flesh, body as body, an organism which consumes and excretes. The dining area of the restaurant strenuously denies its knowledge of body functions, despite Spica's deliberately offensive reminders to Georgina and other diners. It does so by its opulence, by its dressing up of eating and the bodies of those present. "There is a mediaeval-like feeling in *The Cook, the Thief* about this rotten, worm-infested body which is covered in an extraordinary gloss of elaborate clothing, feathered hats and that sort of thing."[14] Even what could be seen as honest carnality in the context of the dining-room's consumerism is depicted as "carnality" demands, in highly physical terms. Greenaway goes so far as to see the lovers' delight in verbal dalliance as a form of intercourse which has associations with fellatio.[15]

The meaning of Greenaway's extraordinary film has been claimed to reside in the director's biography (his revenge on the philistines who refused him financing for this work, for example). His anti-Thatcher sentiments are on record, even if he does not wish the film to be read totally in such political terms. Perhaps the most remarkable element in the film is the way that it shares obsessional concern with the experience of the body with such low-brow genres as horror and "epic war-movie" (though *Born* only seems to be so categorizable at first glance). It shares this also with the Comic Strip's late-eighties morality *Eat the Rich*. Consumption is not abstract in its treatment here. It involves eating, digesting, and evacuating. The body may be sexually arousing as spectacle and, in the case of Alan Howard's, mock-appetizing as a piece of cuisine, but it also decays, diminishes, rots, and smells. Consumerist society knows this but chooses to ignore it and to concentrate on the "acceptable," aesthetically pleasing parts of bodily experience and of consumption. The job of Ron Kovic in the Stone film, of the Wife in the Greenaway, is to make consumerist bourgeois society look hard, unblinkingly, at the body not just for what it is in itself but for what it has been turned into by that society.

Society (Brian Yuzna, 1989)

This movie is the American mainstream horror version, in some obvious senses, of the British art movie from Greenaway just discussed. Both films deal with the amorality of the rich and powerful, or rather of those whom wealth automatically makes powerful in nations which, as Greenaway puts it, know the price of everything but the value of nothing. Both films also deal with conspicuous consumption including, finally, the consumption of human flesh.

Bill Whitney (Billy Warlock), the good-looking teenage hero of *Society,* appears to have a great deal going for him, to be a "winner." He has a rich family, drives a macho black jeep, appears to be a star of the school debating society, and is successful enough with the opposite sex to have a blond cheerleader as his girlfriend. Still, he suffers what appear to be unpleasant hallucinations (about, for example, his sister's anatomy) and is dogged by the anxiety that he does not really belong within the family in which he finds himself. His psychiatrist explains his feelings as an extreme example of teenage alienation and discourages him from crediting his perceptions with any element of veracity.

The movie's narrative sets up the possibility that Bill may indeed be seeing the truth. Confirmation of this possibility appears to be provided in the form of a tape smuggled out by Bill's friend—and his sister's former boyfriend—Blanchard (Tim Bartell). On the tape, Bill hears the aural record of his sister's "coming-out" party, and believes that he now has evidence of incestuous sexual relationships between his parents and their daughter, the party becoming more of an orgy than a debutante's coming out. Yet when he hands the tape over to his psychiatrist, it bears no such evidence of debauchery the next time he listens to it under the doctor's supervision. Moreover, its source, Blanchard, is apparently killed in a car accident, so that his only means of confirming what he heard has gone.

Yet, not for the first time in the horror genre, his "paranoia" is well-founded, his worst fears prove true. Incest is only part of the reality that surrounds him. He is, just as he felt, not truly a blood relation of the family that claims him, but an adopted son, recruited to be the victim rather than the heir of its wealth. As the naked, slime-covered judge informs him at the final orgy of the movie, "You're a different race from us, a different species, a different class. . . . You have to be *born* into Society." The top people, to whom the name "Society" is applied, are the elite of Beverly Hills, and yet they are mutated aliens, not recognizable human beings, or at least not recognizable for long once the "shunting" orgy which forms the film's finale begins. The orgy requires sacrificial victims. Blanchard and Bill are to be those victims on this occasion.

Bill sees, to his horror, that these Society folk can change shape, alter body parts not only in their own bodies but by taking the body parts of others into themselves. His adoptive mother and father, along with his believed sister, not only perform sex together but physically use anatomical details from one another to form new shapes and re-form into still stranger ones. "Society" softens up the flesh of its victims by applying lips to the skin and sucking so voraciously upon it that the mouths become indistinguishable from the victims' flesh. This preparatory element is called "sucking off." The apparently aristocratic schoolmate tormentor of Bill's, Ted Ferguson (Ben Meyerson), helpfully explains, "The rich have always sucked off low-class shit like you." "Shunting" is the name applied to the terminally violent act of turning the victim inside out, quite literally, by means of invasion via the anus. The revoltingly blubbery figure of the judge succeeds in the penetration of Blanchard and reaches his fist into his victim's head. Bill manages to disprove the belief in Society's unfailing dominance by reversing Ted's intentions and turning him inside out instead. As in *The Cook,* the outwardly healthy and handsome appearance of the body belies its worm-infested inner reality, suddenly revealed when the inner becomes the outer in the remarkably unpleasant final minutes of the film.

The connection of the viscerally horrid and the sexual, which underlies much of the horror genre, is rendered with new force in the Yuzna movie. The incest taboo is only one aspect of what is broken within the narrative. As Michael O'Pray observes, "The violation of the incest taboo implies perhaps that the ultimate appetite to be satisfied is beyond sex."[16] This may be only partly right, however. Rather than exploring violations which go beyond sex, the film seems to show that all its violations of "human rules" are rooted in sex. "Sucking off" has its own obvious sexual sense, as a term, but that its sexual basis should not be missed by the audience, the penultimate assault on the sacrificial victims is portrayed in an obviously sexual way. The fastening of wizened, ravening mouths on the chubby naked body of the first victim, Blanchard, looks like part of a sadistic sexual orgy. When the first act in Ted Ferguson's attempted shunting of Bill involves the planting of his mouth on the young hero's, it certainly looks as if they are passionately kissing, whatever the motivation offered within the logic of shunting. Yuzna reports that audiences were more upset by the handsome teenage boys apparently kissing than they were by the violence of the shunting. "Why," he asks, "are people more squeamish about sex than horror?"[17] Perhaps, it could be suggested, because certain sexual dreads underlie many horror movie motifs. Yuzna simply makes the connections much more explicit than usual. What O'Pray terms the "unsettling incoherence" between shunting and sex[18] may be exactly the point.

Just as Greenaway forced attention on the anus by his film's repeated references to excrement and to lavatories and by the Thief's obsessive interest in the lavatorial, shunting in *Society* seems to involve not simply preliminary "sucking off" but an assault on the entire male body by means of penetration of the anus, albeit with fist rather than penis. That "fisting" was, though potentially lethal, a variant on anal intercourse among certain homosexuals before the days of "safe sex" gives credibility to the shunting process. At one level, "sucking off" and "shunting," as demonstrated in *Society,* are bizarre, "impossible," nonhuman acts. At another, they have a basis in the culturally taboo areas of sexuality.

What is particularly repellent about the incestuous couplings of daughter and parents within this movie is not so much the incest per se as the interchangeability of body parts among those who have had sex together. It is as if the opening up of the body to sexual intercourse involves a loss of the borders of the self. Sexual acts may result in the mingling of limbs and faces from different bodies to make up a new whole. A particularly gruesome—shocking enough to produce laughter in the audience—example is the father's mouth appearing between his buttocks so that the authoritative parent is seen, to use the English slang, to be, quite literally, "talking out of his arse." The film is full of similar vulgarities. O'Pray mentions "the hand of the law," indicated when it appears all the way from the victim's anus in his head.[19] A more obvious reference, although the assailant is a judge and not a policeman, must surely be to "the long arm of the law."

Yuzna's inspiration in Salvador Dali and Hieronymus Bosch is evident in the riot of special effects in the final third of the movie. (These are credited to "Screaming Mad George.") The movie is a lengthy version of the sick joke, in such appallingly bad taste that it manages to be almost endearing, over-the-top enough to be less revolting than sober verbal description of the final orgy could suggest. The makers of *Society* have given physical expression, though, to deeply held fears of the eighties. They have gone well beyond the fears of incest that may arguably inspire much of horror, in making intimations of incest seem like unexciting fare. What they have tapped into, with much more contemporary relevance than these matters, includes: the fear that the rich and powerful are a separate species who can defy human conventions by virtue of not being human at all; the terror of losing control of one's physical individuality by the blurring of human boundaries through sex; the fear that outré sexuality and outré sexual acts may have lethal consequences in themselves; the male fear of rape, loss of power by external control over the anus. And, like the Greenaway film and the Stone film of the same year, the movie discovers potential horror in the exposure of corporeality, of the body as body, outwardly prettified to mask the putrefaction within.

Parenthood (Ron Howard, 1989)

Ron Howard's clearly popular movie (made for eighteen million dollars, it took in over ninety million at the box office) centers on families, four generations of them, ending with the birth of a fifth. There are no suggestions of incest, of Roman Catholic sexual repression, or of hysterical fear of communists (as with Ron Kovic's mother) and little concern with other races or creeds, although the movie is "modern" enough to touch on vibrators as masturbatory aids and on premarital sex.

The setting is Saint Louis, a city—as portrayed here—of green-lawned family homes. The patriarch is Frank Buckman (Jason Robards). He has sired two sons, two daughters. Most of the action takes place in the homes of or at least in the company of these four and their offspring. The eldest son, Gil (Steve Martin), married to Karen (Mary Steenburgen), is a responsible, loving father with three children and, it transpires in the course of the narrative, a fourth on the way. The younger son, Larry (Tom Hulce), by contrast is a work-shy, irresponsible man who brings to Frank Buckman's home his son by a black Las Vegas dancer, the son memorably named Cool. One daughter, Helen (Dianne Wiest), is divorced and attempting to bring her two children up in single-parent-family fashion. The other, Susan (Harley Kozak), is married to Nathan (Rick Moranis), who seems obsessed with bringing up their three-year-old daughter so "correctly" that she reads Kafka and is on a vegetarian diet.

There is no shortage of incidents. To recount them all could take several pages. The problems involved in the child-rearing methods of Susan and Nathan are obvious, while Larry's fecklessness in relation to Cool means that the latter is finally left to be brought up by Frank and his wife. Gil's eldest son evidences lack of self-confidence and uncertain abilities at sports. There is also the financial burden of facing up to another birth. Helen has one daughter enjoying an apparently full, but forbidden, sex life with her boyfriend in the family home and a son discovered to be hoarding pornographic magazines. Overall, the qualities of the parents, the problems they face, and their various successes and failures in coping with these problems supply the movie's matter.

The director, a married man with several children of his own, believes that parenthood is heroic. The film has a pleasing quality which helps to account for its notable box-office success. It is sufficiently old-fashioned about parents and children to recall Vincente Minnelli's *Meet Me in St. Louis* (1944), sufficiently "liberated" to raise the possibility of abortion as an answer to Gil's financial anxieties or of masturbation as an indication of Helen's loneliness. The homiletic discourse of *Parenthood* teaches easily absorbed lessons—that parents should beware of repeating their own parents' mistakes, that children need room to find their own way.

A less "innocent" message in 1989, given, say, Oliver Stone's treatment of his hero's relation with family stress, is the emphasis on winning. Gil has fantasies of his son's academic and sporting success. He also has nightmares—that his son will become a mass killer, for example—admittedly. Yet, the fact that the best father of all, in the film's terms, fantasizes in the way he does indicates the crucial importance of success in the acceptability of son to father. It is possibly suggested that the child's awareness of the need to succeed, imposed on him by Gil, could explain his timidity and tearfulness. Gil's wishful expectations are realized, the son's problems solved, by no less than that dreamed-of, long-elusive success in baseball. Ron Kovic's shame in losing the wrestling match and Gil's highly physical expressions of joy in his son's catch form a suggestive dual comment on the stresses of family life among the American middle classes.

The central question which the wealth of incident, the notably successful acting performances, the stellar cast, do not ultimately mask is what the film is about. While there are manifold crises and resolutions in the busy narrative, the central thesis is elusive. That it eludes the filmmakers too is suggested by the inclusion of a twinkling-eyed oldest family member's comments on parenthood and by a final sequence in which the screen fills with newborn babies.

The old lady, a *Reader's Digest* most unforgettable character in conception, drops into her conversation with Gil and Karen her belief that, given a choice between the safe merry-go-round and the scary roller-coaster rides, she would take the roller coaster every time. Gil and Karen recognize that the remark is more profound than it may at first appear, that she is offering them a pearl of wisdom. What does the pearl of wisdom amount to, though? Is risk-taking parenthood more rewarding than "safe" parenting, and how is either variety to be recognized? Or, as seems more probable, is the roller-coaster scariness of taking on the risks of parenthood more rewarding than the (unspecified) dull, safe life of not taking on parenthood? The fact that the speech is delivered late in the movie and that Gil and Karen feel that they have learned something important from it demands that the audience should have access to its importance. Yet the sequence in which blissful generations serenely contemplate the fulfillment that bawling babies promise seems to suggest that the meaning of parenthood is—more parent-hood. The cycle goes on—uncertain beginnings, parental hopes and disappointments, compromise, a new generation of parents, with their own hopes and disappointments, and so on and so on.

Angela McRobbie's approving commentary on *Parenthood* makes the case against it even as she praises it. She notes that the film is sufficiently aware of contemporary mores to realize that different forms of family arrangement may obtain. She continues, "It pokes gentle fun at these new combinations and suggests that, for the good of the child, we lower our expectations. Family love is better than single sex, and who cares if the earth doesn't always move."[20] There is little quarrel with her analysis of the film's messages—that "new combinations" are indulged—as inferior, but valuable, mutant forms of family—that "single sex" (presumably masturbation) is inferior to family love, that lack of sexual excitement is not to be held against the family, that instead we should "lower our expectations."

These, though, are ideologically loaded messages. Feminism's analyses of the family and its power distribution might suggest that a great deal of unhappiness accrues when the earth does not move. Nor should it lightly be conceded that "single sex" or—a possibility that is scarcely raised, let alone dealt with, in this film—sex right outside the approved family ideal is inferior to the familial version. Most significantly, why should "new combinations" of family merit being made fun of? The fact that it is "gentle" fun simply disguises the message implicit in the lighthearted treatment—that the new combination may be trying hard to emulate "real" family life, that it deserves support for that emulation, but that it just cannot be the real thing. It is a short step from such gentle funmaking to the penalization of the promotion of "pretended" family relationships, as in Britain's Clause 28.

McRobbie offers a summation of the movie's ideology when she makes the extraordinary statement that "the family is not romanticised or even celebrated, but is simply asserted as the framework within which people live out their lives."[21] How family is not celebrated when all other forms of close relationship are banished from the account of human lives is a major mystery. If people live out their lives in only this framework, the family scarcely needs romanticizing. If it is the only visible form, familialism has found its voice—the only voice.

The "problems" identified within these particular families' lives are largely created by the family, but any potential criticism is closed down by the solution of the same problems within largely the same families. The pressures on Gil's son are lifted when the family rejoices in his success. Helen's loneliness is solved not by the vibrator but by a biology teacher who is available to make a "proper family" out of Helen's sad, one-parent setup. Larry, whose shiftlessness may have something to do with being Frank Buckman's favorite, edits himself out of the family picture, leaving Cool to grow up in his own parents' house. Larry's problems are occasioned, in immediate terms, by his gangster connections and his financial shadiness. These areas are "out there," beyond the family and therefore invisible. When Larry leaves Cool behind because he has not been reintegrated into the family, he goes off into if not the unknown, at least the unseen. This is an either/or world. Either you are in a family or you are not. If you are not, you are relegated to outer darkness or find visibility and salvation by entering into one. Either you are on the roller-coaster ride or having a dull, uneventful ride on the merry-go-round. All you achieve on that ride is going round and round, never getting anywhere. If that is the case, it is odd that the parents and children who have been on the roller coaster simply reproduce—more of the same, round and round, safe and sound. The final baby-celebrating sequence seems to contradict all that the audience was asked to believe about the futility of lives on the merry-go-round.

Lizzie Francke seems to grasp precisely what *Parenthood* is teaching when she writes, "Family is all you've got . . . so you better make it work. And what better way than to produce yet more babies, and so by the time the credits roll there are more of them on screen than in a Pampers ad. It's not a message to brood on."[22]

Both *Parenthood* and television's *thirtysomething* offer a surprisingly stark picture of human life beneath their warm, gentle exteriors. If you are in a "real" family, your problems deserve sympathetic attention, the solutions to them deserve admiring publicity. If you are not quite in a "real" family but earnestly strive to be, you deserve a helping hand and some encouragement, although you have not yet acquired the maturity and status to gain respectful attention. If you are not in a "real" family and show no wish to be, you are symbolically annihilated. You are, quite literally, nowhere.

Shivers (David Cronenberg, 1974)

Fifteen years before any of the preceding considerations of family, sexuality, or corporeality, David Cronenberg made a modestly budgeted horror film in Canada which uncannily foreshadows the thinking of the eighties on the dangers of "liberated" sex. The film has been variously titled. Apart from the above version of its title, it has been known as *The Parasite Murders*. Possibly the most suggestive of the three titles is *They Came from Within,* in that it signals its relation to fifties horror at the same time as it declares its difference. Where fifties horror movies dealt with alien invasion from far beyond earth *(They Came from Outer Space),* mobilizing and expressing fears about communist takeovers masterminded from Moscow, Cronenberg's film deals with an outwardly secure, self-sufficient human society whose destruction comes from inside each individual human organism.

Richard Combs detects an additional point of comparison with George A. Romero's *Night of the Living Dead* (1969), since both films deal with uncontaminated and contaminated ranks of people, where the contaminated (the living-dead zombies in Romero's version) swell dramatically in numbers as the action proceeds.[23]

Shivers is set in a luxury apartment block located on an island close to Montreal, in which affluent Canadians enjoy a self-sufficient life-style. Their home, Starliner Towers, becomes a breeding ground for parasites which invade their bodies during sex and which act as powerful aphrodisiacs, so that there will be further sex, further transmission of the parasites. The parasites can also leave the body of a host by breaking out through the abdomen or being vomited up. They have the power to slither and ooze through bathroom pipes and hence into victims' baths (and into their unprotected bodies). The parasites originate in a failed experiment by a medical researcher who sought to replace organ transplants with implantation of parasites, originally designed to correct bodily imbalances.

The summary might suggest that the invasion of the residents of Starliner Towers marks them out as innocent victims. A strong connection is suggested, however, from the opening of the film between the "unnatural" lives of these complacent, materialistic people and their succumbing to the parasites. For one critic, the parasites are "literal embodiments of the general malaise attached to the place."[24] Another sees the luxury residence as "already an incubator of deviant forms of behaviour."[25] The fact that the parasites use the very sanitation system or leap out of a washing machine indicates that what the Starliner Towers residents try to shut their eyes to, try to wash out of their awareness, becomes their weak point. Peter Greenaway's diners are no more anxious to hide squalor and wretchedness out in the car-park area than Cronenberg's residents to live their lives uncontaminated by contact with the rest of the world or even with their own bodies. It is when they wash their clothes or their bodies that they seem to be at greatest risk of invasion if, that is, they are not actively engaged in polymorphous-perverse sexual liaisons.

The connection set up in the film between sanitation as wishful denial and, on the other hand, sex may explain why the appearance of the parasites is so disturbing. They have been aptly described as a cross between a slug, a leech, and a "particularly offensive penis,"[26] but they have fecal as well as phallic connotations. They came from within, in truth—from within sexual desires, from within the body itself.

It is not simply the outward appearance of the parasites which makes them disturbing. It is also that, perversely, the parasites represent a form of liberation from the repressed quality of life in Starliner Towers. Don Siegel's body snatchers substituted a passionless "pod" version of the person for the human being thus replaced. In *Shivers,* it is as if the Starliner people are already pods, and as if the parasite invasion represents a distorted version of salvation for them. Their passionless lives are suddenly converted into maelstroms of erotic hunger, their passivity becomes aggressive activity. It is the ambivalence of the parasites which makes the sexual liberation that they represent so ambivalent, and which helps to explain why Robin Wood, for example, finds the movie so detestable. The parasites are given, in the film's context, a "purpose," in that they redeem the soul-dead denizens of Starliner Towers through the libido. Yet the redemption leads to destruction on—to judge by the final moments of the movie—a cosmic scale. Charles D. Leayman finds an explanation for the film's ambivalence about "liberation" in Marcuse's statement in *Eros and Civilization*: "Left to pursue their natural objectives, the basic instincts of man would be incompatible with all lasting association and preservation: they would destroy even where they unite. The uncontrollable Eros is just as fatal as his deadly counterpart."[27]

Like three of the four 1989 films discussed above, *Shivers* is a film about corporeality. Cronenberg explains this as an inevitable consequence of its being a horror film. "The true subject of horror films is death and anticipation of death, and that leads to the question of man as body, as opposed to man as spirit."[28]

Cronenberg's dreams are as suggestive as his films, not surprisingly, since his dreams inform his film scenarios. In relation to *Shivers,* he reports two dreams. "I had a dream. My mouth was open and this thing crawled out. I was lying in bed, absolutely neutral atmosphere, and that was the kernel of the film."[29] Then, later, he dreamed a perhaps more interesting dream for the conception of parasite infestation as illness and even of the experience of film as exposure to disease: "I dreamt I was at a theatre with an audience. Certain members of the audience contracted a disease from the screen and then there was a certain amount of antagonism between those who got the disease and those who were immune. The disease caused extremely fast aging: I watched myself growing old."[30] This last dream account, incidentally, typifies the emphasis in AIDS reporting on the degeneration of the formerly beautiful body, and on the rapid aging, of the youthful sufferer. The parallel with eighties writing about AIDS is strengthened by the connection which Cronenberg makes between sexual license, disease, and destruction.

At the time of the film's exhibition at the Edinburgh Film Festival, Robin Wood objected to *Shivers*'s ideology as being reactionary, in that it portrayed acts of lesbianism, for example, as "monstrous." Wood does detect in the film "a sort of perverse wish-fulfilment," all the same.[31] The reading of the Cronenberg movie in terms of reactionary ideology is feasible, but it may be an oversimplification at the same time. Now, it seems weirdly prophetic, if not of the AIDS complex, of attitudes to it.

In 1976, Alexander Walker wrote of the infestation under the heading of "a parasitic *virus*."[32] The presence of the parasites involves swellings of the throat (and abdomen). The explanation of the infestation within the movie has noticeable connections with the AIDS story as told in terms of popular mythology. Thus, a period of repression is followed by a period of "society-threatening" sexual license, which is followed by a period of danger (of infection) and decay (of those infected). The fear of punishment for "going too far too fast" in the seventies is well illustrated by the movie. So is the dread at the end of the movie that the "general population" may be taken over and contaminated by those already contaminated within their hitherto confined world. So is the explanation of AIDS in terms of a "scientific experiment" gone wrong, even if the experiment of the film is motivated by benignancy, the CIA-inspired experiments of eighties mythology (against central Africa, against sexual deviants) by malignancy. The most overtly reactionary reading of the film is by the British censorship board, who claimed that "the permissive society" might be the result of "this new form of plague."[33] Its reading is scarcely persuasive in itself, or as an interpretation of the film, but it is a strikingly clear revelation of the kind of thinking that *Shivers* exposes and which finds its moment of most confident expression within the AIDS crisis.

Fatal Attraction (Adrian Lyne, 1987)

The plot outline of *Fatal Attraction* is well known, even to those who have not seen the movie. Successful lawyer Dan Gallagher (Michael Douglas) spends "irresponsible" weekend away from his wife Beth (Anne Archer) with apparently independent single woman Alex (Glenn Close). Single woman becomes clingingly dependent, begins to threaten Dan and his family, claims pregnancy. Wife shoots mistress when she invades the bathroom of their home.

Much of the controversy concerning the film rages around the figure of Alex, who, in her representation of the postfeminist single

woman, bears a political burden well beyond the demands of a
thriller menace. The contrast between wife and mistress begins
with their names: "Beth" has connotations of warmth and "homi-
ness," as it did as early as in Louisa May Alcott's *Little Women*;
"Alex," by virtue of its androgyny, appears to be chosen as suitable
for a single woman who, on the film's early evidence, has become a
successful editor. While Beth is associated visually with warm,
suburban interiors, Alex seems to be the spirit of Manhattan at its
most savage and rootless; she lives in an apartment which gives no
clue that she has a past, or any present emotional connections. The
spheres of Beth and Alex must be assumed to exclude each other.
Beth does not attempt to enter Alex's, but when Alex approaches
Beth's sphere, her "proper" exclusion is always marked. Alex is
either looking in through a window at family togetherness,
wretched in her exclusion, or she is violently forcing her presence
upon family members who resist it. Unless, that is, she comes in
disguise, to catch Beth off guard, as she does in one sequence.

If Alex begins as representing the successful single woman, she
quickly becomes witchlike. Whether this means that single careerist women are automatically witchlike is one of the points of
most bitter controversy in the interpretation of the film. Deborah
Raschke believes that her powers of seduction and destruction are
those of an archetypal witch. (To these, she could add her powers of
disguise and dissembling.) She notes her flying hair when she
dances wildly with Dan in the "seduction" part of the film. (Even
when Alex is still, moreover, her hair can aptly be termed Medusa-
like.) To underline the point, she notes that the entrance to Alex's
apartment promises an inferno.[34]

To temper the picture of a deeply reactionary representation of
the career woman as jealously aware of missing out on a woman's
natural destiny as wife and mother, there is a particular reading of
Alex which is worth serious consideration.

The obvious reading of the meaning of Beth and Alex is as
polarized opposites. Their mutual exclusion is strongly suggested in
the visual evidence of their home environments. Beth's home is
cluttered and "friendly." Alex's apartment is almost minimalist.
Moreover, her home is above a meat-packing area of the city, where
flames rise from rusted oil drums to give meager heat to some of the
city's shifting, shapeless itinerants. To reach her apartment, the
visitor has to negotiate a wire-covered elevator whose only lighting
is by means of one swinging red bulb. It is impossible to see a living
area as starkly "other" in these terms except as part of the design of
the movie. There is evidence for this in the director's assertion

concerning the location of Alex's apartment: "It's Fellini down there. It functions as meat market, but on the periphery, you have a motley crew living round the oil drums: transvestites, transsexuals, a mind-boggling collection."[35] (His words suggest that Alex could be taken to bear a burden of representation not only of single women but of all that is deemed "deviant" in terms of sexuality.)

The contrast between Alex and Beth is also marked at the level of what might be termed gaze transactions. The classic "feminine" position with regard to looking is characterized by Laura Mulvey[36] as the object of the male gaze. Beth, by this reckoning, is truly feminine, in that she is always the object of Dan's approving look, as well as the camera's. She represents what a man would "normally" desire in a wife. She has no active desire and is not an active gazer. From her early scenes, though, Alex takes command of the gaze, making Dan an object of it, much as he becomes an object of the camera's gaze when, for example, he is photographed both erotically and parodically with trousers at ankles as he tries to lift his lover across the room. When Alex turns her gaze on Dan's family, the difference in subject/object positions is at its most marked. She looks in at them. The objects of her look are not even aware of being so positioned, but have taken few precautions to prevent that positioning. They are available as a perfect image of family harmony.

Then, too, Alex and Beth fight over the same man, so that their complete separateness and mutual antagonism are especially marked in the film's denouement. At its most obvious level, this denouement is a male fantasy, where he is the desired object with the power of a subject.

However, Barbara Creed suggests a fascinating possibility—that Alex and Beth are not so much separate, mutually antagonistic characters as two warring facets of the same character, that of Dan's wife. She uses as her principal evidence the final bathroom sequence, and particularly the moment where the wife wipes the steam from the mirror, expecting to see her own reassuring wifely image. Instead she sees Alex's face looking back at her. Creed suggests that Alex is Beth's alter ego. The bath in which Alex drowns with so much difficulty and after a supernatural struggle for life has been prepared by Dan. The water has been drawn for Dan's wife, though, even if it is the Fury that dies in it.[37]

Alex as the shock mirror image of Beth is strongly suggested by the emphasis before her appearance on the looks passing between Dan and Beth, as framed images of happy family life. They do not so much look frankly at each other as smile approvingly at each other in the mirror. When Alex's face is framed after the steam is wiped away, a quite different meaning for their mutual exclusion is suggested—that mothers cannot, in Dan's eyes, be allowed to be active and sexual, that his wife must exclude what attracted him to Alex in the first place, her erotic dominance, her illusion of control and "freedom."[38]

Dan, after all, confesses his fear of passion. In his early years, he responded to *Madame Butterfly,* but his reaction to the heroine's suicide was to crawl under the seat to avoid watching it. His marriage seems remarkably lacking in passion, though his domestic environment is womblike, comforting, secure. This is the domain of the mother and child (both actual and metaphorical). Alex's announcement of her pregnancy shakes the security of the domestic image, since it suggests the possibility of the union of passionate woman and mother. Such a creature must, in Dan's eyes, be "monstrous." Perhaps the fears summoned up around the person of Alex are those of a traditional male whose fear of passion and activity in a woman must also be a fear of feminism, or at least of what he takes feminism to represent. Brian De Palma may understand as much when he terms the movie "a post-feminist AIDS thriller."[39]

De Palma's calling it an "AIDS thriller" is curious, since the film at no point refers to that most dreaded of New York afflictions, although in realist terms, it might well have. The silence about AIDS as a deeply feared result of weekend playing around is sufficiently dense as to make the fear audible.

It has been taken to be an "AIDS thriller" by more commentators on the film than De Palma. The connection is made even by those who tread an absolutely traditionalist line on male sexuality (and one which, incidentally, justifies rape at the same time as it attempts to justify "unsafe sex" as a sign of virility): "It does not seem to me that it *[Fatal Attraction]* would put delinquent males off having one-night stands any more than AIDS has done. Sex is rarely subject to rational thought processes."[40] It might be worth noting that the whole notion of "safe sex" is predicated on the feasibility of sex as regularly subject to rational thought processes. Is the writer suggesting that only homosexuals—and women perhaps—can be expected to bring reason to bear on their sexual practices? J. Hoberman, while recognizing that AIDS is not raised specifically as an issue, feels that its omission is only because its mention is not necessary: "society has never needed [a] sexually transmitted killer virus to seek to regulate individual libidos."[41]

Popular belief about HIV transmission may account for the peculiarly horrible effect of the result of Alex's suicide attempt—her dripping fresh blood on to Dan. (Contaminated blood is already part of the association with Alex, thanks to the siting of her apartment above a district where bloody carcasses are carelessly toted about.) It is crystal clear that Dan and Alex did not practice safe sex. If they had, how could she credibly claim pregnancy by him? Their obliviousness to it is, thus, a principal reason for Dan's near downfall.

Perhaps the movie suggests, as Adrian Lyne himself suggests, that there is no such thing as safe sex, even though he puts the idea somewhat obliquely, following the lines of popular prejudice by making Beth the potential "innocent victim" and Dan the only half-guilty means of transmission, with Alex as the clearly culpable, and almost indestructible, source of contagion. Viewed as an "AIDS thriller," *Fatal Attraction* is remarkably ignorant and complacent, confirming the most dangerous attitudes in a public already saturated in them. Seen as a parable about male anxiety and male splitting of the feminine into irreconcilable halves—Madonna/whore, wife/slut, safely passive/dangerously active—it may be explored as a terrifying example of the masculine modes of thought which so easily lead to catastrophe when they are imposed on women in actuality.

Planes, Trains and Automobiles (John Hughes, 1987)

Michael Douglas seems to be one of the peculiarly eighties versions of the male star, embodying male anxiety, a fear of losing authority within the very act of asserting it, thanks to such films as *Fatal Attraction,* or, earlier, *A Chorus Line,* later, *The War of the Roses.* Another kind of quintessentially eighties male star is Steve Martin. Martin can play the perfect husband and father (as in *Parenthood*), but normally he is in retreat from the role, as in Herbert Ross's *Pennies from Heaven* (1981), the film adaptation of Dennis Potter's scripted-for-British-television "musical"/melodrama. In the John Hughes movie, he seems to be occupying a halfway house between these two characterizations, in that he gives every appearance of being, if not the perfect husband, the husband in a perfect home. At the same time, his eventual response to misadventures and people undreamed of in his worst nightmares, while he remained in his perfect home, suggests that that home is more what he feels he ought to desire than what he experiences himself as having.

The shift in public attitudes to business—the energetic fostering of an ideal of "enterprise culture" within Thatcher's Britain, for

example—that helps to delineate the eighties increases expectations that commerce, and the world of finance, should be explored
and indeed heroized in entertainment. It is explored, as in Oliver
Stone's *Wall Street,* though less often heroized than might be anticipated.

America's free-market ideals were in place well before Britain's,
despite the apparent interruptions to that basic philosophy represented by, say, "New Deal" economics or Carter's presidency, at
least as the latter has been portrayed in the eighties. As such,
America could be claimed to be built on selling, individual success
having much to do with successful salesmanship. Yet, salesmen in
overtly serious drama from the United States tend to be insecure
soul searchers (often searching for their souls, in fact). A notable
summation of salesmanship within the context of drama is provided
by Arthur Miller's play *Death of a Salesman,* filmed in 1951 and
then again, as a film version of a theater performance, by Volker
Schlöndorff, in 1985.

Arthur Miller was disappointed with Laslo Benedek's 1951 film
version of *Death of a Salesman.* He believed that the basic reason
for its failure was its "literal" transference of the salesman hero,
Willy Loman, "to the locales he had only imagined in the play."[42]
For Miller, it was important that the audience should see Willy's
immediate surroundings while he was losing consciousness of them
and should continue to see them when he had completely lost
consciousness of them and was conversing with people from other
times and places: "The movie's tendency is always to wipe out what
has gone before. . . . It did not solve, nor really attempt to find a
resolution for the problem of keeping the past constantly alive."[43]
Miller is talking of the Benedek movie here but could as well be
talking of Volker Schlöndorff's 1985 film version (even if it would be
unfair to suggest that it does not *attempt* to find a resolution).

Steve Martin seems a far more plausible choice to play Willy
Loman than either Fredric March or Dustin Hoffman, especially in
the wake of his role as Depression sheet-music salesman of *Pennies
from Heaven.* The eighties movie that seems to be making statements of a kind that Miller was attempting in his celebrated play is
not the film of the play but *Planes, Trains and Automobiles.* Again
and again, as unlikely as it may first appear, the ideas that Miller
was attempting to express, using the devices of Willy Loman, his
wife, Linda, and their two sons, Biff and Happy, are reembodied in
this anxiety-based farce, suggesting that the existential questions
which Miller raised through his salesman (whose abilities at salesmanship are never unambiguously clarified) have become more
immediate in the environment of eighties America.

Willy. Funny, y'know? After all the highways, and the trains, and the appointments and the years, you end up worth more dead than alive.

(p. 192)[44]

There is little doubt that Neal Page (Steve Martin) and Del Griffith (John Candy) in *Planes, Trains and Automobiles* are "real" salesmen, with real selling skills. Neal is, on the evidence of his clothes and home and expectation of a first-class seat on the Chicago-bound flight, successful in his job. This job appears to be at the level of advertising executive. The opening scene involves a silent New York client agonizing over which illustration will work best for his lipstick campaign and Neal exasperated at the thought that he may miss the plane that he must take home to be in good time for Thanksgiving with the family. This scene shows that his selling is a better-organized affair than Willy Loman's. He is part of a team. His success appears to have no relation to his likability or even pretended consideration for others, nor to his self-presentation, unless that be taken to center on the image of success itself.

To judge by the skill that Del, a salesman of shower-curtain rings, has in raising money by later marketing the rings as Czechoslovakian ivory, he too is a good salesman. Salesmanship at this lowly level depends far more, it seems, on plausibility and energy.

Despite their highly disparate personalities, income brackets, and attitudes to others, Neal and Del share an awareness of being sellers in a world like Willy Loman's, composed exclusively—with the exception of Neal's family—of sellers and buyers. They begin their odyssey together in the tourist-class area of a plane and continue, once the flight is diverted to Wichita, on the highways and trains familiar to Willy, as they attempt to get back to Chicago in time for Thanksgiving dinner.

Biff. I'm like a boy. I'm not married, I'm not in business, I just—I'm like a boy.

(p. 139)

Linda. Few men are idolized by their children the way you are.

(p. 149)

Business success and familial happiness through marriage are the only goods aspired to and understood by Willy Loman and his family. There is no other success. Biff is the perpetual adolescent, stuck on the metaphorical frontier, unable to grow up and integrate.

Neal has the kind of family and house which Dan Gallagher of *Fatal Attraction* enjoys. By the Lomans' standards, he has it all. In terms of his lower-class expectations, Del appears to have it all too. Nevertheless, by the end of the movie, we learn that his life is lonely, that he has been unable to admit to the death of his beloved wife and to the absence of a fixed home. An apparent resolution to the absences which threaten audience enjoyment of this screwball comedy is offered by Neal's final invitation to Del to enter his home, for at least Thanksgiving. Neal's plenitude and Del's lack both serve to confirm the centrality and inseparability of success in business and marriage.

Willy. Someday I'll have my own business, and I'll never leave home any more! . . . Bigger than Uncle Charley! Because Charley is not— liked. He's liked, but he's not—well liked.

(p. 144)

Be liked and you will never want.

(p. 146)

. . . they do laugh at me. I know that.

(p. 149)

Willy Loman's vacillation between conviction that he is liked and that he is laughed at, somehow not liked enough, is discoverable in Del. Del insists on his likability at the point where the unrepentantly dislikable Neal lists Del's faults, his off-putting personal habits, and the vacuity of his conversation, in the Wichita hotel bedroom he is persuaded to share with Del. Del's insistence indicates his uncertainty. He does indeed have friends, willing to do him a good turn. It is through old pals of his that they are given a truck ride to the railway station and a train ticket. To this extent, he is demonstrably liked. However, the demonstration is relatively worthless, because they have to sit, freezing, in the back of an open farm truck, and the train ticket gets them only as far as Saint Louis, not Chicago.

Above all, the irrelevance of likability to the higher levels of reward in self-selling is repeatedly demonstrated by Neal's relative affluence and material security. It is only by the loss of his suit, credit cards, and money and by the necessity to start again at zero that Neal can find some use in courtesy—or at least that he can discover the dangers of discourtesy. In one of several parodies of frenzied rudeness, Neal, at the end of his tether, learns that verbal aggression is rewarded with physical aggression, once the differences of class are rendered invisible by the series of catastrophes.

The dichotomies that *Salesman* offers, between love (familial) and likability on one side and business success on the other, are discoverable afresh in the John Hughes movie. There is a subtext also, particularly in the hotel sequences, which introduces a quite other dichotomy, between marriage and business success on one side and extrafamilial love and prolonged adolescence on the other. Hughes was generally associated with the teen pic before this movie. Small surprise, perhaps, that his middle-aged heroes should at times embody Biff's belief that he is "only a boy" (because he is outside marriage and also business). In addition, there is the antinomy of home (supercivilized, a living Christmas card, in the final sequences) and what is "out there," what in Arthur Miller might be "the West." The planes, trains, and automobiles ultimately link New York City with Home, but what may be more interesting is the territory over which they travel, the world beyond Neal's experience in which transient Del feels comfortable.

In a potentially shocking and hilarious bedroom sequence in the Wichita hotel the morning after their first up-front row, Neal is wrapped in Del's embrace. He awakens and protests when Del kisses his ear. But this was done, Del claims, because Neal was holding his hand. "Where's your other hand?" Neal inquires. "Between the pillows." "What pillows?!"—in mounting homophobic panic they leap out of bed in opposite directions, with Neal repeating "Helluva game!" to reassert his virility.

J. Hoberman is impressed by the way that, under the overt contrast of home and homelessness, lies "a hint of conflicted homosex." The hint is given credibility as a reading by Del's endless throat-clearing as he lies beside Neal in the dark, by Neal's later memory of the kiss as pleasurable, and by what Hoberman terms the long ambiguous glance between Del and Neal's wife once he is brought into their home.[45] "Why do I feel like I'm at summer camp?" Neal asks himself, drawing attention once more to the possibility that what is "out there," the territory through which he travels to return home with Del, is as much psychological as geographical, that it is the territory of exclusion, all that is not admitted by familial ideology.

Willy. I'm always in a race with the junkyard! I just finished paying for the car and it's on its last legs. . . .

(p. 174)

Linda. Remember I wrote you that he smashed up the car again? . . . The insurance inspector came. He said that they have evidence. That all these accidents in the last year—weren't—weren't—accidents.

(p. 164)

If the territory is psychological, surely the means by which it is traversed cannot, in its turn, be only physical. All the transport, public and private, aerial and terrestrial, on which Neal has relied to keep him efficiently traveling between home and business breaks down. He loses his first-class seat on the plane which, in any case, is forced by a blizzard at O'Hare to land in Wichita. The railway engine breaks down. The bus goes only as far as Saint Louis. They nearly freeze to death on the farm truck and then a refrigerator truck. When Del takes the wheel, he nearly kills them both by driving on the wrong side of the highway and by allowing his cigarette to set fire to the upholstery. At this point, Neal "sees" Del as the devil incarnate, laughingly driving him to his destruction. Elsewhere, the endless accidents seem less externally motivated and to be at some level as self-willed as when Neal lands in the path of Del's car wheels.

> *Happy.* My own apartment, a car, and plenty of women. And still, godammit, I'm lonely.
> *Biff. (With enthusiasm.)* Listen, why don't you come out West with me?
> (p. 139)

The Hughes movie seems to give this line of Biff's to Del, except that it is to the Midwest "as it really is" that he invites Neal. It is a Midwest peopled by humanoids scarcely able to utter intelligible speech, who wear plastic smiles (reinforced by the plastic devil's head on the customized car), whose idea of a comfortable motel room includes a velvet picture of Roy Orbison. *Planes* takes up the notion of going out West in order to demonstrate that the frontier is firmly closed, that the freedom it promises is illusory, that the cowboys are rhinestone, that the farthest West these salesmen are going to get is Wichita, Kansas.

> *Willy. (With great feeling.)* You're the best there is, Linda, you're a pal, you know that? On the road—on the road I want to grab you sometimes and just kiss the life outa you.
> (p. 149)

Against the nightmare of "the territory," and suggesting the maturity which is shucked off increasingly by Neal as, for example, he speeds away from the motel room which he has just wrecked by reversing the car into it, are the brief images of his beautiful wife, always at the other end of the telephone, a latter-day Penelope awaiting her Odysseus's return. Their daughter may lose faith temporarily, but Neal's wife, like his home, offers an image of perfection which reflects, presumably, his own self-image of perfection as father and husband.

When he returns to his home with Del, the home is, against screwball's generic expectations, intact. His offspring, his parents, his in-laws, his wife greet him. Her faith in him has not wavered, even if she has been weeping softly (without so much as a puffy eyelid). The Return is epic—measured, serene, fulfilling all Neal's expectations. The scene is shot with the loving care meted out by Brian De Palma to those sequences which change to threat, violence, dashed hopes. (A good example is the happy-family sequences of *Obsession* [1976].) For that reason, and because the logic of the bulk of the movie suggests that a Clytemnestra, not a Penelope, will be awaiting Neal, we expect disruption. It is not provided. Not before the end credits, anyhow.

> *Charley.* . . . A salesman is got to dream, boy. It comes with the territory.
>
> (p. 222)

> *Biff.* Will you take that phony dream and burn it before something happens?
>
> (p. 217)

Neal's Return to the paradise of his home is a dream of wish fulfillment, shot as such in the precatastrophe style of De Palma. The bulk of the movie, from Neal's failure to buy his seat in a cab in New York City, all the way to Chicago by plane, train, and automobile, has the inexorable logic of an anxiety dream, a nightmare which perpetually denies its dreamer arrival at his destination. The collision of the nightmare and the cozy dream of Home, marked by its "excessive" mise-en-scène, suggests not so much a surprise happy ending as continuing ideological anxiety. The sting in the tail seems absent, however—except to those who wait through the end credits (a tiny minority of the movie's audience, surely). These spectators may be surprised to find that, at the end of the movie, the silent lipstick-campaign client is still attempting to choose among the three illustrations before him. Is this how he spends his Thanksgiving? Or has the movie ended as it began, with Neal trapped in the boardroom, terrified by his nightmares of being unable to reach home, or wishfully making it to the safe haven with a token of his sojourn in "the territory" in the person of Del?

A man is still only as good as his salesmanship some four decades after Miller's now-classic play was written. What is new, and more pessimistic, is that the frontier, with its irresponsibility and untamed colts, has gone, leaving plastic and tackiness in the place of Nature. If the salesman has got to dream, as Arthur Miller's Uncle Charley believes, he may awaken to find that Linda, Biff, and his lovely home were just another part of that dream.

13
Some Conclusions

In view of the lengthy treatment of the subjects announced in the preceding chapter titles, the concluding chapter ought to be brief. Conclusions about familialism and views on sexuality in the eighties have already been drawn, a potted history of the understanding of AIDS in the eighties as, primarily, a disease associated with a particular form of sexuality already offered.

What may usefully be attempted before the book's end, however, is some consideration of the information that films seem to provide about the principal ideological concerns and questions of the eighties.

One way of looking at movies in the light of ideological evidence is to claim certain broad trends as indicating a right-wing or left-wing tendency. Thus, both Robin Wood and Andrew Britton have provided a range of useful insights into "Reaganite entertainment" on the basis of a number of films not only made in the eighties but, in Wood's case, highly popular in the eighties and just previous to those years. There is indeed clear enough evidence for a revival of militaristic macho attitudes in such successes as *An Officer and a Gentleman* or *Top Gun* or for the sort of entertainment that by-passes the head for the heart in the huge commercial success of *E.T.* and other allegedly Reaganite movies. Films such as *Ordinary People* and *Terms of Endearment* do indeed indicate a strengthening of the traditional nuclear family and a hardening of attitudes against "unfeminine" or else unmotherly, careerist women.

Yet it may be too circular to outline certain trends in political thinking as Reaganite and then to pick out those films which illustrate those trends, although the emphasis on particular box-office appeal helps to establish the credibility of the links suggested. (The demonstrable box-office appeal of *Parenthood* at the end of the eighties surely helps to establish that family values remain a crucial concern of the American public at that time.) Because the Reagan victory in 1980 ushers in a period of marked conservatism, just as with the Thatcher success in 1979 Great Britain undergoes a time of "radical conservatism" (if this is not a contradiction in terms), these political leaders have clearly had an effect on public policy and individual thinking. Yet the question remains of what might be termed "permeation." In other words, because Thatcherist change permeated institutions, did national thinking follow the pattern of her thinking—making "Victorian values" dearly held national values, for example? Commentators have analyzed the Reagan election to show that it is not quite the triumph of conservatism that benefactors of the election have claimed. Despite her three terms, Margaret Thatcher's party was at no point elected on a majority vote of the British electorate. Indeed, with the system of proportional representation which is the rule in most of continental Europe, her program of radical reform would have been unlikely to have been carried forward with such profound results for, say, the National Health Service of Great Britain.

Because a country does not become uniformly conservative in the way that its national politics may become, and because the desire for financial return at the box office alone requires that movies appeal to wide audiences, it is perhaps misleading to home in on the most obviously Reaganite American or Thatcherite British movies. For one thing, there are notable exceptions. Oliver Stone's movies seem, at some level, oppositional, or at least critical of the "official" ideology. For another, the reading of movies is a far more complex matter than their categorization in terms of Left or Right politics might suggest. I have argued elsewhere, for example, that the "self-evident" antifeminism of certain Brian De Palma movies should not easily be conceded, since active reading suggests that quite other patterns of thinking than the blatantly misogynist may be discovered in his major box-office successes.[1] Take another controversial director, David Cronenberg; his *Shivers* can be seen by one set of cogent arguments as reactionary. Yet meaning and ideological significance alter with time. The advent of AIDS in later years makes *Shivers* today seem like a remarkable prophecy of attitudes to come, just as one of Cronenberg's dreams (about infection and immunity in a theater audience watching his movie) seems applicable to attitudes in the eighties, without elaborate argument or abstruse dream interpretation.

It may be truer to the film experience in general to abstain from labeling in the party-political fashion and, instead, to focus attention on ideological conflict. Labeling rests on resolutions, largely. The opposing sides in a conflict are treated as being of less significance than the "winning" side. A comedy such as *Planes, Trains and Automobiles* thus is capable of being labeled as a profamily film because of its resolution, or at least its pre-final-titles resolution. The hero returns to his ideal home and his ideal wife and ideal family in the company of the lonely, fat "loser" who has become his friend for what remains of Thanksgiving. The significance of the return and of the "excessive" picture of family bliss is altered, however, by attention to what has preceded—the anxiety nightmare that makes the dream itself a product of ideological anxiety which continues beyond the safe return, from "the territory" outside the home, to home itself.

In any case, Thomas Schatz[2] would argue that the function of genre movies is not so much to resolve conflict as to explore afresh the oppositions which underlie all generic conflict. He thinks of genre as, at one level, a ritual in which irresoluble contradictions are, in the denouement, closed down with a particular resolution but which cannot close down the continuing concern with their irresolubility. Thus, another genre film quickly surfaces which puts the oppositions back into play and which may this time "resolve" them in a different manner. *An Officer and a Gentleman* must suggest a range of nonmacho, antimilitarist forms of behavior (the hero's early rootlessness and lack of ambition or even of self-discipline, his friend's suicide, the attitudes of the suicide's former girlfriend) in order that militaristic machismo be given meaning and something to triumph over. The values which are contrasted in this 1982 movie can be seen to inform, in 1989, *Born on the Fourth of July*. The quite different ending of the Stone movie, with militarism, as it were, discredited in the interests of a different kind of masculine self-assertion, may well indicate a new mood. On the other hand, it may not, since such force as the ending has rests upon the power which the unseated values have exerted on the hero and on the film's audience. (That militarism does not retire defeated from the national consciousness because one movie suggests that perhaps it should is shown in, for example, the support for President Bush in the Gulf War of 1991.)

What consideration of eighties and late seventies movies may indicate is not so much which popular successes are Reaganite or Thatcherite but what concerns have become paramount, how certain key terms, such as "family," have come to be understood. (Far from being self-evident, as if the word "family" had a universally accepted, unified meaning, its usage can be grasped by observation of those areas or phenomena with which contrasts are made. Politicians may want to use the term as if it were unified and admitted no other interpretation, but the work of examining its acquisition of the meaning which they wish to give to it has a political relevance, in that it allows consideration of what is constructed as "common sense," therefore beyond rational question, by party politics.)

An audience is not manipulable in the simple way that categorization of movies as Right or Left would suggest. Differences in class, age, gender, race, all modify the totalizing picture that some accounts of movies' effects would seek to paint. The notion of the unassailably correct reading seems untenable.

If we follow the suggested method of looking at dominant cinema less for the "message" of its resolved endings as for what it reveals of competing meanings and messages, some strands could be identified as particularly eighties. They may be so called either because they intensify already existing oppositions or because they represent new sorts of antitheses. The following is a suggested list of particular obviousness, in no particular order:

THE BESIEGED FAMILY. The importance of the family (as well as its "natural" form) is suggested by the range of threats to it. It may be the object of violent threat, from criminals, as in *Someone to Watch over Me,* or from a crazed, rejected woman, as in *Fatal Attraction.* The violence to the family, while obviously physical in terms of these films' narratives, is also metaphorical. The Other Woman in Adrian Lyne's movie does not need to wield a knife in order to represent a threat to this family, since the husband seems afraid to tell his wife of her existence and since the marriage has been built on lines that would seem to exclude frenzied passion.

The image of contamination is powerful. The nuclear family's increasing "perfection" of image in films of the eighties calls into question its very credibility as the only natural form of close relationship—since, otherwise, it would not *need* the carefully fostered images of bliss. *Parenthood* works in the interests of child-producing nuclear families by featuring threats to them and then "containing" these threats. Thus, the unfatherly father is made good by the reformed patriarch becoming surrogate father. The daughter who disobeys her mother by having premarital sex in the parental home sets up a home of her own with the man who made her pregnant. The son who seems too sensitive and insecure to be manly simply achieves manliness by his sudden baseball success. He can go on to form a family of his own, it is implied. Parenthood seems ultimately to be defined by what has at the end been excluded or else recuperated in familial terms.

The power of what is not recognized as familial is constantly rehearsed in eighties movies—the appeal of the independent, sexually active woman; male bonding; "excitement" in general, whether it comes from contact with grand opera or exploring the hinterlands of America by its highways and railroads. The vigor with which alternatives to, or supplements of, the family are eliminated or recuperated suggests a heightened ideological anxiety about the feasibility of the traditional family in the late-twentieth century.

CAPITALISM AND FAMILY. The emphasis which both Reagan and Thatcher publicly put on traditional families is especially interesting in that the emphasis came from devout free-market apologists. Whether or not these spokespersons for the family were conscious of it, the traditional family is most threatened by capitalism. In other words, as several commentators have notices, patriarchy and capitalism, while being mutually supportive, are far from equatable systems.

Parenthood shows awareness of this when it has the perfect father, Gil, passed over at work because of his refusal to put the company's interests over his family's. The threats to the family in *Someone to Watch over Me* and *Fatal Attraction* come from the contacts which men doing their jobs have in the world outside the family home. The fact that they are attracted to experiences beyond the home, and that the attraction is "fatal," indicates the profundity of the gap between capitalism's demands and those of the stable nuclear family, with its renewed emphasis on monogamy and fidelity.

While *Fatal Attraction* may show that it is "just" sex which threatens to undermine the family, *Someone to Watch over Me* suggests that "serious" entanglements have a chance to turn into something more threatening than sexual pleasure can for long be. This in turn would suggest that the security of home life depends partly on the domestication of desire, its being tamed from the obsessional into the quotidian. *Planes, Trains and Automobiles* goes farther. It brings its hero some awareness of the vast range of people and, here, places that have not made it into the bourgeois life-style, which is all that he recognizes as valid (and which is, noticeably, once again threatened by the demands of business, since it is his job which nearly wrecks his family Thanksgiving). By allowing the hero to give way to the affection and tenderness that Del, the representative of these people and places, embodies, the film signals the narrowness of family life, the necessity of its narrowness and blinkering of vision so that it may survive in a world which is not, after all, designed to protect it.

ACCEPTABLE AND UNACCEPTABLE SEXUALITY. The preceding sections ought to clarify that only the sexuality which is tamed into the marital and domestic and which supports patriarchal power positions is "officially" approved in most eighties movies. They ought also to clarify that, precisely by making other forms threatening and scary, the disruptive potency of these is eloquently attested. *Born on the Fourth of July* seems to argue in another direction by making the brothels of Mexico, while unsatisfactory as a long-term solution, at least recognize the hero's needs while all the home environment can do is to shut its eyes to them and forbid even the word *penis* to be used within the household. *Shivers* in the middle seventies gives expression to the dichotomies between safe monogamy and wildly irresponsible, but exciting, promiscuity by showing the greater appeal of the latter even as it suggests its deadliness. In other words, while attraction is as fatal in *Shivers* as in the Adrian Lyne movie, it is also unavoidable, given the deadening effect of "decency" in the Starliner Towers environment.

THE LONGING FOR A BORDER. In order that a line be drawn and maintained between the acceptable and unacceptable forms of sexuality, the quest for a demarcating borderline is central to many eighties movies. The quarantine that once existed in the space vessel, keeping the alien world at bay in *Alien,* is one of the most succinct expressions of this fundamental need. While the line is sometimes difficult to identify in eighties movies, the need for it is manifested in the fear of contamination, most vividly illustrated in *Fatal Attraction*. Here, the husband's dalliance in the city becomes threatening only when the line between suburb and city is crossed by an element unacceptable to the former. The dread with which Alex's invasion of the family is viewed shows that, for the survival of the family, there must be areas alien to it, and that those areas must remain unacknowledged. The daring of *Planes, Trains* is that it forces the hero to acknowledge them by forcing him to live among the alien in their own territory.

CONSUMPTION AS PLEASURE AND DANGER. In the age of consumer capitalism, it is not surprising that conspicuous consumption, always an element of fan magazines' portraits of their stars' lives, should be treated as pleasurable. What may be new is the reversibility of consumption, so that chief consumers can chiefly be consumed, or where the appetite for consumption crosses its own particular borderline into the monstrous and "unnatural." Both notions are economically illustrated by the final "shunting" sequences of *Society,* in which Beverly Hills's elite expose their fondness for the absorption of flesh of lesser beings and where one of the invincible elite is vanquished by means of the anus—his "weak spot," demanded by the very patterns of consumption on which he bases his life. Albert Spica, the Thief of Peter Greenaway's Jacobean drama, graduates to the eating of human flesh before his life is snuffed out, as punishment for turning the books which nourished the Lover's mind into fodder force-fed to him by Spica's henchmen.

What is suggested in these films is that, where consumer capitalism rules and justifies all other forms of behavior and organization, there is no easily discernible limit set upon the processes of consumption. If consumption is the imperative, all can be consumed, including that which previously was secure as consumer.

EIGHTIES MOVIES AND THINKING ABOUT AIDS. It is remarkable in itself that AIDS did not become the overt subject of a major eighties movie—remarkable, but explicable, given the prevailing conception of AIDS and the prestige accorded to borderlines between the acceptable and unacceptable. Despite the absence of AIDS, the very silence about it except in the context of embarrassed jokiness bespeaks the terror that it represents.

Study of eighties movies allows us to see one aspect of what must be a circular, mutually supporting process. All the energy which goes into defining family, acceptable sexuality, and the border between it and the unacceptable sexuality of Alex or Del or the Mexican brothels, augments the fear of passage from one area to the other and helps to allow the defects within the acceptable explanation in terms of contamination, despite precautions, from the other area. The frame preexists the picture. When AIDS is "understood" by the mideighties, the frame in which it is henceforth to be pictured in the West is ready for it. The frame had evidently been waiting from at least the midseventies. The lethal consequences of the actively gazing heroine's life-style in *Looking for Mr. Goodbar,* or of the cruising in the film of that name, the death of *Dressed to Kill's* heroine, linked perhaps for the first time explicitly with venereal disease, seem to await concretization. In the early eighties, the media's enthusiasm for identifying a precise exemplification of the punitive process was indicated by the attempt to make genital herpes into the scourge. It was somehow inadequate to play the full role demanded of it. AIDS was not. Its understanding has been so deeply embedded in the scenario that apparently awaited it that it may have fixed the minds of medical experts on certain tracks which may or may not prove to be the only feasible ones.

The concerns of eighties entertainment films with establishing lines of demarcation between pure and impure, ideal and vile, those who belong and those who are alien, make it almost impossible for there to be an "objective" look at AIDS, once it is identified with, as well as IV-drug users and Haitians, male homosexuals. Moreover, the conceptions of the syndrome and its "causes" are not only shaped by the movies but continue to be reinforced by them—just as the movies gain their power from popular understanding of the meanings of AIDS.

If this were all that eighties movies had achieved, it would still be a formidable contribution to our history, not only in dealing with matters of life and death but in helping to bring them about. Because of a set of beliefs about contamination and its source in an epoch when the watchword of purification has been taken from fundamentalists and commandeered by politicians, the deaths of thousands are at issue. The ideological power of popular entertainment can seldom have been illustrated as so terrible.

Notes

Chapter 1. Introduction

1. Michael Paul Rogin, *Ronald Reagan, the Movie, and Other Episodes in Political Demonology* (Berkeley and Los Angeles: University of California Press, 1987), 296.

2. Richard M. Perloff, Jane Delano Brown, and M. Mark Miller, "Mass Media and Sex-Typing: Research Perspectives and Policy Implications," *International Journal of Women's Studies* 5: 269.

3. Caroline Sheldon, "Lesbians and Film: Some Thoughts", in *Gays and Film,* ed. Richard Dyer (London: British Film Institute, 1977, 1980), 5.

4. Gaye Tuchman, "Introduction: The Symbolic Annihilation of Women by the Mass Media," in *Hearth and Home: Images of Women in the Mass Media,* ed. Gaye Tuchman, Arlene Kaplan Daniels, and James Benét (New York: Oxford University Press, 1978), 8.

5. Stuart Hall, "Media Power and Class Power," in *Bending Reality: The State of the Media,* ed. James Curran, Jake Ecclestone, Giles Oakley, and Alan Richardson (London: Pluto Press, 1986), 12.

6. Lorraine Gamman and Margaret Marshment, eds., *The Female Gaze: Women as Viewers of Popular Culture* (London: The Women's Press, 1988), 1–2.

7. Kenneth MacKinnon, *Hollywood's Small Towns* (Metuchen, N.J.: Scarecrow, 1984).

8. Kenneth MacKinnon, *Misogyny in the Movies: The De Palma Question* (Newark: University of Delaware Press, 1990).

Chapter 2. The Reagan-Thatcher Epoch

1. Lawrence Grossberg, *It's a Sin: Essays on Postmodernism, Politics and Culture* (Sydney: Power Publications, 1989), 44.

2. Ibid., 38.

3. Ibid.

4. Ibid., 32.

5. Ibid., 38.

6. Andrew Britton, "Blissing Out: The Politics of Reaganite Entertainment," *Movie* 31–32: 3.

7. Jeffrey Weeks, *Sex, Politics and Society: The Regulation of Sexuality since 1800* (London: Longman, 1981), 281, 282.

8. Stuart Hall and Martin Jacques, *The Politics of Thatcherism* (London: Lawrence and Wishart, 1983), 9, 10.

9. Ibid., 9.

10. One aspect of this question that suggests itself is whether the Left was *potentially* capable of commandeering popular allegiance in the British 1979

election—albeit a Left that would have had to have transformed and re-presented itself after the manner of the Thatcherite Right. It would be a mistake to conflate the phenomena of Reaganism and Thatcherism, since there are observable differences in, for example, the extent of interference in the state by religious fundamentalists in the two countries' politics. Nevertheless, the relevance of postmodernity to an analysis of Reaganism's appeal may be worth considering in relation to the populist appeal of Thatcherism at the end of the seventies. The major question may be whether the ascendancy of Britain's Right was "inevitable," given the difficulties of the Labour government in the late seventies, or whether the national "mood" made the popular ripe for exploitation by a certain kind of political party, a certain kind of passionate politics, from either end of the political spectrum.

11. Randy Shilts, *And the Band Played On: Politics, People, and the AIDS Epidemic* (London: Penguin, 1987), 44.

12. Zillah Eisenstein, "Antifeminism in the Politics and Election of 1980," *Feminist Studies* 7, no. 2 (Summer 1981): 187.

13. Ibid., 189.

14. Alan Crawford, *Thunder on the Right: The "New Right" and the Politics of Resentment* (New York: Pantheon, 1980), 5.

15. Ibid., 5, 34.

16. Jerry G. Pankhurst and Sharon K. Houseknecht, "The Family, Politics, and Religion in the 1980s," *Journal of Family Issues* 4, no. 1 (March 1983): 21.

17. Ibid., 11.

18. Andrea Dworkin, *Right-Wing Women: The Politics of Domesticated Females* (London: The Women's Press, 1983), xii.

19. Erling Jorstad, *The Politics of Moralism: The New Christian Right in American Life* (Minneapolis, Minn.: Augsburg Publishing House, 1981), 7.

20. Ibid., 93–94; cf. Jeffrey K. Hadden and Anson Shupe, *Televangelism: Power and Politics on God's Frontier* (New York: Henry Holt and Co., 1988), 27.

21. Hadden and Shupe, *Televangelism*, 29.

22. Ibid., 28.

23. Dworkin, *Right-Wing Women*, xi.

24. Grossberg, *It's a Sin*, 31.

25. Ibid., 27.

26. Ibid., 28.

27. In this regard, it is surely interesting that Ronald Reagan chose a famous line spoken by himself in that movie—"Where's the rest of me?"—to be the title of his autobiography.

28. Lloyd deMause, *Reagan's America* (New York: Creative Roots, 1984), 38.

29. Rogin, *Reagan, the Movie, and Other Episodes*, xiii, xiv.

30. Susan Sontag, *Illness as Metaphor* (Harmondsworth: Penguin, 1977), 18.

31. Rogin, *Reagan, the Movie, and Other Episodes*, xvii.

32. Ibid., xv.

33. deMause, *Reagan's America*, 119.

34. Ibid., 120.

35. See, for example, Roberta McGrath, "Dangerous Liaisons: Health, Disease and Representation," in *Ecstastic Antibodies: Resisting the AIDS mythology*, ed. Tessa Boffin and Sunil Gupta (London: Rivers Oram Press, 1990), 144.

36. Arthur Kroker and Marilouise Kroker, "Panic Sex in America," in *Body Invaders: Sexuality and the Postmodern Condition*, ed. Arthur and Marilouise Kroker (London: Macmillan, 1988), 12.

37. Zillah R. Eisenstein, "The Sexual Politics of the New Right: Understanding the 'Crisis of Liberalism' for the 1980s," *Signs: Journal of Women in Culture and Society* 7 (1982); 573.

38. Eisenstein, "Sexual Politics of the New Right," 586.

39. Margaret Thatcher, quoted in Jeffrey Weeks, *Sexuality and Its Discontents: Meanings, Myths and Modern Sexualities* (London: Routledge and Kegan Paul, 1985), 18.

40. Weeks, *Sexuality and Its Discontents,* 19.

41. Weeks, *Sex, Politics and Society,* 250.

42. Rogin, *Reagan, the Movie, and Other Episodes,* xvii–xviii.

43. Martin Jacques, "Thatcherism: Breaking out of the Impasse," in Hall and Jacques, *Politics of Thatcherism,* 53.

44. Hall and Jacques, *Politics of Thatcherism,* 10.

45. Ibid.

46. Stuart Hall, *The Hard Road to Renewal: Thatcherism and the Crisis of the Left* (London and New York: Verso, 1988), 8.

47. The use of the term may be interestingly compared with the New Christian Right's employment of "the collectivists" as an appellation not simply for communists, whom they no longer name as such, but secular humanists, who are saddled by it with responsibility for threatening the family and, thereby, the country (Hadden and Shupe, *Televangelism,* 60).

48. The Right Reverend Professor James White, quoted in Mark Douglas Home, "Moderator Criticises 'Thatcher Theology,'" *Independent,* 18 February 1989.

49. deMause, *Reagan's America,* 159–60.

50. Grossberg, *It's a Sin,* 49–50.

51. Andy Metcalf and Martin Humphries, *The Sexuality of Men* (London: Pluto Press, 1985), 11.

52. The puppet representing her in Independent Television's satirical series "Spitting Image" was dressed as a man and smoked a cigar.

53. Casper G. Schmidt, "The Group-Fantasy Origins of AIDS," *Journal of Psychohistory* 12 (1984): 60.

54. deMause, *Reagan's America,* 1.

55. Ibid., 91.

56. Jeffrey Weeks, "Decades of Desire," *Gay Times* (December 1989): 30.

57. Eisenstein, "Sexual Politics of the New Right," 587.

Chapter 3. Movies and the Reagan-Thatcher Epoch

1. Steve Jenkins, "*An Officer and a Gentleman,*" *Monthly Film Bulletin* 50 (1983): 75.

2. Ibid.

3. Britton, "Blissing Out," 1–42.

4. Robin Wood, *Hollywood from Vietnam to Reagan* (New York: Columbia University Press, 1986), 69.

5. Ibid., 163–82.

6. Ibid., 207.

7. Dennis Altman, *The Homosexualization of America, The Americanization of the Homosexual* (New York: St. Martin's Press, 1982), 29.

8. Vito Russo, *The Celluloid Closet: Homosexuality in the Movies,* rev. ed. (New York: Harper and Row, 1987), 276.

9. Britton, "Blissing Out," 2.

10. Ibid., 9.

11. A similar reluctance to be associated with homosexual male admirers is evidenced by Donna Summer, although her success—like the Village People's—is unimaginable without her original connection in the seventies with gay discos.

12. Richard Combs, "*Working Girl*," *Monthly Film Bulletin* 56 (1989): 100.

13. Chris Auty, "*Poltergeist*," *Monthly Film Bulletin* 49 (1982): 206.

14. David Hare, quoted in *Monthly Film Bulletin* 56 (1989): 212.

15. Derek Jarman, "Britannia on Trial," *Monthly Film Bulletin* 53 (1986): 101.

16. Ibid.

17. Ibid.

18. Mark Finch, "*What Can I Do with a Male Nude?*" *Monthly Film Bulletin* 53 (1986): 159.

19. Pam Cook, "*Near Dark*," *Monthly Film Bulletin* 55 (1988): 3.

Chapter 4. Familialism

1. Weeks, "Decades of Desire," 31.

2. John Scanzoni, Karen Polonko, Jay Teachman, and Linda Thompson, *The Sexual Bond: Rethinking Families and Close Relationships* (Sage Library of Social Research, vol. 170, Newbury Park, Calif.: 1989), 18.

3. Ibid., 9.

4. Ibid.

5. Ibid., 19.

6. Eli Zaretsky, *Capitalism, the Family and Personal Life* (London: Pluto Press, 1976), 73.

7. Weeks, "Decades of Desire," 31.

8. Cf. Simon Watney, *Policing Desire: Pornography, AIDS and the Media* (London: Methuen, 1987), 48.

9. This seems precisely what the 1988 Act attempts to do.

10. Sar A. Levitan and Richard S. Belous, *What's Happening to the American Family?* (Baltimore and London: Johns Hopkins University Press, 1981), 4.

11. See, for example, Pankhurst and Housekneckt, "Family, Politics, and Religion," 28.

12. Levitan and Belous, *What's Happening to Family?* 126.

13. Weeks, *Sex, Politics and Society*, 278.

14. Crawford, *Thunder on the Right*, 144.

15. Schmidt, "Group-Fantasy Origins of AIDS," 67.

16. Betty Friedan, *The Second Stage* (London: Michael Joseph, 1982), 28.

17. Weeks, *Sexuality and Its Discontents*, 34.

18. Eisenstein, "Antifeminism," 188.

19. Friedan, *Second Stage*, 109.

20. Michele Barrett and Mary McIntosh, *The Anti-Social Family* (London: Verso Editions/NLB, 1982), 27.

21. Michel Foucault, *The History of Sexuality*, vol. 1, trans. Robert Hurley (Harmondsworth: Penguin, 1981), 108.

22. Anita Bryant, *The Anita Bryant Story* (Old Tappan, N.J.: Fleming H. Revell Company, 1977), 53–54.

23. Ibid., 54.

24. Weeks, *Sex, Politics and Society*, 279.

25. See Watney, *Policing Desire*, 16.

26. Sonja Ruehl, "Sexual Theory and Practice: Another Double Standard," in *Sex and Love: New Thoughts on Old Contradictions,* ed. Sue Cartledge and Joanna Ryan (1983; reprint, London: The Women's Press, 1987), 212.

27. Ferdinand Mount, *The Subversive Family: An Alternative History of Love and Marriage* (London: Jonathan Cape, 1982), 1.

28. Ibid., 46.

29. Ibid.

30. Levitan and Belous, *What's Happening to Family?* vii.

31. Hadden and Shupe, *Televangelism,* 60.

32. Barbara Ehrenreich, *The Hearts of Men: American Dreams and the Flight from Commitment* (London: Pluto Press, 1983), 145.

33. Eisenstein, "Sexual Politics of the New Right," 575.

34. Ibid., 579.

35. Ibid., 585.

36. Margaret Thatcher, quoted in Lynne Segal, ed., *What Is to Be Done about the Family?* (Harmondsworth: Penguin, 1983), 9.

37. Ibid., 21.

38. Ibid., 11.

39. Ibid., 22.

40. Ibid., 223.

41. Barrett and McIntosh, *Anti-Social Family,* 80.

42. Levitan and Belous, *What's Happening to Family?* 8.

43. Carolyn Faulder and Sandra Brown, "Introduction to the British Edition," in Friedan, *Second Stage,* 16.

44. Barrie Gunter and Michael Svennevig, *Behind and in Front of the Screen: Television's Involvement with Family Life* (London and Paris: John Libbey, 1987), 3.

45. Lynne Segal, "The Heat in the Kitchen," in Hall and Jacques, *Politics of Thatcherism,* 209.

46. Eisenstein, "Sexual Politics of the New Right," 581.

47. Faulder and Brown, "Introduction," 17.

48. Altman, *Homosexualization of America,* 89–90.

49. Ibid., 89.

50. Zaretsky, *Capitalism,* 29, 33.

51. Ibid., 29.

52. Mark Poster, *Critical Theory of the Family* (London: Pluto Press, 1978), 3–4.

53. Segal, *What Is to Be Done?* 10.

54. Levitan and Belous, *What's Happening to Family?* 183.

55. Jeffrey Weeks, *Coming Out: Homosexual Politics in Britain, from the Nineteenth Century to the Present* (1977; reprint, London: Quartet Books, 1983), 144–45.

56. Mary McIntosh, "The Family in Socialist-Feminist Politics," in *Feminism, Culture and Politics,* ed. Rosalind Brunt and Caroline Rowan (1982: reprint, London: Lawrence and Wishart, 1986), 111.

57. Ibid., 109.

58. Ibid., 111.

59. Ibid., 123.

60. Linda Gordon and Allen Hunter, "Sex, Family and the New Right: Anti-Feminism as a Political Force," *Radical America* 12, no. 1 (1978): 25.

61. Friedan, *Second Stage,* 109–10.

62. Gordon and Hunter, "Sex, Family, and New Right," 19.

63. Grossberg, *It's a Sin*, 54.

Chapter 5. Movies and Familialism

1. Britton, "Blissing Out," 24.
2. Philip Brophy, "Horrality: the Textuality of Contemporary Horror Films," *Screen 27*, no. 1 (January–February 1986): 7.
3. Ibid.
4. Ibid.
5. Cynthia Rose, "*The Funhouse*," *Monthly Film Bulletin* 48 (1981): 66.

Chapter 6. Sexuality

1. Mount, *Subversive Family*, 46.
2. Bryant, *Anita Bryant Story*, 107.
3. Watney, *Policing Desire*, 50.
4. Pat Caplan, "Introduction," in *The Cultural Construction of Sexuality* (London and New York: Tavistock, 1987), 2.
5. Weeks, *Sex, Politics and Society*, 3.
6. Ibid., 10.
7. Ibid., 12.
8. Weeks, *Sexuality and Its Discontents*, 56.
9. Ibid., 17.
10. Ibid., 20.
11. Ibid.
12. Victoria Greenwood and Jock Young, "Ghettos of Freedom: An Examination of Permissiveness," in *Permissiveness and Control: The Fate of the Sixties Legislation*, ed. National Deviancy Conference (London: Macmillan, 1980), 149.
13. Schmidt, "Group-Fantasy Origins of AIDS," 60.
14. Sheldon, "Lesbians and Film," 6.
15. Weeks, *Coming Out*, (London: Quartet Books, 1977, repr. 1983), 4.
16. Ibid., 5.
17. Foucault, *History of Sexuality*, 5.
18. Ibid., 6.
19. See, for example, Eisenstein, "Sexual Politics of the New Right," 582.
20. Gordon and Hunter, "Sex, Family, and the New Right," 13.
21. Ibid., 25.
22. Altman, *Homosexualization of America*, 90–91.
23. Zaretsky, *Capitalism*, 68.
24. Altman, *Homosexualization of America*, 81, 82, 85.
25. Ibid., 88.
26. Ibid., 89.
27. Weeks, *Sex, Politics, and Society*, 287.
28. Gregg Blachford, "Male Dominance and the Gay World," in *The Making of the Modern Homosexual*, ed. Kenneth Plummer (London: Hutchinson, 1981), 198.
29. Gordon and Hunter, "Sex, Family, and the New Right," 18–19.
30. Mariana Valverde, *Sex, Power and Pleasure* (Toronto: The Women's Press, 1985), 15.
31. Ibid., 15, 17.

32. Richard von Kraft-Ebbing, in *Nationalism and Sexuality: Respectability and Abnormal Sexuality in Modern Europe,* by George L. Mosse (New York: Howard Fertig, 1985), 10–11.

33. Ibid., 134.

34. Herbert Marcuse, quoted in Poster, *Critical Theory,* 59.

35. Victor J. Seidler, "Reason, Desire, and Male Sexuality" in Caplan, *Cultural Construction,* 99.

36. Metcalf and Humphries, *Sexuality of Men,* 148.

37. Ibid.

38. Sheldon, "Lesbians and Film," 10.

39. Weeks, *Sex, Politics, and Society,* 12.

40. Foucault, *History of Sexuality,* 49.

41. Weeks, *Sex, Politics and Society,* 7.

42. Ibid.

43. Michel Foucault, quoted in Caplan, *Cultural Construction,* 7.

44. Weeks, *Sex, Politics and Society,* 8.

45. Ibid., 8–9.

46. Poster, *Critical Theory,* 8.

47. Sheila Jeffreys, *The Spinster and Her Enemies: Feminism and Sexuality, 1880–1930* (London: Pandora, 1985), 3.

48. Foucault, *History of Sexuality,* 44.

49. Ibid., 45.

50. Michel Foucault, quoted in the preface to Plummer, *Making of the Modern Homosexual.*

51. Weeks, *Coming Out,* 28.

52. Dyer, "Postscript (1980)" in *Gays and Film,* 4.

Chapter 7. Movies and Sexuality

1. David Shipman, *Caught in the Act: Sex and Eroticism in the Movies* (London: Elm Tree Books, 1985), 151.

2. Ibid.

3. Wood, *Hollywood,* 56.

4. E. Ann Kaplan, *Women and Film: Both Sides of the Camera* (New York and London: Methuen, 1983), 80.

5. For an extended discussion of negative judgments and of counterreadings which would destabilize the orthodoxy on *Dressed To Kill,* see Kenneth MacKinnon, *Misogyny in the Movies: The De Palma Question* (Toronto and London: Associated University Presses, 1990), 138–60.

6. Wood, *Hollywood,* 57.

7. Ibid., 58.

8. Ibid.

9. Ibid.

10. Geoffrey Nowell-Smith, "Minnelli and Melodrama," *Screen* 18, no. 2 (1977).

11. Barbara Creed, "Horror and the Monstrous Feminine: An Imaginary Abjection", *Screen* 27, no. 1 (January–February 1986): 48–49.

12. Robert Brown, "*Terror Eyes,*" *Monthly Film Bulletin* 48 (1981): 144.

13. Pam Cook, "*Love Letters,*" *Monthly Film Bulletin* 53 (1983): 134.

14. Friedan, *Second Stage,* 147.

15. Ibid., 148.

16. Ibid., 141.
17. Ibid., 146–47.
18. Ibid., 147.
19. Ibid., 146.
20. Ehrenreich, *Hearts of Men,* 137.
21. Ibid., 137, 138–39.
22. Jill Forbes, *"Heartbreakers," Monthly Film Bulletin* 53 (1986): 146–47.
23. Bobby Roth, quoted in ibid. 147.
24. Ibid.
25. Lizzie Borden, quoted in Sylvia Paskin, *"Working Girls," Monthly Film Bulletin* 54 (1987), 69.

Chapter 8. Homosexuality

1. Foucault, *History of Sexuality,* 38.
2. Ibid., 39.
3. Ibid., 43.
4. Both Mary McIntosh and Kenneth Plummer take 1869 as the date of birth for the homosexual, on the other hand, since, as Plummer claims, the term was coined in that year by Benkert. See Kenneth Plummer, "Sexual Diversity: A Sociological Perspective," in *The Psychology of Sexual Diversity,* ed. Kevin Howells (Oxford: Basil Blackwell, 1984), 234.
5. Weeks, *Sex, Politics and Society,* 12.
6. Ibid.
7. Ibid.
8. Weeks, *Coming Out,* 25.
9. Ibid., 31.
10. Greenwood and Young, "Ghettos of Freedom," 159.
11. Frank Pearce, "How to Be Immoral and Ill, Pathetic and Dangerous, All at the Same Time: Mass Media and the Homosexual," in *The Manufacture of News: Social Problems, Deviance and the Mass Media,* ed. Stanley Cohen and Jock Young (London: Constable, 1973), 290.
12. Ibid.
13. Edwin M. Schur, *The Politics of Deviance: Stigma Contests and the Uses of Power* (Englewood Cliffs, N.J.: Prentice-Hall, 1980), xi.
14. Ibid., 40.
15. Barry D. Adam, *The Survival of Domination: Inferiorization and Everyday Life* (New York: Elsevier, 1978), 13.
16. Mordechai Rotenberg, *Damnation and Deviance: The Protestant Ethic and the Spirit of Failure* (New York: Free Press, 1978).
17. See, for example, Mary McIntosh, "The Homosexual Role," in Plummer, *Making of the Modern Homosexual,* 32.
18. Weeks, *Sex, Politics, and Society,* 10.
19. Richard Dyer, "Getting over the Rainbow: Identity and Pleasure in Gay Cultural Politics," in *Silver Linings: Some Strategies for the Eighties,* ed. George Bridges and Rosalind Brunt (London: Lawrence and Wishart, 1980), 58.
20. Mike Brake, "Sexuality as Praxis: A Consideration of the Contribution of Sexual Theory to the Process of Sexual Being," in *Human Sexual Relations: A Reader in Human Sexuality,* ed. Mike Brake (Harmondsworth: Penguin, 1982), 18.
21. Richard Dyer, "Stereotyping," in Dyer, *Gays and Film,* 27.

22. Ibid., 31.
23. Emmanuel Reynaud, *Holy Virility: The Social Construction of Masculinity,* trans. Ros Schwartz (London: Pluto Press, 1983), 55.
24. Sheldon, "Lesbians and film," 10.
25. Seidler, "Reason, Desire and Male Sexuality," 99.
26. See Pearce, "How to Be Immoral," 284.
27. Richard Liebmann-Smith, *The Question of AIDS* (New York: New York Academy of Sciences, 1985), 88.
28. Altman, *Homosexualization of America,* xi.
29. Weeks, *Coming Out,* 7.
30. Dyer, "Getting over the Rainbow," 59.
31. Altman, *Homosexualization of America,* 18.
32. Susan Sontag, "Notes on 'Camp,'" in *Against Interpretation, and Other Essays* (London: Eyre and Spottiswoode, 1967), 275.
33. Ibid., 290.
34. Ibid., 280.
35. Ibid., 290.
36. Dyer, "Getting over the Rainbow," 61.
37. Andrew Britton, "FOR Interpretation: Notes against Camp," *Gay Left* 7 (1978–79): 11.
38. Britton, "FOR Interpretation," 14.
39. Liebmann-Smith, *Question of AIDS,* 89.
40. Gordon and Hunter, "Sex, Family, and the New Right," 20.
41. See Weeks, "Decades of Desire," 31–32.
42. See Greenwood and Young, "Ghettos of Freedom," 164.
43. Gordon and Hunter, "Sex, Family, and the New Right," 11.
44. Ehrenreich, *Hearts of Men,* 157.
45. Gordon and Hunter, "Sex, Family, and the New Right," 14.
46. Dworkin, *Right-Wing Women,* 135.
47. Stuart Hall, "Deviancy, Politics and the Media," (Birmingham: University of Birmingham, Centre for Contemporary Cultural Studies, 1971), 21–22.
48. Altman, *Homosexualization of America,* 92.
49. Ibid., 67–68.
50. Michael Tracey and David Morrison, *Whitehouse* (London: Macmillan, 1979).
51. Ibid., 17, 18.
52. Ibid., 15.
53. Mary Whitehouse, in ibid., 18.
54. Whitehouse, in ibid., 18.
55. Ibid., 18.
56. Ibid., 19.
57. Dworkin, *Right-Wing Women,* 34.
58. Bryant, *Anita Bryant Story,* 21.
59. Ibid., 13.
60. Ibid., 21.
61. Ibid., 59.
62. Ibid., 38.
63. Ibid.
64. Ibid., 35.
65. Ibid., 55.
66. Ibid., 14–15.
67. Ibid., 15.

68. Crawford, *Thunder on the Right,* 37.
69. Bryant, *Anita Bryant Story,* 146.
70. Ibid., 17.
71. Ibid., 107.
72. Ibid., 35–36.
73. Ibid., 43
74. Ibid., 126.
75. Ibid., 52.
76. British Local Government Act, 1988, quoted in Boffin and Gupta, *Ecstatic Antibodies,* 2.
77. Weeks, "Decades of Desire," 31.
78. Ibid.
79. Mosse, *Nationalism and Sexuality,* 135.
80. Ibid., 165.
81. Bryant, *Anita Bryant Story,* 42.
82. Edward Albert, "Acquired Immune Defiency Syndrome: The Victim and the Press," in *Studies in Communications: News and Knowledge,* ed. Thelma McCormack, vol. 3 (Greenwich, Conn. and London: JAI Press, 1986), 151.
83. Richard Goldstein, quoted in Simon Watney, "The Rhetoric of AIDS: A Dossier," comp. Simon Watney, *Screen* 27, no. 1 (January–February 1986): 79.

Chapter 9. Movies and Homosexuality

1. Stuart Marshall, "Picturing Deviancy," in Boffin and Gupta, *Ecstatic Antibodies,* 19–20.
2. Ibid., 20.
3. Dyer, *Gays and Film.*
4. Russo, *Celluloid Closet.*
5. Marshall, "Picturing Deviancy," 20.
6. Ibid., 20–21.
7. Ibid., 21.
8. Watney, *Policing Desire,* 98.
9. Ibid., 100.
10. Armistead Maupin, quoted in Lon G. Nungesser, *Epidemic of Courage: Facing AIDS in America* (New York: St. Martin's Press, 1986), 211.
11. Wood, *Hollywood,* 58.
12. Ibid., 59–60.
13. Ibid., 59.
14. Steve Neale, "Masculinity as Spectacle: Reflections on Men and Mainstream Cinema," *Screen* 24, no. 6 (November–December 1983): 15.
15. Ibid.
16. Russo, *Celluloid Closet,* 47, 48.
17. Ibid., 249.
18. Perhaps it might have been safer to have written "are sometimes taken to reflect."
19. Russo, *Celluloid Closet,* 250.
20. Ibid., 251, 255.
21. Wood, *Hollywood,* 238.
22. Ibid.
23. Ibid., 241.

24. Ibid., 242.
25. Ibid., 243.
26. Ibid., 237.
27. Ibid., 237–38.
28. Ibid., 243.
29. Ibid., 242.
30. Suzanne Moore, "Here's Looking at You, Kid!" in Gamman and Marshment, *Female Gaze,* 44.
31. Ibid., 52–53.
32. Jack Babuscio, "Camp and the Gay Sensibility," in Dyer, *Gays and Film,* 45.
33. Andrew Britton, *Cary Grant: Comedy and Male Desire* (Newcastle upon Tyne: Tyneside Cinema, 1983), n.p.
34. Ibid.
35. Mandy Merck, "*Veronica 4 Rose,*" *Monthly Film Bulletin* 51 (1984): 215.
36. Kobena Mercer, "*Looking for Langston,*" *Monthly Film Bulletin* 57 (1990): 45.
37. Steve Jenkins, "*Desert Hearts,*" *Monthly Film Bulletin* 53 (1986): 227.
38. Mark Finch, "*Torch Song Trilogy,*" *Monthly Film Bulletin* 56 (1989): 155.
39. Wood, *Hollywood,* 234.
40. Kim Newman, "*Kiss of the Spider Woman,*" *Monthly Film Bulletin* 53 (1986): 9.
41. See chapter 8.
42. Russo, *Celluloid Closet,* 7.
43. Wood, *Hollywood,* 64.
44. Altman, *Homosexualization of America,* 198.
45. Wood, *Hollywood,* 66.
46. Ibid., 68.

Chapter 10. AIDS

1. Sander L. Gilman, *Disease and Representation: Images of Illness from Madness to AIDS* (Ithaca: Cornell University Press, 1988), 246.
2. Jan Zita Grover, "AIDS: Keywords," in *AIDS: Cultural Analysis/Cultural Activism,* ed. Douglas Crimp (Cambridge: MIT Press, 1988), 18.
3. Weeks, *Sexuality and Its Discontents,* 46.
4. Gilman, *Disease and Representation,* 247.
5. Grover, "AIDS: Keywords," 18.
6. Weeks, *Sexuality and Its Discontents,* 46.
7. Gilman, *Disease and Representation,* 247.
8. Ibid., 258.
9. Weeks, *Sexuality and Its Discontents,* 46.
10. Kevin M. Cahill, M.D., *The AIDS Epidemic* (New York: St. Martin's Press, 1983), 2.
11. Ibid.
12. Celia Hall, "AIDS Cases among Heterosexuals Have Doubled in a Year," *Independent* (12 April 1990): 3.
13. Grover, "AIDS: Keywords," 19.
14. Gilman, *Disease and Representation,* 246.
15. Shilts, *And The Band Played On,* 191.

16. Ibid., 214.

17. Schmidt, "Group-Fantasy Origins of AIDS," 37.

18. Harry Schwartz, "AIDS in the Media," in *Science in the Streets: Report of the Twentieth Century Fund Task Force on the Communication of Scientific Risk* (New York: Priority Press, 1984), 95.

19. Liebmann-Smith, *Question of AIDS*, 1.

20. Graham Hancock and Enver Carim, *AIDS: The Deadly Epidemic* (London: Victor Gollancz, 1986), 17.

21. Shilts, *And the Band Played On,* xxi.

22. Hancock and Carim, *AIDS: Deadly Epidemic,* 17, 21.

23. Edward Albert, "Acquired Immune Deficiency Syndrome: The Victim and the Press," in *Studies in Communications,* 136.

24. Eve K. Nichols, *Mobilizing against AIDS: The Unfinished Story of a Virus* (Cambridge: Harvard University Press, 1986), 2.

25. Hancock and Carim, *AIDS: Deadly Epidemic,* 10.

26. Ibid.

27. Crimp, *AIDS,* 7–11.

28. C. Hall, "Aids Cases among Heterosexuals," 3.

29. Grover, "AIDS: Keywords," 20.

30. See ibid., 20, 21.

31. Albert, "Acquired Immune Deficiency Syndrome," 137.

32. Nichols, *Mobilizing against AIDS,* 5.

33. Nungesser, *Epidemic of Courage,* 35.

34. Schmidt, "Group-Fantasy Origins of AIDS," 38.

35. Duncan Campbell, "AIDS: The Duesberg Myth," *New Scientist* 122, no. 1663 (6 May 1989): 60–61.

36. Bruce Dessau, "Critical Immunity," *Time Out* (13–20 June 1990): 48.

37. Schmidt, "Group-Fantasy Origins of AIDS," 38–39.

38. Ibid., 39.

39. Ibid.

40. Ibid., 43.

41. Ibid., 48–49.

42. Ibid., 50.

43. Ibid., 68.

44. Ibid., 49–50.

45. Ibid., 56.

46. Ibid.

47. Ibid., 57.

48. Ibid.

49. Ibid., 60.

50. Ibid., 63.

51. deMause, *Reagan's America,* 125.

52. Jeffrey Weeks, "Post-Modern AIDS?" in Boffin and Gupta, *Ecstatic Antibodies,* 134.

53. Susan Sontag, *AIDS and Its Metapors* (New York: Farrar, Straus and Giroux, 1988), 63.

54. Weeks, "Decades of Desire," 31.

55. Shilts, *And the Band Played On,* 183.

56. Ibid., 495.

57. Ibid., 596.

58. Rogin, *Reagan, the Movie, and Other Episodes,* xvii.

59. Hancock and Carim, *AIDS: Deadly Epidemic,* 38–39.

60. Crimp, *AIDS*, 6.
61. Mayor Edward I. Koch, "Welcome," in Cahill, *AIDS Epidemic*, xv.
62. Cahill, *AIDS Epidemic*, 2.
63. Schwartz, "AIDS in the Media," 88.
64. Ibid., 96.
65. Shilts, *And the Band Played On*, 303.
66. Hancock and Carim, *AIDS: Deadly Epidemic*, 35.
67. Sontag, *AIDS and Its Metaphors*, 73.
68. Shilts, *And the Band Played On*, 492.
69. Bill Margold, quoted in David Hebditch and Nick Anning, *Porn Gold: Inside the Pornography Business* (London: Faber and Faber, 1988), 115.
70. Nichols, *Mobilizing against AIDS*, 3.
71. Ibid., 4.
72. Crimp, *AIDS*, 3.
73. Sontag, *AIDS and Its Metaphors*, 20–21.
74. Ibid., 28.
75. Nungesser, *Epidemic of Courage*, 29.
76. Michael Lynch, quoted in Marshall, "Picturing Deviancy," in Boffin and Gupta, *Ecstatic Antibodies*, 31.
77. Nungesser, *Epidemic of Courage*, 33.
78. Marshall, "Picturing Deviancy," 31.
79. Ibid., 52.
80. Sontag, *AIDS and Its Metaphors*, 62.
81. Gilman, *Disease and Representation*, 263.
82. Albert, "Acquired Immune Deficiency Syndrome," 151.
83. Sontag, *AIDS and Its Metaphors*, 61–62.
84. Schwartz, "AIDS in the Media," 88.
85. Weeks, *Sexuality*, 46.
86. Albert, "Acquired Immune Deficiency Syndrome," 139.
87. Ibid., 146.
88. Ibid., 147.
89. Ibid., 150.
90. Ibid., 154.
91. Marshall, "Picturing Deviancy," 21.
92. Sontag, *Illness as Metaphor*, 68–70.
93. Ibid., 63.
94. Sontag, *AIDS and Its Metaphors*, 11.
95. Ibid., 17.
96. Ibid., 18.
97. Ibid., 67.
98. Gilman, *Disease and Representation*, 259, 262.
99. Weeks, *Sexuality*, 48.
100. Viper, quoted in Hebditch and Anning, *Porn Gold*, 115.
101. Hancock and Carim, *AIDS: Deadly Epidemic*, 15.
102. Sontag, *AIDS and Its Metaphors*, 66.
103. Hancock and Carim, *AIDS: Deadly Epidemic*, 13.
104. Sontag, *AIDS and Its Metaphors*, 72–73.
105. Ibid., 73.
106. Ibid., 45.
107. Sontag, *Illness as Metaphor*, 26, 27.
108. Ibid., 62.
109. Hancock and Carim, *AIDS: Deadly Epidemic*, 40.

110. Weeks, *Sex, Politics and Society,* 14.
111. Hancock and Carim, *AIDS: Deadly Epidemic,* 24.
112. Albert, "Acquired Immune Deficiency Syndrome," 152.
113. Dennis Altman, *AIDS and the New Puritanism* (London: Pluto Press, 1986), 8.
114. Hancock and Carim, *AIDS: Deadly Epidemic,* 22.
115. Ibid., 23.

Chapter 11. Movies and AIDS

1. B. Ruby Rich, quoted in Crimp, *AIDS,* 14.
2. Crimp, *AIDS,* 7.
3. Ibid., 15.
4. Philip Core, "Unseen Enemy," *Independent* (14 April 1989): 18.
5. E. Ann Kaplan, *Rocking around the Clock: Music Television, Postmodernism, and Consumer Culture* (New York and London: Methuen, 1987), 84.
6. Crimp, *AIDS,* 14.
7. Martha Gever, "Pictures of Sickness: Stuart Marshall's *Bright Eyes,*" in Crimp, AIDS, 113–14.
8. Altman, *AIDS and the New Puritanism,* 23.
9. Hancock and Carim, *AIDS: Deadly Epidemic,* 38.
10. Altman, *AIDS and the New Puritanism,* 18.
11. Watney, *Policing Desire,* 113.
12. Ibid., 114.
13. Gever, "Pictures of Sickness," in Crimp, AIDS, 111.
14. Ibid., 112.
15. Altman, *AIDS and the New Puritanism,* 20–21.
16. Bill Margold, quoted in Hebditch and Anning, *Porn Gold,* 115.
17. Jane Root, "*Parting Glances,*" *Monthly Film Bulletin* 53 (1986): 341.
18. Kim Newman, "*Skin Deep,*" *Monthly Film Bulletin* 56 (1989): 215.
19. Brophy, "Horrality," 9.
20. Pete Boss, "Vile Bodies and Bad Medicine," *Screen 27,* no. 1 (January–February 1986): 15.
21. Ibid.
22. Ibid., 17.
23. Ibid., 16.
24. Weeks, *Sex, Politics and Society,* 10.
25. Boss, "Vile Bodies," 19.
26. Ibid., 20.
27. Ibid., 21.
28. Ibid., 18.
29. Ibid.
30. Hancock and Carim, *AIDS: Deadly Epidemic,* 13.
31. David Cronenberg, in Anne Billson, "Cronenberg on Cronenberg: A Career in Stereo," *Monthly Film Bulletin* 56 (1989): 5.
32. Kim Newman, "Dracula Has Risen from the Grave . . . Again," *Monthly Film Bulletin* 55 (1988): 5.
33. Anne Billson, "*Sea of Love,*" *Monthly Film Bulletin* 57 (1990): 77.
34. Rock Hudson and Sara Davidson, *Rock Hudson. His Story* (London: Weidenfeld and Nicolson, 1986).

35. Ibid., 13, 110.
36. Ibid., 34, 40.
37. Ibid., 35.
38. Ibid., 36.
39. Ibid., 35.
40. Ibid., x, xiii.
41. Ibid., 63, 64.
42. Ibid., xi, 169.
43. Ibid., xii, 169.
44. Phyllis Gates and Bob Thomas, *My Husband, Rock Hudson: The Real Story of Rock Hudson's Marriage to Phyllis Gates* (London: Angus and Robertson, 1987).
45. Ibid., 46, 45.
46. Ibid., 225, 87–88, 128.
47. Ibid., 23, 51, 56, 64, 69, 129, 138, 190.
48. Ibid., 200.
49. Ibid., 34, 35, 38, 67, 127.
50. Ronald Reagan, quoted in Hancock and Carim, *AIDS: Deadly Epidemic,* 39.
51. Dean Dittman, quoted in Hudson and Davidson, *Rock Hudson,* 188.
52. Watney, *Policing Desire,* 88.
53. Mark Miller, quoted in Hudson and Davidson, *Rock Hudson,* 221.
54. Shilts, *And the Band Played On*, xxi.

Chapter 12. Some Key Films

1. Jill Feldman, "*Born on the Fourth of July,*" *Rolling Stone* (22 September 1989): 45.
2. J. Hoberman, "The Worst Years of Our Lives," *Village Voice* (26 December 1989): 99.
3. Ibid.
4. Robert Richardson, quoted in Bob Fisher, "*Born on the Fourth of July,*" *American Cinematographer* 71, no. 2 (February 1990): 27.
5. Peter Greenaway, "*The Cook, the Thief, His Wife and Her Lover,*" *Films and Filming* 420 (October 1989): 43.
6. Peter Greenaway, quoted in Gary Indiana, "Peter Greenaway," *Interview* 29, no. 3 (March 1990): 120.
7. Adam Mars-Jones, "Architectural Bellies," *Independent* (12 October 1989): 17.
8. Sean French, "*The Cook, the Thief, His Wife and Her Lover,*" *Sight and Sound* 58, no. 4 (1989): 277.
9. Indiana, "Peter Greenaway," 121.
10. Brian McFarlane, "Peter Greenaway," *Cinema Papers* 78 (March 1990): 68.
11. Peter Greenaway, "Cannibalism on the Corso," *Guardian* (12 October 1989): 29.
12. Ibid.
13. Peter Greenaway, quoted in William Green, "One Man's Meat," *Sunday Telegraph* (1 October 1989): 216.
14. Peter Greenaway, quoted in McFarlane, "Peter Greenaway," 41.
15. Peter Greenaway, in ibid.
16. Michael O'Pray, "Carnival Time: Cinema, Society and the Body Busi-

ness," *Monthly Film Bulletin* 57 (April 1990): 92.

17. Brian Yuzna, quoted in Alan Jones, "Brian Yuzna's *Society,*" *Starburst* 140 (April 1990): 12.

18. O'Pray, "Carnival Time," 92.

19. Ibid., 93.

20. Angela McRobbie, "Putting Sex Back in Its Place," *New Statesman and Society* (5 January 1990): 44.

21. Ibid.

22. Lizzie Francke, "*Parenthood,*" *The Face* (January 1990): 19.

23. Richard Combs, "*Shivers,*" *Monthly Film Bulletin* 43, no. 506 (March 1976): 62.

24. Charles D. Leayman, "*They Came from Within* . . . Siegel's 'Pods' Have in Fact Won Out . . .," *Cinefantastique* 5, no. 3 (1976): 22.

25. Combs, "*Shivers,*" 62.

26. Natalie Edwards, "*The Parasite Murders,*" *Cinema Canada* 22 (October 1975): 44.

27. Robert Marcuse (*sic*), quoted in Leayman, "*They Came from Within,*" 22.

28. David Cronenberg, quoted in Combs, "*Shivers,*" 62.

29. David Cronenberg, quoted in Stephen Chelsey, "it'll bug you," *Cinema Canada* 22 (22 October 1975): 25.

30. David Cronenberg, quoted in ibid.

31. Leayman, "*They Came from Within,*" 23.

32. My emphasis. Alexander Walker, *Evening Standard* (29 April 1976).

33. Ibid.

34. Deborah Raschke, "*Fatal Attraction,*" *Cinéaste* 6, no. 3 (1989): 44.

35. Adrian Lyne, quoted in Louise Tanner, "Adrian Lyne and Patricia Rozema," *Films in Review* 38, no. 12 (December 1987): 598.

36. Laura Mulvey, "Visual Pleasure and Narrative Cinema," in Laura Mulvey, *Visual and Other Pleasures* (London: Macmillan, 1989).

37. Barbara Creed, "*Fatal Attraction,*" *Cinema Papers* 68 (March 1986): 43.

38. See Raschke, "*Fatal Attraction,*" 45.

39. Brian De Palma, quoted in *Guardian* (17 December 1987): 11.

40. Peter McKay, "*Fatal Attraction,*" *Evening Standard* (7 March 1988): 9.

41. J. Hoberman, "The Other, Woman," *Village Voice* (29 September 1987): 68.

42. Arthur Miller, *Collected Plays,* vol. 1 (London: Secker and Warburg, 1967): 26.

43. Ibid., 27.

44. Page-number references to quotations from Miller's play relate to the Secker and Warburg publication cited in note 42.

45. J. Hoberman, *Village Voice* (1 December 1987).

Chapter 13. Some Conclusions

1. MacKinnon, *Misogyny in the Movies.*

2. Thomas Schatz, *Hollywood Genres* (New York: Random House, 1981).

Select Bibliography

Adam, Barry D. *The Survival of Domination: Inferiorization and Everyday Life,* New York: Elsevier, 1978.

Altman, Dennis, *AIDS and the New Puritanism.* London: Pluto Press, 1986.

———. *The Homosexualization of America, The Americanization of the Homosexual.* New York: St. Martin's Press, 1982.

Ariès, Philippe, and André Béjin, eds. *Western Sexuality: Practice and Precept in Past and Present Times.* Translated by Anthony Poster. Oxford: Basil Blackwell, 1985.

Bamigboye, Baz. "Changing the Face of Tom Cruise." *Daily Mail* (28 March 1989): 20.

Barrett, Michele, and Mary McIntosh. *The Anti-Social Family.* London: Verso Editions/NLB, 1982.

Bergan, Ronald. *"The Cook, the Thief, His Wife and Her Lover." Films and Filming* 420 (October 1989): 43.

Blanchot, Maurice. *The Writing of the Disaster.* Translated by Ann Smock. Lincoln and London: University of Nebraska Press, 1986.

Boffin, Tessa, and Sunil Gupta, eds. *Ecstatic Antibodies: Resisting the AIDS mythology.* London: Rivers Oram Press, 1990.

Boss, Pete. "Vile Bodies and Bad Medicine." *Screen* 27, no. 1 (January–February 1986): 14–24.

Brake, Mike, ed. *Human Sexual Relations: A Reader in Human Sexuality.* Harmondsworth: Penguin, 1982.

Bridges, George, and Rosalind Brunt, eds. *Silver Linings: Some Strategies for the Eighties.* London: Lawrence and Wishart, 1981.

Britton, Andrew. "Blissing Out: The Politics of Reaganite Entertainment." *Movie* 31–32: 1–42.

———. *Cary Grant: Comedy and Male Desire.* Newcastle upon Tyne: Tyneside Cinema, 1983.

———. "FOR Interpretation: Notes against Camp." *Gay Left* 7 (1978–79): 11–14.

Brophy, Philip. "Horrality: The Textuality of Contemporary Horror Films." *Screen* 27, no. 1 (January–February 1986): 2–13.

Brunt, Rosalind, and Caroline Rowan, eds. *Feminism, Culture and Politics,* 1982. Reprint. London: Lawrence and Wishart, 1986.

Bryant, Anita. *The Anita Bryant Story.* Old Tappan, N.J.: Fleming H. Revell Company, 1977.

Cahill, Kevin M., M.D., ed. *The AIDS Epidemic.* New York: St. Martin's Press, 1983.

Campbell, Duncan. "AIDS: The Duesberg Myth." *New Scientist* 122, no. 1663 (6 May 1989).

Caplan, Pat, ed. *The Cultural Construction of Sexuality*. London and New York: Tavistock, 1987.

Cartledge, Sue, and Joanna Ryan, eds. *Sex and Love: New Thoughts on Old Contradictions*. 1983. Reprint. London: Women's Press, 1987.

Chelsey, Stephen. "it'll bug you." *Cinema Canada* 22 (October 1975): 23–25.

Cohen, Stanley. *Folk Devils and Moral Panics: The Creation of the Mods and Rockers*. Oxford: Martin Robertson, 1980.

Cohen, Stanley, and Jock Young, eds. *The Manufacture of News: Social Problems, Deviance and the Mass Media*. London: Constable, 1973.

Combs, Richard. "*Shivers*." *Monthly Film Bulletin* 43, no. 506 (March 1976): 62.

Conover, Pamela Johnston, and Virginia Gray. *Feminism and the New Right: Conflict over the American Family*. New York: Praeger, 1983.

Cook, Pam. "Masculinity in Crisis?" *Screen* 23, nos. 3–4 (September–October 1982): 39–46.

Core, Philip. "Unseen Enemy." *Independent* (14 April 1989): 18.

Coveney, Lal, Margaret Jackson, Sheila Jeffreys, Leslie Kay, and Pat Mahony. *The Sexuality Papers: Male Sexuality and the Social Control of Women*. London: Hutchinson: Explorations in Feminism Collective, 1984.

Coward, Rosalind. *Female Desire*. 1984. Reprint. London: Paladin, 1987.

Crawford, Alan. *Thunder on the Right: The "New Right" and the Politics of Resentment*. New York: Pantheon, 1980.

Creed, Barbara. "*Fatal Attraction*." *Cinema Papers* 68 (March 1988): 42–44.

———. "Horror and the Monstrous-Feminine: An Imaginary Abjection." *Screen* 27, no. 1 (January–February 1986): 44–70.

Crimp, Douglas, ed. *AIDS: Cultural Analysis/Cultural Activism*. Cambridge: MIT Press, 1988.

Curran, James, Jake Ecclestone, Giles Oakley, and Alan Richardson, eds. *Bending Reality: The State of the Media*. London: Pluto Press, 1986.

deMause, Lloyd. *Reagan's America*. New York: Creative Roots, 1984.

Dessau, Bruce. "Critical Immunity." *Time Out* (13–20 June 1990): 48–49.

Dworkin, Andrea. *Right-Wing Women: The Politics of Domesticated Females*. London: The Women's Press, 1983.

Dyer, Richard. "Rock: The Last Guy You'd Have Figured?" *Body Politic* (December 1985): 27–29.

———, ed. *Gays and Film*. London: British Film Institute, 1977, 1980.

Edwards, Natalie. "*The Parasite Murders*." *Cinema Canada* 22 (October 1975): 44–45.

Ehrenreich, Barbara. *The Hearts of Men: American Dreams and the Flight from Commitment*. London: Pluto Press, 1983.

Eisenstein, Zillah. "Antifeminism in the Politics and Election of 1980." *Feminist Studies* 7, no. 2 (Summer 1981): 187–205.

———. "The Sexual Politics of the New Right: Understanding the 'Crisis of Liberalism' for the 1980s." *Signs: Journal of Women in Culture and Society* 7, no. 3 (1982): 567–88.

Fettner, Ann Giudici, and William A. Check, Ph.D. *The Truth about AIDS: Evolution of an Epidemic*. New York: Henry Holt and Co., 1985.

Fisher, Bob. *"Born on the Fourth of July."* *American Cinematographer* 71, no. 2 (February 1990): 26–33.

Formations Editorial Collective, eds. *Formations of Pleasure.* London: Routledge and Kegan Paul, 1983.

Foucault, Michel. *The History of Sexuality.* Vol. 1. Translated by Robert Hurley. Harmondsworth: Penguin, 1981.

Francke, Lizzie. *"Parenthood."* *The Face* (January 1990): 19.

Friedan, Betty. *The Second Stage.* London: Michael Joseph, 1982.

Gamman, Lorraine, and Margaret Marshment, eds. *The Female Gaze: Women as Viewers of Popular Culture.* London: The Women's Press, 1988.

Gates, Phyllis, and Bob Thomas. *My Husband, Rock Hudson: The Real Story of Rock Hudson's Marriage to Phyllis Gates.* London: Angus and Robertson, 1987.

Gay Left Collective, eds. *Homosexuality: Power and Politics.* London: Allison and Busby, 1980.

Gilman, Sander L. *Disease and Representation: Images of Illness from Madness to AIDS.* Ithaca: Cornell University Press, 1988.

Gordon, Linda, and Allen Hunter. "Sex, Family and the New Right: Anti-Feminism as a Political Force." *Radical America* 12, no. 1 (1978): 9–25.

Gove, Walter R. *The Labelling of Deviance: Evaluating a Perspective.* 2d ed. Beverly Hills: Sage, 1980.

Green, William. "One Man's Meat." *Sunday Telegraph* (1 October 1989): 216–17.

Greenaway, Peter, "Cannibalism on the Corso." *Guardian* (12 October 1989): 29.

Grossberg, Lawrence. *It's a Sin: Essays on Postmodernism, Politics and Culture.* Sydney: Power Publications, 1989.

Gunter, Barrie. *Television and Sex Role Stereotyping.* London and Paris: John Libbey, 1986.

Gunter, Barrie, and Michael Svennevig. *Behind and in Front of the Screen: Television's Involvement with Family Life.* London and Paris: John Libbey, 1987.

Hadden, Jeffrey K., and Anson Shupe. *Televangelism: Power and Politics on God's Frontier.* New York: Henry Holt and Co., 1988.

Hall, Celia. "Aids Cases among Heterosexuals Have Doubled in a Year." *Independent* (12 April 1990): 3.

Hall, Stuart. "Deviancy, Politics and the Media." Birmingham: University of Birmingham, Centre for Contemporary Cultural Studies, 1971.

———. *The Hard Road to Renewal: Thatcherism and the Crisis of the Left.* London, New York: Verso, 1988.

Hall, Stuart, and Martin Jacques. *The Politics of Thatcherism.* London: Lawrence and Wishart, 1983.

Hancock, Graham, and Enver Carim. *AIDS: The Deadly Epidemic.* London: Victor Gollancz, 1986.

Hartsock, Nancy C. M. *Money, Sex, and Power: Toward a Feminist Historical Materialism.* New York: Longman, 1983.

Hebditch, David, and Nick Anning. *Port Gold: Inside the Pornography Business.* London: Faber and Faber, 1988.

Hibbert, Ray Eldon, and Carol Reuss. *Impact of Mass Media: Current Issues.* New York: Longman, 1985.

Hoberman, J. "The Other, Woman." *Village Voice* (29 September 1987): 68.

———. "The Worst Years of Our Lives." *Village Voice* (26 December 1989): 99.

Home, Mark Douglas. "Moderator Criticises 'Thatcher Theology,' " *Independent* (18 February 1989): 3.

Howells, Kevin, ed. *The Psychology of Sexual Diversity.* Oxford: Basil Blackwell, 1984.

Hudson, Rock, and Sara Davidson. *Rock Hudson: His Story.* London: Weidenfeld and Nicolson, 1986.

Indiana, Gary. "Peter Greenaway." *Interview* 20, no. 3 (March 1990): 120–21.

Jeffreys, Sheila. *The Spinster and Her Enemies: Feminism and Sexuality, 1880– 1930.* London: Pandora, 1985.

Jones, Alan. "Brian Yuzna's *Society.*" *Starburst* 140 (April 1990): 9–12.

Jones, Ann. *Women Who Kill.* New York: Holt, Rinehart and Winston, 1980.

Jorstad, Erling. *The Politics of Moralism: The New Christian Right in American Life.* Minneapolis, Minn.: Augsburg Publishing House, 1981.

Kaplan, E. Ann. *Rocking around the Clock: Music Television, Postmodernism, and Consumer Culture.* New York and London: Methuen, 1987.

———. *Women and Film: Both Sides of the Camera.* London: Methuen, 1983.

Kappeler, Susanne. *The Pornography of Representation.* Minneapolis: University of Minnesota Press, 1986.

Kroker, Arthur, and Marilouise Kroker, eds. *Body Invaders: Sexuality and the Postmodern Condition.* London: Macmillan, 1988.

Lasch, Christopher. *The Culture of Narcissism: American Life in an Age of Diminishing Expectations.* New York: W. W. Norton and Co., 1978.

Leayman, Charles D. "*They Came from Within* . . . Siegel's 'Pods' Have in Fact Won Out . . ." *Cinefantastique* 5, no. 3 (1976): 22–23.

Levitan, Sar A., and Richard S. Belous. *What's Happening to the American Family?* Baltimore and London: Johns Hopkins University Press, 1981.

Liebmann-Smith, Richard. *The Question of AIDS.* New York: New York Academy of Sciences, 1985.

Lippe, Richard. "*Rock Hudson: His Story.*" *CineAction* (Fall 1987): 47–54.

McCormack, Thelma, ed. *Studies in Communications: News and Knowledge.* Vol. 3, Greenwich, Conn., and London: JAI Press, 1986.

McFarlane, Brian. "Peter Greenaway." *Cinema Papers* 78 (March 1990): 38–43, 68–69.

MacKinnon, Kenneth. *Misogyny in the Movies: The De Palma Question.* Newark: University of Delaware Press, 1990.

McRobbie, Angela, "Putting Sex Back in Its Place." *New Statesman and Society* (5 January 1990): 44, 46.

Mars-Jones, Adam. "Architectural Bellies." *Independent* (12 October 1989): 17.

Metcalf, Andy, and Martin Humphries. *The Sexuality of Men.* London: Pluto Press, 1985.

Miller, Arthur. *Collected Plays.* London: Secker and Warburg, 1967.

Monthly Film Bulletin 46–57 (1979–90).

Morris, N. A. "In Defence of *Fatal Attraction.*" *Movie* 33 (Winter 1989): 53–55.

Mosse, George L. *Nationalism and Sexuality: Respectability and Abnormal Sexuality in Modern Europe.* New York: Howard Fertig, 1985.

Mount, Ferdinand. *The Subversive Family: An Alternative History of Love and Marriage*. London: Jonathan Cape, 1982.

Mulvey, Laura. *Visual and Other Pleasures*. London: Macmillan, 1989.

National Deviancy Conference, ed. *Permissiveness and Control: The Fate of the Sixties Legislation*. London: Macmillan, 1980.

Neale, Steve. "Chariots of Fire, Images of Men." *Screen* 23, 3–4 (September–October 1982): 47–53.

———. "Masculinity as Spectacle: Reflections on Men and Mainstream Cinema." *Screen* 24, no. 6 (November–December 1983): 2–16.

Nichols, Eve K. *Mobilizing against AIDS: The Unfinished Story of a Virus*. Cambridge: Harvard University Press, 1986.

Nowell-Smith, Geoffrey. "Minnelli and Melodrama." *Screen* 18, no. 2 (1977).

Nungesser, Lon G. *Epidemic of Courage: Facing AIDS in America*. New York: St. Martin's Press, 1986.

Ortner, Sherry B., and Harriet Whitehead, eds. *Sexual Meanings: The Cultural Construction of Gender and Sexuality*. Cambridge, New York, and Melbourne: Cambridge University Press, 1981.

Pankhurst, Jerry G., and Sharon K. Houseknecht. "The Family, Politics, and Religion in the 1980s." *Journal of Family Issues* 4, no. 1 (March 1983): 5–34.

Peachment, Chris. "Food and Death." *The Times* (19 May 1989): 20.

Perloff, Richard M., Jane Delano Brown, and M. Mark Miller. "Mass Media and Sex-Typing: Research Perspectives and Policy Implications." *International Journal of Women's Studies* 5: 265–273.

Plummer, Kenneth (ed.) *The Making of the Modern Homosexual*. London: Hutchinson, 1981.

Poster, Mark. *Critical Theory of the Family*. London: Pluto Press, 1978.

Raschke, Deborah, "*Fatal Attraction*." *Cinéaste* 6, no. 3 (1989): 44–45.

Reynaud, Emmanuel. *Holy Virility: The Social Construction of Masculinity*. Translated by Ros Schwartz. London: Pluto Press, 1983.

Rogin, Michael Paul. *Ronald Reagan, the Movie, and Other Episodes in Political Demonology*. Berkeley and Los Angeles: University of California Press, 1987.

Rose, Jacqueline. *Sexuality in the Field of Vision*. London: Verso, 1986.

Rotenberg, Mordechai. *Damnation and Deviance: The Protestant Ethic and the Spirit of Failure*. New York: Free Press, 1978.

Russo, Vito. *The Celluloid Closet: Homosexuality in the Movies*. Rev. ed. New York: Harper and Row, 1987.

Sayers, Janet. *Biological Politics: Feminist and Anti-Feminist Perspectives*. 1982. Reprint. London and New York: Tavistock, 1983.

———. *Sexual Contradictions: Psychology, Psychoanalysis, and Feminism*. London and New York: Tavistock, 1986.

Scanzoni, John, Karen Polonko, Jay Teachman, and Linda Thompson. *The Sexual Bond: Rethinking Families and Close Relationships*. Sage Library of Social Research, vol. 170, Newbury Park, Calif.: 1989.

Schatz, Thomas. *Hollywood Genres*. New York: Random House, 1981.

Schmidt, Casper G. "The Group-Fantasy Origins of AIDS." *Journal of Psychohistory* 12 (1984): 37–78.

Schur, Edwin M. *The Politics of Deviance: Stigma Contests and the Uses of Power.* Englewood Cliffs, N.J.: Prentice-Hall, 1980.

Science in the Streets: Report of the Twentieth Century Fund Task Force on the Communication of Scientific Risk. New York: Priority Press, 1984.

Segal, Lynne, ed. *What Is to Be Done about the Family?* Harmondsworth: Penguin, 1983.

Seggar, John F., Jeffrey K. Hafen, and Helena Hannonen-Gladden. "Television's Portrayals of Minorities and Women in Drama and Comedy Drama, 1971–1980." *Journal of Broadcasting* 25: 277–88.

Shilts, Randy. *And the Band Played On: Politics, People, and the AIDS Epidemic.* London: Penguin, 1987.

Shipman, David. *Caught in the Act: Sex and Eroticism in the Movies.* London: Elm Tree Books, 1985.

Signorielli, Nancy, comp. and ed. *Role Portrayal and Stereotyping on Television: An Annotated Bibliography of Studies Relating to Women, Minorities, Aging, Sexual Behavior, Health and Handicaps.* With the assistance of Elizabeth Milke and Carol Katzman. Westport, Conn.: Greenwood Press, 1985.

Slater, Philip. *Footholds: Understanding the Shifting Family and Sexual Tensions in Our Culture.* Edited by Wendy Slater. New York: Dutton, 1977.

Smart, Carol, and Barry Smart, eds. *Women, Sexuality and Social Control.* London: Routledge and Kegan Paul, 1978.

Sontag, Susan. *Against Interpretation, and Other Essays.* London: Eyre and Spottiswoode, 1967.

———. *AIDS and Its Metaphors.* New York: Farrar, Straus and Giroux, 1988.

———. *Illness as Metaphor.* Harmondsworth: Penguin, 1977.

Tajima, Renee. "*Parenthood.*" *Village Voice* (8 August 1989): 63.

Tanner, Louise. "Adrian Lyne and Patricia Rozema." *Films in Review* 38, no. 12 (December 1987): 597–99.

Tracey, Michael, and David Morrison, *Whitehouse.* London: Macmillan, 1979.

Tuchman, Gaye, Arlene Kaplan Daniels, and James Benét, eds. *Hearth and Home: Images of Women in the Mass Media.* New York: Oxford University Press, 1978.

Valverde, Mariana. *Sex, Power and Pleasure.* Toronto: The Women's Press, 1985.

Vance, Carole S. *Pleasure and Danger: Exploring Female Sexuality.* Boston: Routledge and Kegan Paul, 1984.

Watney, Simon. *Policing Desire: Pornography, AIDS and the Media.* London: Methuen, 1987.

———. "The Rhetoric of AIDS: A Dossier Compiled by Simon Watney, with photographs by Sunil Gupta." *Screen* 27, no. 1 (January–February 1986): 72–85.

Weeks, Jeffrey. *Coming Out: Homosexual Politics in Britain, from the Nineteenth Century to the Present.* 1977. Reprint. London: Quartet Books, 1983.

———. "Decades of Desire." *Gay Times* (December 1989): 30–32.

———. *Sex, Politics and Society: The Regulation of Sexuality since 1800.* London: Longman, 1981.

———. *Sexuality.* London: Ellis Horwood, 1986.

———. *Sexuality and Its Discontents: Meanings, Myths and Modern Sexualities.* London: Routledge and Kegan Paul, 1985.

Williamson, Judith. "Nightmare on Madison Avenue." *New Statesman* (15 January 1988): 28–29.

Wilson, Elizabeth. *What Is to Be Done about Violence against Women?* Harmondsworth: Penguin, 1983.

Wood, Robin. *Hollywood from Vietnam to Reagan.* New York: Columbia University Press, 1986.

Zaretsky, Eli. *Capitalism, the Family and Personal Life.* London: Pluto Press, 1976.

Index